Social Theory and Social Movements

Jochen Roose · Hella Dietz
Editors

Social Theory and Social Movements

Mutual Inspirations

 Springer VS

Editors
Jochen Roose
Willy Brandt Center for German and
European Studies, University of Wrocław
Wrocław
Poland

Hella Dietz
Institut für Soziologie
Georg-August University of Göttingen
Göttingen, Lower Saxony
Germany

ISBN 978-3-658-13380-1   ISBN 978-3-658-13381-8   (eBook)
DOI 10.1007/978-3-658-13381-8

Library of Congress Control Number: 2016937375

Springer VS

Lektorat: Dr. Cori Mackrodt

This Springer VS imprint is published by Springer Nature
The registered company is Springer Fachmedien Wiesbaden GmbH

Contents

Editors and Contributors

About the Editors

Dr. Jochen Roose is professor for social sciences at the Willy Brandt Center for German and European Studies, University of Wrocław, and researcher at the Institute for Protest and Social Movement Studies (ipb). His research interests are participation, Europeanization, and research methodology. Recent publications are „Empirische Kultursoziologie" (edited with J. Rössel, Springer VS 2015), "Culture and Movement Strength from a Quantitative Perspective" (in Baumgarten et al. Conceptualizing Culture, Palgrave 2014), "How European is European Identification?" (Journal of Common Market Studies 2013), and „Fehlermultiplikation und Pfadabhängigkeit" (Kölner Zeitschrift für Soziologie und Sozialpsychologie 2013).

Dr. Hella Dietz is postdoctoral research associate at the Georg-August University of Göttingen. Her research focuses on social change and collective action, protest movements, truth commissions, and human rights. She currently explores the potential of a narrative sociology. Recent publications are „Polnischer Protest. Zur pragmatistischen Fundierung von Theorien sozialen Wandels" (Campus 2015), „Prozesse erzählen oder was die Soziologie von der Erzähltheorie lernen kann" (in Schützeichel/Jordan: Prozesse – Formen, Dynamiken, Erklärungen, Springer VS 2015), and „Theorien erzählen: Überlegungen im Anschluss an John Dewey" (in Farzin/Laux: Gründungsszenen soziologischer Theorie, Springer VS 2014).

Contributors

Britta Baumgarten, CIES, ISCTE IUL, Lisbon, Portugal

Nick Crossley, University of Manchester, Manchester, UK

Thomas Kern, University of Bamberg, Bamberg, Germany

Isabel Kusche, Aarhus University, Aarhus, Denmark

Dorothea Reinmuth, Universität Erfurt, Erfurt, Germany

Jochen Roose, University of Wrocław, Wrocław, Poland

Lars Schmitt, Hochschule Düsseldorf, Düsseldorf, Germany

Annette Schnabel, Heinrich-Heine-Universität, Düsseldorf, Germany

Peter Ullrich, Technische Universität Berlin, Berlin, Germany

Paths of Innovation in Social Movement Research Theory

Jochen Roose

Social movement research, like all research in the social sciences, needs theory. Of course, it needs not only theory. The main interest of scientific analysis is explaining and understanding social reality. Accordingly, empirical analysis should be at the fore. We want to learn about reality, not about books.

However, a naïve positivist approach was discarded a long time ago for two reasons (Chalmers 1990, pp. 42ff). First, reality is always too complex and the human ability to gather information is too limited to simply be open and collect everything for our analysis. We necessarily have to focus our attention and this implies that we concentrate on some more important aspects of reality while disregarding other less important aspects. We have to choose and this choice is inescapable. Second, and directly connected to the first point, the choice of what we consider important is guided by a priori assumptions, and that means by theory. We use this theory regardless of whether we want to or not. The use of implicit and therefore uncontrollable steps in scientific analysis runs counter to the grand rule, that each step can be reproduced by others. Thus, we are called to explicate our theory. However, the explication of theory goes beyond the mere documentation of selection criteria for others. It also enables researchers themselves to reflect on the assumptions, test them for plausibility and logical consistency, and expose them to debate. Theoretical debate is a necessary and important part of research. It paves the way to sound and enlightening work.

As innovation and the production of new findings is a core task of science, the question arises of how innovation in the important part of theory production and

J. Roose (✉)
Willy Brandt Center for German and European Studies,
University of Wrocław, Wrocław, Poland
e-mail: jochen.roose@fu-berlin.de

© Springer Fachmedien Wiesbaden 2016   1
J. Roose and H. Dietz (eds.), *Social Theory and Social Movements*,
DOI 10.1007/978-3-658-13381-8_1

modification occurs. We argue that there are four ways of theoretical innovation: (a) empirical findings, (b) innovation of methods, (c) theoretical debate, and (d) changes in general perspectives. These paths are not mutually exclusive but partly reinforce or enable each other. In the following, we will discuss each of these four ways and illustrate it with regards to social movement research. Then we show in which way this volume chose to contribute to innovation in the study of social movements, including a short introduction to the chapters. Finally, we shortly introduce the project behind this volume.

1   Theory Innovation by Empirical Findings

Empirical findings can irritate theory. If assumptions cannot be confirmed, this points to the necessity to modify or even dismiss a theory. This was Popper's idea of critical rationalism (Popper 1959). He even championed the falsification of theory as the main aim of empirical research. As theory could never be verified he suggested targeting research to the falsification of theory, which leads to theoretical improvement.

The logic of falsification has three problems. The first problem is a result of theory-driven research in the first place. As the empirical investigation is guided by theory and the theory determines which aspects of social reality are observed and considered in the study, the research is sheltered from aspects of reality that may be also relevant but neglected by the theory.

The research paradigms subsumed under the heading of interpretative or qualitative approaches (see, for example, Creswell 1998) opt for openness in their research. The idea behind these approaches is to be inclusive in data collection and consider a broad range of alternatives. Openness for unexpected information and alternative explanations should enhance the probability of new findings. However, the fundamental problem of theory-guided research is not solved by this approach. Still, observation is necessarily selective, and explicit or implicit theories on what is relevant or important influence empirical work. Also, in practice, the distinction between open qualitative and theory-driven, deductive, quantitative approaches is often exaggerated. Further, in quantitative studies, inductive elements are included when possible "control variables" are used, the analysis experiments with correlations between various available variables, or statistical results are used to spot possible influences and modify theory. In sum, the problem remains that prior theoretical assumptions necessarily limit the possibility of innovation by unexpected empirical findings.

The second problem was described by Popper himself. Not only is verification of theory impossible as always there might be or might have been a case contradicting the theory that has not been observed or is not yet observed; falsification is also impossible. We can never compare the theory directly with reality. Rather, we compare the results of empirical analysis in its verbalized form with theory. Hence, a contradiction of theory and the verbalized finding can stem from the wrong theory or wrong empirical findings or from a wrong representation of empirical findings. We never actually know whether a theory has been falsified or if the empirical findings are wrong. Thus, there is always a defense line for theory under attack.

This chance to escape falsification is particularly relevant in connection with the third problem. Irrespective of the idea of critical rationalism, Kuhn (1963) argued that the history of science clearly shows the stability of paradigms. According to Kuhn, the grand logic of theories remains stable for a long time and across findings that do not fit with the initial logic of the theory. Instead of discarding or fundamentally revising the theory, it is rather amended step-by-step and contradictory findings are either questioned with regard to methodological problems or they are integrated with minor additional assumptions. Only if these theoretical problems pile up is the theory changed.

For empirical scientific disciplines, reality is the apparent source for information. However, empirical information alone seems to be limited in its ability to change theory and thereby our understanding of reality. Findings contradicting dominant theoretical ideas may lead to minor changes but are not overly likely to change the theoretical perspective as a whole. Possibly these findings are even considered to be a contribution to methodological debate that intends to overcome a supposed flaw of research techniques. There is no direct automatic correspondence between theoretical and empirical developments.

However, this also applies to the reverse situation. Developments in reality can have a strong impact on theoretical debates even if the developments could in principle be covered in the hitherto dominating theoretical framework. The turn from a collective behavior perspective to the rational choice-inspired resource mobilization approach is a case in point (McCarthy and Zald 1977; Neidhardt and Rucht 1991). The current debate on the role of deprivation for the protest in Southern European countries in relation to the Eurozone crisis and austerity policy is another (della Porta 2015; Roose 2016). In these cases there was not an outright contradiction between empirical findings and theory but rather an uneasiness with the general outline and basic assumptions of a theoretical framework. If social phenomena of a different kind become important, basic theoretical assumptions can be questioned.

2   Innovation of Methods

Another source for theoretical development also comes from the empirical side, though not from empirical findings but changes in methods. These can be methods of data generation or analytical methods. The establishment of new methods enlarges the field that can be accessed by research. These possibilities also encourage theoretical reasoning to cover the newly accessed spaces.

Innovation of methods can be found in various forms. Methods of statistical analysis are invented or become feasible by developments in information technology and increased calculation power. Principle component analysis or multi-level models developed into widely used techniques simply because computers became more powerful and the software was easier to use. Other innovations are developed in the field itself like the spread of protest event analysis, political claims analysis, or surveys among demonstrators (for an overview, see della Porta et al. 2014).

Innovation of methods enhances theory development in two ways. First, methods enable an approach to reality. Accordingly, innovations provide new empirical insights that inform theory. Even if the limitations mentioned above (Sect. 1) apply, the findings still enlarge our knowledge and support further theoretical insights. Second, new methods and their application result in a need for corresponding theory. To make sense of empirical findings provided by new techniques, theory is needed. Theory may be invented from scratch to be tested by the newly available means, or it is theory that is inductively obtained through interpretation of the newly available material. In either case, new approaches to data collection or data analysis create the need and pave the way to the development of new theory.

3   Theoretical Debate

While the first two paths for theoretical innovation are linked to empirical findings, the third path remains in the realm of theory itself. Theory can be developed from theoretical debates in three ways. First, scientific theory is expected to be logically coherent. Debating the internal consistency of a theory is therefore an important part of scientific work. Of course, such a debate can not only spot problems of consistency but also develop solutions and thereby change and improve theory. The debate about the political opportunity structure approach is one example (Meyer and Minkoff 2004; Roose 2003, pp. 33–44, 64–88 and the debate in the Sociological Forum 1999, vol. 14, issue 1).

Second, the combination of approaches is another avenue of theoretical pro-gress. The approaches in social movement research, namely deprivation, resource mobilization, framing, political opportunity structure, and identity (see, for example, della Porta and Diani 1999; Hellmann 1998; Müller 2016; Snow et al. 2007), have been deemed compatible with each other and various combinations have been discussed. We find suggestions to apply one approach to the other, like the framing of opportunities (Diani 1996; Gamson and Meyer 1996) or the impact of political opportunities on organizational structures (Koopmans et al. 2005; Rucht 1996). More inclusive concepts, combining several or all of these approa-ches have been suggested inter alia by Neidhardt and Rucht (1991, 2002), Opp (2009), Kern (2007), Roose (2003), or most famously and including approaches of revolution studies by McAdam et al. (2001).

These combinations use theoretical approaches that were developed for the very same research object, namely the field of social movements. Initially, these approaches were suggested as alternatives, highlighting different aspects as the crucial dimension for explaining the mobilization of social movements. However, this debate argued more and more for their compatibility and integration.

The third path of the theoretical debate is to combine a specific theory, such as social movement theory, with theory from other realms. Because social movement research is dominated by middle range theories, the link to social theory seems a particularly promising path. Very different social theories have been used to understand social movements and/or revise the middle range theories of movement research. For example, Pettenkofer (2010) revised insights about social movements from a pragmatist perspective, Hellmann (1996) applied Luhmann's system theory to social movements, Roose (2003) modified the theories by using Giddens' structuration approach, and Opp (2009) integrated the middle range theories from a rational choice perspective. Less holistic theoretical approaches can also be fruitful to elaborate the social movement theory. It is this third path of theory innovation that is used in this volume (see Sect. 5).

4   Changes in Perspective

A fourth path of theoretical innovation is a mixture of the aforementioned. Theory can be improved by absorbing general tendencies in the scientific community. From time to time general trends emerge or far-reaching developments influence a broad range of debates in a discipline. The discussion of globalization is an example. The observation of broad social change became influential for various debates and also influenced the analysis of social movements. While the phenomenon as such developed in a long and gradual process, in politics as well as societies, the attention was drawn to this issue in the second half of the 1990s (see, for example, della Porta et al. 1999; Guidry et al. 2001; Hamel et al. 2001; Keck and Sikkink 1998; Smith et al. 1997). Of course, in these years the United Nations and international conferences gained political importance and highlighted the relevance of transnational developments for social movement studies. So we could argue that it was these empirical phenomena that triggered the attention of social movement scholars. However, if we take a look at publications in social science in general, it becomes apparent that the whole discipline discussed phenomena of globalization, and social movement studies was part of this trend.

Maybe even more influential are "turns" in the general theoretical and methodological perspective of the discipline. The cultural turn influenced a broad range of fields. It not only became highly influential but also so diverse that Bachmann-Medick (2016) identifies a number of cultural turns. The career of the framing approach within and beyond social movement studies (Benford and Snow 2000; Chong and Druckman 2007; Scheufele 1999; Snow 2007) could possibly be linked to this development. But also beyond framing, cultural approaches inspired social movement analysis in various ways (Baumgarten et al. 2014; Jasper 2010).

The spatial turn (Döring and Thielmann 2008; Warf and Arias 2009) is only now about to fully exert its influence on social movement studies (Daphi 2014; Martin 2015, pp. 153ff). Again, the widespread occupations of urban central squares are an empirical phenomenon attracting attention (for example, Farro and Demirhisar 2014; Said 2015). However, the interest in space and its connection to social movements goes beyond these cases and is rather embedded in the general attention towards space and spatial phenomena in social sciences.

These turns and general highlighted topics in a discipline and often even beyond one discipline are a source of inspiration for theory development. They draw attention to phenomena that were previously sidelined and call for the consideration and integration of these aspects. At times this may require only minor amendments but in other cases a reconsideration of basic ideas may be necessary.

5   Walking a Path: Contributing to Theory Innovation

As outlined, social science takes different paths for innovation in theory development. This volume takes a specific path: It confronts social movement theory with specific theorists or theoretical traditions. Thus, it chooses the path of theoretical debate (see Sect. 3) by combining social movement theory with other theoretical approaches. Our intention is twofold: On the one side, we want to advance theories in the field of social movements. Systematically introducing the respective perspectives can help to advance our theoretical understanding of social movements, highlight aspects that received only minor attention up to now, or enable us to theoretically grasp aspects that had been at the margin. On the other side, we contribute to the discussion of the respective research tradition. Social movements are or could be a research object in the context of various theories and often the phenomena of social movements are at least marginally integrated, especially in the discussions on social change. However, social theory seldom makes use of insights in the field of social movement studies and therefore these considerations of social movement in the broader theoretical framework is only partly consistent with established findings. Therefore it is also fruitful to contribute to more general theoretical debates from a social movement perspective.

The authors in this volume follow a similar outline. They were asked to briefly present the most relevant ideas of their respective theory or theoretical tradition and then discuss both the implications of this theory to social movement studies and the implication of social movement analysis on the theory.

Britta Baumgarten and *Peter Ullrich* draw on Foucault's rich theory and show insights on mobilization practices as well as on the likeliness of mobilization itself. Concerning the ways and forms of mobilization, Foucault helps us to go beyond the framing tradition and to develop an understanding of discursive opportunities that makes use of Foucault's concepts of power, dispositives, and the actor's restrictions in interpretation and arguing. The concepts of governmentality and subjectivity help us to understand why (and when) people protest and, even more so, abstain from protest. By undermining the legitimacy of critique, protest becomes less likely. However, the mechanisms of governmentality can also become issue of protest. Movements may even incorporate governmentality's idea of individual self-control in their concepts of an alternative world, thereby using the very same concept to change society by changes in the way of life.

Annette Schnabel uses rational choice theory, which inspired some early works of social movement research but then was sidelined in its explicit form. She describes this early history and lays out the fundamental explanatory problem for a rational choice perspective: As social movements produce public goods there is no motivation for the individual to contribute to mobilizations. Rational choice offered some suggestions to solve this problem, such as iteration, reputation, selected incentives, and threshold models. Open questions are in particular the role of movement aims and ideology because the relevance of these is by and large undisputed, but its role is not systematically integrated in the theory. Similarly, emotions are a big challenge for rational choice theory.

Lars Schmitt builds on the work of Pierre Bourdieu, who was active in protest mobilization and also analyzed social movements, but most fruitful is Bourdieu's concept of the societal (symbolic) struggle to understand social movements. The concept of a habitus-structure conflict focuses our attention on how social movements challenge the constellation of symbolic conflicts in a society and voice calls for the recognition of marginalized groups. Regarding the internal structure of movements, Bourdieu's theory is an instrument to understand hierarchies and symbolic orders among protesters.

Isabel Kusche draws on Niklas Luhmann's theory of autopoietic systems. Initially, Niklas Luhmann did not consider social movements, but the phenomenon was so highly visible that a discussion of the role of social movements became inevitable. For the theory, centrally building on functional differentiation, social movements are a major challenge. Isabel Kusche argues that social movements play an important role as they spot and criticize the problematic consequences of functional differentiation. At the same time, the permanent need for explicit decisions in modern societies leads to the continuous proliferation of causes for protest, as all these decisions can be challenged by social movements.

Thomas Kern discusses the theory of Jeffrey Alexander. Alexander also presents a theory based on functional differentiation, however he conceptualizes differentiation as a conflictive process. Social movements play a central role in this constellation. They continuously challenge motives, relationships, and institutions. Functional differentiation leads to inequalities and other externalized problems. Social movements voice these problems in the civic sphere. In this role Alexander regards social movements as powerful in changing patterns of exclusion.

Jochen Roose starts from the observation of similarity or isomorphism among movement organizations. In a Weberian tradition and in line with social movement theory, similarity among movement organizations can be explained by the convergence of movement tactics to the most rational way. This explanation, however, is not convincing because causes of successful behavior are so unclear. Neo-institutionalism, in the tradition of Meyer and Rowan, suggests a different argument, which is compliance with institutionalized rules and scripts that describe the "normal" or "modern" behavior. Thereby, movement organizations gain legitimacy, which is also vital, even if the strategies are not very promising for achieving the movement's main objective. A neo-institutionalist perspective improves our explanatory possibilities but also redirects attention to processes of diffusion among movement organizations.

Dorothea Reinmuth uses Judith Butler's concepts of recognition and performativity to improve social movement theory. Butler identifies recognition as a human need, but recognition can be positive or negative. Performative acts signal these recognitions. Social movements are in an inherently contradictive situation because they call for the recognition of norms that they want to change at the same time. Ironic performance is a way to deal with this ambiguous situation. Thus, Butler's theory helps us to understand an important development in movement action.

Nick Crossley uses relational sociology for the understanding of social movements. Networks have long been recognized as important for social movements but their actual analysis is rare. Crossley argues that the network configuration is crucial to understand recruitment processes and the shape of collective action.

Overall, the contributions offer a wide array of theoretical approaches that are discussed in respect to their contribution to social movement theory. Unquestionably there are more theoretical approaches that provide fruitful insights. The path of innovation by theory combination is still full of promises.

6 The Project Behind the Book

This volume is the product of a series of workshops that were conducted by the researchers network "New perspectives on protest and social movements." Funded by the German Research Foundation (Deutsche Forschungsgemeinschaft), a group of movement researchers met regularly and discussed virulent questions in their field. We received the support of guests who joined our discussions and helped to improve the papers.

Two of the workshops circled around the combination of social movement theory and social theory, resulting in this book. The discussions and thereby also the chapters of this book profited by comments of the workshop participants: Britta Baumgarten, Nick Crossley, Priska Daphi, Hella Dietz, Marion Hamm, Swen Hutter, Andrea Pabst, Andreas Pettenkofer, Dorothea Reinmuth, Jochen Roose, Lars Schmitt, Simon Teune, Peter Ullrich, Mundo Yang, and Sabrina Zajak.[1] All of them invested more than most conference discussants to improve the products of our debate. A special thanks goes to Mundo Yang who initiated the network in the first place, the Deutsche Forschungsgemeinschaft for the generous funding, and

---

[1]A second volume from the network was published by Britta Baumgarten, Priska Daphi, and Peter Ullrich: "Conceptualizing Culture in Social Movement Research" (Palgrave 2014). Most members of the network continue their cooperation in the Institute for Protest and Social Movement Studies (Institut für Protest– und Bewegungsforschung, protestinstitut. eu).

Peter Ullrich, who continuously insisted on the finalization of this volume against various difficulties.

The contributions to this volume take very different perspectives and highlight different aspects of social movements. However, they converge in one important point: Social movements are an important force that shapes societies. Their analysis is a crucial part of theorizing in the social sciences and needs continuous attention.

References

Bachmann-Medick, Doris. 2016. *Cultural turns. New orientations in the study of culture*. Berlin, New York: de Gruyter.

Baumgarten, Britta, Priska Daphi, and Peter Ullrich (eds.). 2014. *Conceptualizing culture in social movement research*. Houndmills, Basingstoke: Palgrave Macmillan.

Benford, D.R., and David Snow. 2000. Framing processes and social movements. An overview and assessment. *Annual Review of Sociology* 26(1): 611–639.

Chalmers, Alan F. 1990. *Science and its fabrication*. Minneapolis: University of Minnesota Press.

Chong, Dennis, and James N. Druckman. 2007. Framing theory. *Annual Review of Political Science* 10(1): 103–126.

Creswell, J.W. 1998. *Qualitative inquiry and research design. Choosing among five traditions*. Thousand Oaks, London, New Delhi: Sage.

Daphi, Priska. 2014. Movement space: A cultural approach. In *Conceputalizing culture in social movement research*, ed. Britta Baumgarten, Priska Daphi, and Peter Ullrich, 165–185. Houndmills: Palgrave.

della Porta, Donatella. 2015. *Social movements in times of austerity. Bringing capitalism back into protest analysis*. Cambridge: Polity Press.

della Porta, Donatella, and Mario Diani. 1999. *Social movements. An introduction*. Oxford: Blackwell Publishers.

della Porta, Donatella, Hanspeter Kriesi, and Dieter Rucht. 1999. *Social movements in a globalizing world*. London, New York: Routledge.

della Porta, Donatella, et al. 2014. *Methodological practices in social movement research*. Oxford: Oxford University Press.

Diani, Mario. 1996. Linking mobilization frames and political opportunities: Insights from regional populism in Italy. *American Sociological Review* 61(1): 1053–1069.

Döring, Jörg, Tristan Thielmann, et al. 2008. *Spatial Turn. Das Raumparadigma in den Kultur- und Sozialwissenschaften*. Bielefeld: Transcript.

Farro, A.L., and Deniz Günce Demirhisar. 2014. The Gezi Park movement. A Turkish experience of the twenty-first-century collective movements. *International Review of Sociology* 24(1): 176–189.

Gamson, William A., and David S. Meyer. 1996. Framing political opportunity. In *Comparative Perspectives on Social Movement Research. Political Opportunities,*

Mobilizing Structures, and Cultural Framings, eds. Doug McAdam, John D. McCarthy, and Mayer N. Zald, 275–290. Cambridge: Cambridge University Press.

Guidry, John A., Michael D. Kennedy, and Mayer N. Zald (eds.). 2001. *Globalizations and social movements: Culture, power, and the transnational public sphere*. Ann Arbor: University of Michigan Press.

Hamel, Pierre, Henri Lustiger-Thaler, Jan Nederveen Pieterse, and Sasha Roseneil (eds.). 2001. *Globalization and social movements*. Basingstoke, New York: Palgrave.

Hellmann, Kai-Uwe. 1996. *Systemtheorie und neue soziale Bewegungen*. Identitätsprobleme in der Risikogesellschaft. Opladen: Westdeutscher Verlag.

Hellmann, Kai-Uwe. 1998. Paradigmen der Bewegungsforschung. Forschungs- und Erklärungsansätze—ein Überblick. In *Paradigmen der Bewegungsforschung. Entstehung und Entwicklung von neuen sozialen Bewegungen*, eds. Kai-Uwe Hellmann, and Ruud Koopmans, 9–30. Opladen: Westdeutscher Verlag.

Jasper, James M. 2010. Cultural approaches in the sociology of social movements. In *Handbook of social movements across disciplines*, ed. Bert Klandermans, and Conny Roggeband, 59–109. New York: Springer.

Keck, Margaret E., and Kathryn Sikkink. 1998. *Activists beyond borders. Advocacy networks in international politics*. Ithaca: Cornell University Press.

Kern, Thomas. 2007. *Soziale Bewegungen. Ursachen, Wirkungen, Mechanismen*. Wiesbaden: VS Verlag für Sozialwissenschaften.

Koopmans, Ruud, Paul Statham, Marco Giugni, and Florence Passy. 2005. *Contested citizenship. Immigration and cultural diversity in Europe*. Minneapolis, London: University of Minnesota Press.

Kuhn, Thomas S. 1963. *The structure of scientific revolutions*. Chicago: Chicago University Press.

Martin, Greg. 2015. *Understanding social movements*. London, New York: Routledge.

McAdam, Doug, Sidney Tarrow, and Charles Tilly. 2001. *Dynamics of contention*. Cambridge: Cambridge University Press.

McCarthy, John D., and Mayer N. Zald. 1977. Resource mobilization and social movements: A partial theory. *American Journal of Sociology* 82(6): 1212–1241.

Meyer, David S., and Debra C. Minkoff. 2004. Conceptualizing political opportunity. *Social Forces* 82(4): 1457–1492.

Müller, Melanie. 2016. *Die Welt zu Gast. Internationale Konferenzen und ihre kurz- und mittelfristigen Auswirkungen auf soziale Bewegungen. Eine Untersuchung am Beispiel der 17. Conference of the Parties der United Nations Framework Convention on Climate Change in Südafrika*. Berlin: Freie Universität Berlin, unpublished Dissertation.

Neidhardt, Friedhelm, and Dieter Rucht. 2002. Towards a 'movement society'? On the possibilities of institutionalizing social movements. *Social Movement Studies* 1(1): 7–30.

Neidhardt, Friedhelm, and Dieter Rucht. 1991. The Analysis of Social Movements: The State of the Art and Some Perspectives for Further Research. In *Research on Social Movements. The State Of the Art in Western Europe and the USA*, ed. Dieter Rucht, 421–464. Frankfurt/M., New York: Campus.

Opp, Karl-Dieter. 2009. *Theories of political protest and social movements. A multidisciplinary introduction, critique, and synthesis*. London, New York: Routledge.

Pettenkofer, Andreas. 2010. *Radikaler Protest. Zur soziologischen Theorie politischer Bewegungen*. Frankfurt/M., New York: Campus.

Popper, Karl R. 1959. *The Logic of scientific discovery*. London: Hutchinson.

Roose, Jochen. 2003. *Die Europäisierung von Umweltorganisationen. Die Umweltbewegung auf dem langen Weg nach Brüssel*. Wiesbaden: Westdeutscher Verlag.

Roose, Jochen. 2016. Was lernt die Bewegungsforschung aus der Eurozonen-Krise? Was lernt die Bewegungsforschung aus der Eurozonen-Krise. *Forschungsjournal Soziale Bewegungen* 29 (1), in print.

Rucht, Dieter. 1996. The impact of national contexts on social movement structures: A cross-movement and cross-national comparison. In *Comparative perspectives on social movements. Political opportunities, mobilizing structures, and cultural framings*, eds. Doug McAdam, John D. McCarthy, and Mayer N. Zald, 185–204. Cambridge: Cambridge University Press.

Said, Atef. 2015. We ought to be here: Historicizing space and mobilization in Tahrir Square. *International Sociology* 30(4): 348–366.

Scheufele, Dietram A. 1999. Framing as a theory of media effects. *Journal of Communication* 14(4): 103–122.

Smith, Jackie, Charles Chatfield, and Ron Pagnucco (eds.). 1997. *Transnational social movements and global politics. Solidarity beyond the state*. Syracuse: Syracuse University Press.

Snow, David. 2007. Framing processes, ideology, and discursive fields. In *The Blackwell companion to social movements*, ed. David Snow, Sarah Soule, and Hanspeter Kriesi, 380–412. Malden, Oxford: Blackwell.

Snow, David, Sarah A. Soule, and Hanspeter Kriesi. 2007. Mapping the terrain. In *The Blackwell companion to social movements*, ed. David Snow, Sarah Soule, and Hanspeter Kriesi, 3–16. Malden, Oxford: Blackwell.

Warf, Barney, and Santa Arias (eds.). 2009. *The Spatial turn. Interdisciplinary perspectives*. London, New York: Routledge.

Author Biography

Dr. Jochen Roose is Professor for Social Sciences at the Willy Brandt Center for German and European Studies, University of Wrocław and researcher at the Institute for Protest and Social Movement Studies (ipb). His research interests are participation, Europeanisation and research methodology. Recent publications are „Empirische Kultursoziologie" (edited with J. Rössel, Springer VS 2015), „Culture and Movement Strength from a Quantitative Perspective" (in: Baumgarten et al. Conceptualizing Culture, Palgrave 2014), „How European is European Identification?" (Journal of Common Market Studies 2013), „Fehlermultiplikation und Pfadabhängigkeit" (Kölner Zeitschrift für Soziologie und Sozialpsychologie 2013).

Discourse, Power, and Governmentality. Social Movement Research with and beyond Foucault

Britta Baumgarten and Peter Ullrich

Foucault and the rich field of theoretical and empirical work inspired by his thinking currently play a prominent role in the social sciences. It is therefore more than surprising that, with a few exceptions (e.g. Death 2010; Sandberg 2006; Ullrich 2008, 2010; Baumgarten 2010; Heßdörfer et al. 2010; Ullrich and Keller 2014; Snow et al. 2014), this research tradition has scarcely impacted on the mainstream of research into social movements and protest until recently.[1] In this article we outline some ideas on how protest research can be stimulated, enriched, and reformulated out of the vast quarry of (post-)Foucauldian thinking.

It is Foucault's analysis of power, not least his concept of power as a productive force, that helps to bring societal macrostructures back into social movement research, helping to improve our understanding of the boundaries and sometimes even the non-appearance of protest. Power cannot be easily located in certain actors or institutions. Power creates knowledge and forms subjects who are restricted as well as enabled by its omnipresent force (Foucault 1979). Social movements are actors that by definition challenge power (Raschke 1991).

---

[1] This article was submitted and reviewed in September 2011; more current literature could only be inserted selectively.

B. Baumgarten (✉)
CIES, ISCTE IUL, Lisbon, Portugal
e-mail: britta.baumgarten@gmail.com

P. Ullrich
Technische Universität Berlin, Berlin, Germany
e-mail: ullrich@ztg.tu-berlin.de

© Springer Fachmedien Wiesbaden 2016
J. Roose and H. Dietz (eds.), *Social Theory and Social Movements*,
DOI 10.1007/978-3-658-13381-8_2

13

Consequently, developments in the scientific conceptualization of power are especially important for the study of social movements. Foucault's concept of power is central to his studies of discourse and governmentality. The two concepts will be discussed in connection with various questions raised by the study of social movements, protest, and contentious politics. From this vantage point it is possible to highlight non-strategic aspects of protest, such as its discursive and subjectifying preconditions and the world views of (potential) social movement actors. It contradicts the idea of rational movement actors, focuses on long-term processes and pays more attention to the diverse aspects of the action context of social movements than mainstream social movement research does. These new perspectives also engender several new research questions.

Following the development of Foucault's thinking, we first broach the issue of the knowledge–power complex. The social movement researcher, asking with Foucault what societies consider to be "normal" (or not), what they are able to communicate (or cannot even imagine) due to the discursive regulation of knowledge production, gains new insights into the discourse in which social movements are embedded and thus into the context of their ideational processes. Yet, later—our second main issue—Foucault combined this interest in the social production of knowledge with another perspective. Analyzing neoliberalism, Foucault and others showed how knowledge and related practices are spread and maintained by "governmental" or "biopolitical" techniques of subjectification and especially through techniques of governing the self. Thus, we propose a specific link between micro and macro levels, or between structure and subjectivity.

With discourse, power, and governmentality, we focus only on the aspects of Foucault's complex and disparate opus that we consider particularly fruitful for social movement research, necessarily ignoring other facets. We will go beyond Foucault's theory, drawing on the vast field of governmentality studies, Boltanski's sociology of critique, and the concepts of cultural opportunity structures.

At least four types of processes can be analyzed from a Foucauldian perspective (see Fig. 1) within the common distinction of macro (society), meso (movements, networks), and micro levels (individual constituents and bystanders).

1. Discourses define the boundaries of what can be thought of and communicated at a given time in a given society. The suffragettes of the late 19th and early 20th centuries, for example, did not demand equal distribution of childcare between men and women, because at that time it was still generally unthinkable. They did, however, call for equal political rights, e.g. the right to vote.

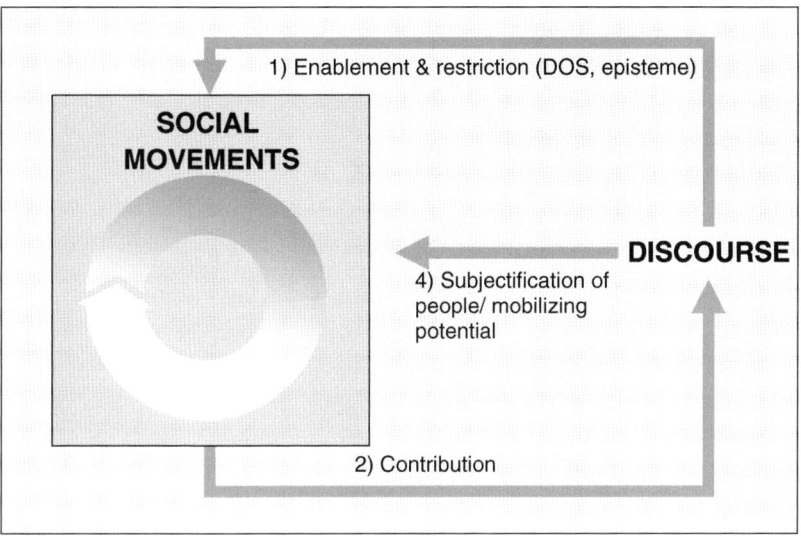

Fig. 1 Connecting social movement and (post-)Foucauldian concepts. *Source*: Figure by the authors

These claims fit well into the historical context of institutional reforms that extended the franchise.[2]

Discourse as *a room for maneuver* for social movements thus restricts and enables specific worldviews. Social movements not only observe discourse and strategically shape their communication accordingly. They *are* the product of discourse, too.

2. Within the boundaries of what is generally conceivable we can analyze framing efforts of social movements and how they contribute to the *discourse*. The resonance of frames depends not only on cultural factors but also on the arenas and the roles of speakers. In a long-term perspective we observe shifts in discourse and in how movements' communication strategies relate to these shifts. We can observe *how movements* influence the boundaries of what is generally conceivable, either by promoting thinking that is not established in

---

[2]The first substantive parliamentary debate on women's suffrage in England took place in May 1867, when women supported by John Stuart Mill insisted that women's suffrage should become part of the electoral reform agenda (Offen 2000, p. 142). But only in 1919 were British women (over the age of 30) granted the vote (Offen 2000: xxvi).

the mainstream discourse or is even antagonistic to it, or by creating new issues and concepts through their practices. One example is the partial success of post-structuralist feminism and queer theory with their ideas of (social) gender and many biological sexes (Butler 1993) in challenging the hegemonic idea of only two (biologically determined) sexes.

3. Furthermore, there are internal communicative practices of movement knowledge generation. These can be seen as a set of both productive and restrictive discursive regularities, which emerge at the movement level in the course of a movement's history. Such a sociology of knowledge approach to discourse regards the communication of social movements, e.g. their leaflets, symbols, not merely as goal-oriented, instrumental action, but as expressing their identity and thus their internal system of knowledge (Ullrich 2013; Ullrich and Keller 2014). It is important to point out that internal discourses are more than strategic power games played by actors within a movement. Movements develop their own specific discursive mechanisms that enable but also restrict the framing of actors within these movements. To capture the nonstrategic aspects, it is important to reconstruct the development of internal discourse over time.

4. Discourses and other practices in power regulation, such as practices of government and the government of the self, shape the subjectivity of the people. In Foucauldian terms, they shape the individual's relations to her-/himself and thus affect the mobilization potential of social movements. With regard to governmentality studies, we show how rationalities of advanced liberal government influence the likelihood of social critique and protest through subjectification processes. These processes are initiated through discourses that see the social in economic terms only, individualize responsibility, and which may thus form subjects that see all plight as individual fault—which delegitimizes protest.

Although we distinguish these *four* basic processes (and respective layers of analysis), our detailed discussion will be *bi*sected in accordance with the two focal points of Foucault's thinking:

- Section 1 focuses on the first three points mentioned above. It links the *communication of social movements* with the concept of discourse. For this purpose we borrow from earlier works by Foucault (1974, 2002).
- The subsequent Sect. 2 deals with the fourth point mentioned. It reflects on Foucault's work from the late seventies onwards and its lively reception over the past two decades under the heading "governmentality studies." Addressing the discursive formation of subjects, it gives insight into the *emergence, strength, or absence of protest*, thus providing a link between the macro and micro level.

1   Social Movements and Discourse

A constructivist approach is the basis of Foucault's oeuvre. He was interested in how knowledge is generated. Among his most basic questions were: What is considered "normal" and what is not? What can be thought of and communicated and what cannot? What (discursive) practices produce these restrictive as well as enabling structures? According to Foucault, modern societies create "regimes of truth": in particular times and spaces something is considered as true and this is the result of discourses—systems of ordered procedures for the production, regulation, distribution, circulation, and operation of statements. Every society thus has its own "police"—mechanisms that distinguish "true" from "false" statements (Foucault 1980, p. 38). Within this Foucauldian view, one specific locus for this "police" cannot be identified. Discursive formations concern *all* actors. They nevertheless result in some actors resonating better than others. In what follows, we argue that discourse should be considered an action guidance for social movements. Actors do not reflect on most of the aspects of the discourse guiding their action, and some things are beyond their imagination. To some extent, however, a movement can relate its framing to discourses in a rational way. This applies for aspects of the discourse that movement actors reflect upon. We refer to Foucault's (1974) "Archaeology of Knowledge" and a number of his ideas in "The Order of Things" (Foucault 2002) as useful for social movement scholars in specifying relations between movement communication and their framework conditions (including its effects on the actor) and thus in overcoming some of the shortcomings of research on social movements. We argue that Foucault helps specify the concepts of cultural/discursive opportunity structure or "discursive contexts" (Ullrich and Keller 2014) and provides strong arguments against the existing bias in social movement research that favors a rational actor concept (Ullrich et al. 2014, see also Schnabel and Roose in this volume).

1.1   Discursive Mechanisms

Foucault investigated long-term processes in the development of discursive structures in search of regularities that affect all statements in a discourse— discursive formations (Foucault 1974). Discursive formations break the concept of the discourse down into different aspects and thus draw our attention to aspects of the discourse that are often omitted in analyzing a social movement's context of action. In "The Archaeology of Knowledge" Foucault distinguishes four discursive formations that help us understand the power of discourse to create what we consider truth: the formation of (1) objects, (2) enunciative modalities, (3) concepts, and (4) strategies (Foucault 1974). "Objects" are what talking is about. The formation of objects describes rules for shaping objects, e.g. their initial creation, the authorities responsible for the objects and their relation to other authorities, their classification and their relation to other objects. "Unemployment" for example is an object that did not emerge in Germany until the late 19th century. It was simply not regarded as a problem until the beginning of industrialization and the population growth that led to an increased number of people without a job that created a need for political action. So there was a growing need for political measures dealing with unemployment. The definition of the "problem" is important, because the way the problem is treated differs according to the concepts of unemployment (e.g. foundation of workhouses or implementation of unconditional basic income). Thus who is regarded as unemployed and how to deal with unemployment have been very controversial and have changed over time and from area to area (Zimmermann 2006).

The "formation of enunciative modalities" refers either to the speakers or the arenas where discourse takes place or to the position of the subject. The status of speakers is particularly important, as it authorizes speakers to have their say in a specific way and determines the issues that can be raised. Discourse arenas and speakers' roles are closely connected. A hospital, for example, authorizes a doctor to speak about an illness in a specific way (Foucault 1974, pp. 50–55) and it has become a commonplace that the status of a professor enhances the impression of expertise. Thus far, these Foucauldian insights add nothing new to the field of social movement research (Ferree et al. 2002; Gerhards 1992, 1995), but Foucault's analysis of discourse goes beyond this observation. He also analyzed the "formation of concepts," which addresses the question of how statements are connected: their dependence on rhetorical schemata of combining statements, how things are ordered in other discursive fields, and the field of presence (all statements that have been made in the past) (Foucault 1974, pp. 56–63). It includes, for example, the dominant way of describing and specifying objects at a certain time and place. In recent years, to give an example, the unemployed were mainly discussed in terms of activation, and debates on the welfare state were dominated by economic rationality (Baumgarten 2010). This way of discussing the problem authorizes speakers to participate in the debates on unemployment who are experts in macro-economic conditions but not interested in the problems of the unemployed themselves (e.g. the employers organizations) (Lahusen and Baumgarten 2010).

The concept "formation of strategies" describes the mechanisms that connect the grand theories of a society. We can observe, for example, that many grand theories are today strongly influenced by the concept of the rational individual. The idea of divine providence instead has lost its importance in Western Europe. We thus find the concept of the rational individual not only in many scientific theories, resulting in a turn which excludes incompatible other models. It has also diffused to everyday knowledge. We thus consider discursive formations to be important factors within the episteme. Episteme are the historical a priori of discourse (including the grand theories), allowing for a certain structure of knowledge and basic modes of thinking in a certain epoch, e.g. the establishment of science over and against a pre-scientific level. They affect the thinking of subjects, but their impact does not have to be reflected on a conscious level (Foucault 1974, pp. 189–192). These concepts remind the social movement researcher of social movements' embeddedness in their time and culture. Some ideas of modern social movements where unthinkable in the past, as historical studies of social movements show.

Discursive formations delimit the totality of all possible statements—the archive (Foucault 1974). But there is room for maneuver within the limits set by discursive mechanisms. To capture how these mechanisms exert power, Foucault chooses a long-term perspective. For analytical reasons, he proposes to look for *points of diffraction of discourses, points of incompatibility,* and alternatives that are both equivalent and incompatible (Foucault 1974, p. 65). Diffractions point to societal change and alternatives to the dominant worldviews.[3]

1.2   Implications for Research on the Communication of Social Movements

The communication of social movements is predominantly examined by framing approaches. Such approaches have been developed to highlight the importance of interpretation processes (often in a strategic sense) within social movements to explain mobilization (Snow 2004, pp. 382–384; Snow and Benford 1988, p. 198). Framing processes are always situated in a specific context, which is specified in various ways. One crucial methodological question is how to connect the discourse level of context (macro) with the framing of social movements at the meso level (Sandberg 2006). In research on social movements the level that we call the

---

[3]In some cases social movements are able to alter what can be imagined: E.P. Thompson, for instance, although he did not work in a Foucauldian tradition, showed how the concept of the working class was created by the worker's movement. The idea of such a collective had not previously existed. It was spawned by the expression of common interests (Thompson 1968).

"discourse level" is usually taken into account as a cultural or discursive opportunity structure (both concepts derived from "political opportunity structures", McAdam 1994; Snow 2004, p. 403) or discursive context (Ullrich and Keller 2014).[4] Culture in framing research is conceptualized in various ways, but mostly not systematically specified (Hart 1996, p. 88; Swidler 1986; d'Anjou and van Male 1998; Benford and Snow 2000; McCammon et al. 2007; Ullrich et al. 2014). The concept of discursive opportunity structures builds on the concept of culture as a toolkit: opportunities for mobilization are seen as deriving from cultural factors, such as dominant values or ideological contradictions (McAdam 1994; Koopmans and Olzak 2004; Ferree et al. 2002; Roose 2014). Discursive or cultural opportunity structures function as incentives for, or restrictions on, choosing frames. Regrettably, the terms tend to be used as underspecified catch-all expressions and are thus not very useful.[5] Furthermore, the strong bias towards rational action inherent in this concept is criticized (Pettenkofer 2010, p. 48; Ullrich and Keller 2014). In what follows we take the concepts of discursive and cultural opportunity structures as a starting point and show how the study of social movement communication can be elaborated in Foucauldian terms.

(1) Foucault contributes to explaining why some frames are more resonant than others.

In order to be successful, most social movement researchers argue that a movement's framing has to be "culturally resonant," e.g. in correspondence to a "master frame" (Swart 1995, p. 466),[6] by addressing central values, or

---

[4]Following Ullrich and Keller (2014) we prefer the term "discursive context" over "opportunity structure," because the latter has a strong strategic bias and is mainly interested in analyzing movement success, while the former notion neutrally covers formative conditions in the discourse movements are embedded in and it allows us to ask all kinds of questions about movement culture, discourse and effects—outcomes and "success" only being two aspects among many.

[5]Approaches of this kind limit the context to some selected factors favorable to mobilization. Benford and Snow, for example, list the following aspects as important contextual factors for social movements: "counter framing by movements' opponents, bystanders, and the media; frame disputes within movements; and the dialectic between frames and events" (Benford and Snow 2000, p. 625). McCammon et al. (2007) speak about legal and traditional gendered discursive opportunity structures to describe aspects of the discursive opportunity structure that were important for the success of the US women's movement.

[6]Some researchers in the field of radical movements, however, stress that radical movements are successful because of their radicalism (Fitzgerald and Rodgers 2000). The degree of radicalism of action and rhetoric versus resonance necessary for success and the definition of success differ in the literature.

through the social position of its actors (Benford 1997, pp. 418ff.). The criteria for the selection of macro phenomena considered important for framing remain largely obscure (Pettenkofer 2010, pp. 71–74). In research practice, the connection between movements' strategies and discursive opportunity (or context) structure is drawn without specifying the broader range of possible structures. Framing processes are often investigated at the movement level and then placed in relation to selected macro level phenomena, solely relying on the plausibility of the established connection (Ferree et al. 2002; Gamson 1988; Gusfield 1996; Neidhardt 1994; Oliver and Johnston 2005; Snow 2008).[7] Foucault does not provide factors decisive for the cultural resonance of a movement. However, his analysis of the formation of concepts, the formation of strategies, and his concept of episteme, which we have described above, helps to specify the context that contributes to framing success, e.g. a specific structure of knowledge or specific ways of connecting statements, etc.

(2) The analysis of discursive opportunity structures can profit from Foucault by considering power relations and dispositives.
A thorough description of the discursive mechanisms for a given time and space is one possibility for embedding a social movement's framing in this specific context of action.[8] Although it is impossible to describe in detail social movement actors' room for maneuver, Foucault helps us to define some important structures that are usually left out of consideration. It contributes mainly to the question of legitimacy of a speaker's position and could thus be used in addition to other approaches structuring opportunity structures (e.g. Ferree et al. 2002). Taking Foucault's concept of discourse, context analysis in social movement research could be guided by the following questions: (1) what can be adequately stated, (2) by whom, (3) in what discursive arena, and (4) how. The communication of a social movement may influence and be influenced by all four aspects. Movements can, for example, shape an issue to fit the discourse, avoid aspects of an issue that have no chance of positive response, or provoke other actors by raising non-adequate issues. They can focus on their speaker position, for example by claiming

---

[7]In many empirical studies the framing as well as the context is restricted to the media discourse (Gusfield 1981; Gamson 1988; Gerhards 1992; Donati 1992).

[8]Discourse according to Foucault is a macrostructure in its own right. This contrasts with the concept of ideology, which is basically (though in a dialectic relationship) understood as an expression of an underlying (e.g. economic) structure, which it conceals or interprets from a particularistic perspective. Discourse does not conceal reality—it is reality.

expertise or by increasing their threat potential. They can adjust the framing of their claims with regard to the arena, e.g. a demonstration or a congress. They can choose the arenas for placing their claims but they are often also denied access. Thus using Foucault also helps to understand why movement actors are sometimes excluded from certain arenas. By specifying the context of framing this way, Foucauldian approaches help empirical research into framing across movements, time, and space (Marullo et al. 1996; Mooney and Hunt 1996; Ellingson 1995). Shifts and national differences can be observed in a more structured way with regard to the four aspects mentioned above (Baumgarten 2014). Integrating Foucault in the mainstream research on framing this way seems quite unproblematic. It is just a way to specify different aspects that determine success of a movement's communication efforts. The movement itself might even be conceptualized as a strategic actor if we use Foucault only with regard to the discursive opportunity structure this way. Following Foucault's concept of discourse, however, we should be aware of the shortcomings of such a strategic actor concept.

(3) The notion of episteme and Foucault's stress on structural elements point to the strong constraints on actors' freedom.

The framing approach has been criticized for not taking seriously enough the cultural constraints of movement framing, the influence of the context on the actors' worldviews, and the actors' interpretation of this context (Swidler 1986; Hart 1996; d'Anjou and van Male 1998; Crossley 2002, pp. 139–142; Ullrich et al. 2014). Owing to the strategic bias of most social movement research, movements' ideologies and framing are seen as outcome-oriented variables. As a result, cultural opportunities are mostly conceptualized as something interpreted and used strategically by a rational actor. This conception is criticized because actors cannot freely choose how they perceive the world (Steinberg 1999; Sandberg 2006; Ullrich and Keller 2014). In the light of this objection, it is worth asking what frames have a chance of being selected because of their cultural or discursive roots. This shifts attention to the conditions for forming movements' world views and not their success. Steinberg, for example, uses the concept "discursive fields" (Steinberg 1999: 748). He systematically contextualizes frames with reference to Foucault's ideas. His discursive fields are framework conditions comprising cultural factors and the actor constellation. Actors create and shape meaning within the boundaries of these framework conditions. Social movement actors also largely take for granted what can be adequately stated, by whom, in what discursive arena, and how.

Following Foucault we must also keep in mind that social movements are not only driven by the expected success of their claims. Social movements as a field with its own inner dynamics in producing world views has largely been neglected (see Kern in this volume for a different approach on this subject). Such a movement is nevertheless also a knowledge system based on specific societal conditions that emerge from and develop during discussion of contested issues (Spillmann 1995, p. 139; Wuthnow 1989, p. 13). With reference to Foucauldian concepts, Ullrich (2008, 2013) shows how different discursive opportunity structures in Germany and Great Britain led to different frames regarding the Israeli–Palestinian conflict. These frames—far from being strategically adapted to the movements' aims—are highly disputed and contradictory within the German left (as is the mainstream discourse due to its interconnectedness with the discourse on the German past) while there is relative unanimity within the British left, where no other discourse causes ruptures. Foucault thus directs our attention to internal processes of movement communication that follow from their society's discursive structure.

The following chapter deals with another aspect of social movement research, namely changes in the mobilizing potential of a movement due to changes in discourse. There is no smooth linearity in Foucault's thinking between the concepts dealt with in the next section and this section. The two chapters belong to two different phases of his work, which he has not connected explicitly. There is some continuity, however, due to the notion of productive power and there are further arguments against the strategic bias. We argue that research can gain new insights and ask new questions with the aid of Foucauldian approaches that show how protest movements are embedded in societies' episteme owing to subjectification of their constituents under given circumstances. Thus, with Foucault, we propose a specific link between the micro and macro levels of the social, or between structure and subjectivity.

2   Governmentality and Subjectivity, or: Why (not) Protest?

Among the most thriving fields of research heavily influenced by Michel Foucault apart from discourse analysis there are the so-called governmentality studies with their concern for the *strategies, techniques, programs, and rationalities of government and the respective subject positions.*[9] It is surprising that governmentality studies have not yet had much impact on theorizing social movements and protest.[10] The popularity of governmentality as a part of the "Foucault industry" has hardly been reflected in mainstream movement and protest research. The occasional mention of the term governmentality in protest-related literature mostly refers to a very general idea without elaborating the concept's specific implications. Yet the governmentality perspective helps us to see the strong interconnectedness of movements and power. Consequently it facilitates overcoming the presupposition implicit in the mainstream literature on protest and social movements that the contester and the contested in the field of protest be separated as two distinct or antagonistic social entities. In this we rely upon the notion presented above that the discursive structures of a society have a strong impact on social movements.

Studies in modern governmentality are strongly interested in programs promoting subtle techniques of government. They recently note the growing importance of self-governing in modern neo-liberal, advanced-liberal (Rose 1996), or neo-social (Lessenich 2008) societies, which most likely affects grievances, critique, and mobilization.[11] In the following sub-section we discuss the concept of governmentality from its origins in Foucault's notion of panoptism to the lively post-Foucauldian debate on the subjectifying processes of "governing the self". The subsequent section analyses implications for protest research, especially the potential of neo-social subjectification processes for hindering protest. We especially posit that specific modes of subjectification may infringe upon the likelihood of protest by creating subjects trained to attribute the causes of problems to the individual rather than to society. These subjects thus tend to forego social critique and making demands on society.[12]

---

[9]It is important to note that Foucault's analyses concentrated on the governing aspects, while the (post-)Foucauldian governmentality studies increasingly valued the subjectivity aspects, which were part of Foucault's thinking, but not so much of his thorough analysis.

[10]Cf. Rose et al. (2006, p. 100); for the few exceptions see the reader by Heßdörfer et al. (2010; especially Ullrich (2010), where the perspective presented here was outlined for the first time) and Death (2010).

[11]To mark the difference from the classic neo-liberalism of the Chicago school and to make clear that the societal changes observed are not a withdrawal of the (welfare) state but an enormous restructuring of state activities, we follow Lessenich's (2008) recommendation for calling this "neo-social", although "neo-liberal" is a common attribute in this discourse.

[12]We will not focus on governmentality within movements. In our view this runs the risk of overstretching the meaning of the term and weakening its inherent relation to government.

2.1 Governmentality and Subjectivity: Two Key Concepts

The concept of governmentality should be traced back to Foucault's (1979) groundbreaking work "Discipline and Punish." In this book he describes the panoptic principle of the unequal distribution of seeing and being seen as a core mechanism by which modern societies provide discipline. As prototypical for this he considers Jeremy Bentham's *Panopticon*, an architectural solution for optimizing surveillance. The disciplining effects of the tower-like structure, designed for prisons as well as factories, hospitals, or schools, stems from its regime of visibility. The prisoners under surveillance are situated in cells located in a circle around a tower in the building's center. While prisoners are unable to look into the tower, the surveillant situated there is able to look into the cells. In such a setting round-the-clock surveillance is not necessary to establish discipline, Foucault argues, because of the implicit uncertainty of the object of surveillance whether it is momentarily under surveillance. It is this uncertainty that makes inmates reflect on the potential costs of misbehavior, leading to the slow incorporation of the surveillant's gaze and thus discipline.

Although Foucault is preoccupied in this book predominantly with understanding discipline in the modernizing societies of the 18th and 19th centuries, he also provides the conceptual basis for more recent forms of (self-)control to which he later turns his attention. The Panopticon produces a somewhat active, reflexive subject that functions properly. (Reflexive) panoptic discipline needs to be distinguished from the older sovereign power as well as from discipline achieved by direct force or threat. In a way, what later became governmentality studies—with its broad concept of government analyzing the "linkages between abstract political rationalities and empirical micro-techniques of everyday life"[13] (Lemke 2000, p. 31)—examines the generalization of this principle (to govern the people with their taking an active role in it) in modern societies.[14] This important role of the governed individuals' reflexivity and incorporation of the social is described by the term subjectivity—the second central concept of governmentality studies and

---

[13]Own translation (PU).

[14]Governmentality studies' scope of interest reaches much farther back in history. Foucault analyzed political thought from ancient times and government back to feudal regimes to specify its modern form. Within this field he was particularly interested in the development of liberalism, the development of the policy, the emergence of the reason of state and the newly discovered problem of population. Here we rely more on the post-Foucauldian shape that governmentality studies took from the early nineties, focusing on techniques of governing at a distance and governing the self (Rose et al. 2006, p. 89).

the other side of government. Foucault argues against the older philosophical discourse on subjects that there is no substance or universal form of the subject which, on the contrary, has to be conceived as historically contingent. It is the practices of an epoch that make the specific subject type.

For Foucault, subjectification is always subjection, too. His research hence concentrated on the power relations in which the subject's body and soul are formed (Foucault 1998).[15] For governmentality studies it is central to explore the forms of subjectivity that are produced in accordance with changing forms of power regulation, whether these subjectivities are conventional and conformist, resistant, or perhaps hybrid in this respect. And this is where social movement and protest research comes in. The governmentality studies' concept of subjectivity provides a micro–macro link between social structure and/or change on the one hand and motivation to protest—or not—on the other.

There is a lively scientific discourse on *current modes of government* among scholars strongly affected by Foucauldian thinking, which is relevant for protest research. Following Foucault's analysis of the rise of neo-liberalism, much effort was invested in analyzing government of contemporary Western societies, which are characterized by the ever-increasing commodification of the social,[16] the retreat of the welfare state from formerly guaranteed social spending, obeisance to the free market, and orientation on the principles of activation, responsibilization, auton-omy, and (self-)management, thus tapering developments Foucault had already observed.

Current processes of subjectification can no longer be completely explained by the panoptic model, because it represents a relatively fixed arrangement. Subjec-tification today corresponds to a more subtle, more incoherent, more complex, more infinite, indeed more productive type of government and regime of visibility. Neo-social governmentality creates subjects that consider themselves managers of their market performance or, as Bröckling put it, enterprising selves (Bröckling 2005). On the state level, the transformations observed signify changes *within* welfare states, changing their character fundamentally. The character of state intervention changed from a mode of guaranteed provision oriented on solidarity to intervention focusing on activating citizens to feel responsible for their own well-being, and incorporating mid-level regulators as relatively autonomous agents

---

[15]For a detailed elaboration of Foucault's subject theory see Foucault (1982), Paulus (2009), and Lembke (2005).

[16]Foucault describes this liberal rationality as "the inversion of the relationships of the social to the economic" (Foucault 2008, p. 240).

(though still also acting in heteronomy, because they are governed "at a distance" (Miller and Rose 1990, p. 9).

Many current governmental measures are inherently ambiguous, comprising both choice and force.[17] For this reason such modes of government have been described as "governing through freedom" (Rose 1996). Subjects are free to take decisions (and bear the consequences) and are sometimes even left in relative uncertainty about the demands of power (cf. Heßdörfer and Bachmann 2009), which again aims to make subjects think and act on their own—enabled by a higher level of reasoning, the incorporation of the demands of power and the obligation to be free (Rose et al. 2006, p. 89). These logics of governing through self-government are exactly what much of governmentality studies is concerned with. For protest research, this basically poses the question of how much of the power side (in the traditional "power vs. contester" view) is to be found on the side of movements and activists themselves.

2.2 Implications for Protest Research

If such specific neo-social subjectification forms exist as a reflection of specific forms of current governmentality, it is necessary to investigate their implications for protest. Drawing on the rich work outlined in Sect. 2.1, protest research will find many aspects likely to affect protest. The task is to link the observed forms of governmentality, related subjectivity or their development, enforcement, and change with protest motivation, behavior, likelihood, and success.

In a certain manner, the new perspective we would like to suggest here ties in with older currents in social movement research. Despite tremendous theoretical disparities scholars often focused on macro societal conditions to explain protest, notably its emergence. This holds true for analysis of movements as phenomena of mass societies, the break-down model, structural functionalist, Marxist and collective behavior approaches. They all emphasized the current social structure or social change as causes for the existence of social movements, which was often

---

[17]Typical examples are the British and German unemployment regulation and healthcare reforms following the activating "rights and responsibilities" paradigm of the Blair/Schröder Manifesto of 1999. Many measures contain disciplinary measures (= negative incentives): cuts and restrictions of services in general and all the more in the case of non-compliance, as well as extensive control mechanisms on the one hand, and activating strategies like rewards for good behavior (= positive incentives), expanding rights of information access, co-determination, further education, training programs, etc. on the other.

seen as grounded in social grievances, dissatisfaction, or anomie (Buechler 2004). The New Social Movement (NSM) debate (esp. Tourraine, cf. Buechler 1999; Roth and Rucht 1987) was particularly interested in the subjectivity of (potential) protesters. This debate was constituted by the emergence of movements that made their subjectivity the reason per se for protest and that seem to have come into being in reaction to cultural conflicts in (post-)industrial societies. This focus on subjectivity as a way to perceive and handle structural change, hence a way to link structure and agency, provides a link to the governmentality approach.

However, governmentality studies draw our attention to different questions. They highlight specific aspects of the structural context of a social movement and not only help find answers to why protest developed but may also help us understand why protest is weak or even absent.

It seems obvious that current societal transformations give rise to much discontent, especially in global justice movements or the anti-austerity movements, protesting against privatization and cuts in the welfare state. And there have been eruptions of protest when aspects of neo-social reforms have lacked public legitimacy. In Germany, for instance, a wave of protest emerged in 2004 against new unemployment legislation that suddenly imposed severe cuts and accelerated the regime of control and activation (Lahusen and Baumgarten 2010). On the other hand, the protest quickly ebbed. Are the causes also to be found in the social conditions against which protest was directed? Can governmentality studies help understand this?

To begin with, our proposal to link governmentality studies with protest research opens up a perspective for examining social movements together with conditions for protest. Yet, several kinds of relations are conceivable between neo-social government of the self and the field of protest, yielding various and even opposing effects.

(1) *Neo-social governmentality infringes on the likelihood of protest by under-mining one of its elementary preconditions: the existence and legitimacy of social critique* (Boltanski and Chiapello 2001) *and the legitimacy of addressing it vis-à-vis society.*

Neo-socially activated subjects who see all their conduct as an investment in their future performance may prefer the economic question whether their wishes are affordable or realizable to whether they are worth pursuing. The question required to generate protest of "what is wrong in society" may to some extent have been replaced by the question "what have I done wrong". Heteronomous and often excessive demands for prevention and activation may be internalized and taken personally by people who are exposed to a discourse that stresses the need of individual effort. Workfare, activation programs, fitness training, healthy food, lifelong learning, active ageing, etc., illustrate this shift. Crucially, little of this is perceived as imposed upon actors, because it is presented as being in their own interest, as an investment in the personal self.[18] Protest and critique, in the Foucauldian sense of affirming negation (Pickett 1996, p. 451), would have to transcend this economic framework that is the underlying principle of modern governmentality. Yet, the specificities of the liberal, and even more so the neo-social relationship between government and the governed, make this difficult.

(2) *Neo-social governmentality might be a source of dissatisfaction and low-level forms of protest.*
    Never-ending demands for prevention, activation, and responsibilization may also breed protest if these demands are perceived as excessive. But the high degree of control and self-control as well as the individualization associated with precarious work and living conditions give such protest a specific form. These multiple reactions, more likely situated on the sub-movement level, have been analyzed under the Foucauldian term counter-conduct (Hechler and Philipps 2008; Kastner 2008). They may be resistant or even just hesitant behavior. Philipps (2008) reports such tactics by people obliged to work in workfare programs. For example, they worked extremely slowly or did not dress properly (they were not provided with work wear) and thus could avoid outdoor work in bad weather. Counter-conduct is the resistant behavior that appears on the borders of the governed space. It is the form of protest still possible despite the regime of control.

(3) *Protest can even be a source of and support for neo-social transformations.*
    Boltanski and Chiapello (2001) showed the share autonomist "artistic" critique of the protest movements had since the seventies in the precarization of working conditions through the production of an individualizing "freedom discourse" that was taken up by the managerial discourse and helped in delegitimizing social critique.[19] Especially sobriety and healthy living

---

[18]See, for example, Ullrich (2010) for a more detailed account of the subjectification effects of medical preventionism or Bröckling (2003) on contemporary feedback techniques and how these discourses undermine social critique. See Bröckling (2005) for the general perspective of the enterprising self.

[19]Though from a different theoretical background than Foucault, Boltanski, and Chiapello share a common interest in the question why people find the state of modern capitalist society legitimate or even desirable (Boltanski and Chiapello 2001, pp. 462, 463; Lorey 2006; Kastner 2008, p. 50).

movements come into one's mind as an example (although they may have more characteristics of lifestyles than of movements). Community policing and vigilante groups such as the self-organized anti-immigration Minuteman border patrols may be another expression of such neo-social governmental-ization from below (Walsh 2008). This perspective raises the question of the presuppositions of society and those who do (not) protest to change it. "Prevention", for example, is one of the most salient facets of neo-social governmentality and decisive for its subjectifying powers (Ullrich 2010). Yet, social movements—at least those not primarily aiming to redistribute material goods or life chances, like the environmental and the peace movements—often use the same (preventive) rhetoric. They are thus clearly designated as sharing that episteme of their context society and reiterate or even strengthen it.

All three aspects need further theoretical and empirical elaboration. There are protest-theorizing approaches with which they can be linked. This applies espe-cially for the "discursive" or "cultural opportunity structure", which take into consideration the impact of deeply rooted cultural patterns on protest and their change over time (Ullrich 2008). Although he does not mention the term gov-ernmentality, Goldberg (2001) gives us ideas about how to link questions of governmentality with protest through opportunity structures. In his case, neo-social subjectification caused empowering group coherence and had an impact on the perception of workers' rights. Goldberg investigated the regulation of unemploy-ment in New York, which had shifted from welfare to workfare. The older welfare system had been based on the distinction between workers and welfare recipients. The transformation challenged this common distinction because of the growing dependence of the city on "non-workers" and because of a change in their self-perception. Although workfare staff were poorly paid and equipped in com-parison with normal workers, their fields of operation have tended to converge, enhancing the self-esteem of workfare staff. They have hence increasingly felt legitimized to organize in their interest. This example shows that neo-social governmentality (of which workfare is a central feature) does not necessarily only hinder protest. It depends on concrete conditions whether protest is caused or hindered. But it is obvious how important a role legitimacy plays for organizing protest and it is highly probable that changes in governmentality can have a sig-nificant effect on the perceived legitimacy of protest.

It seems practical and fruitful to investigate the emergence and non-emergence of protest under neo-social governmentality in limited spaces as demonstrated by

Goldberg (2001).[20] But it is much more challenging to investigate the general macro-level hypothesis of neo-social governmentality as a condition for hindering protest by undermining the legitimacy of social critique.[21]

One empirical problem of such a macro perspective is the isolation of neo-social governmentality as a cause within the variety of social developments. This holds especially true due to the structural ambivalence of these changes composed of liberation and discipline. The continuous uncertainty of governmental demands also makes uniform reactions in the field of protest unlikely. So this question is more of the nature of a theoretically inspired perspective to be applied in a variety of research designs. Within its scope, research on the individual level of activists and non-activists is necessary. Researchers would have to explore to what extent the subjectivities promoted by neo-social governmentality (to be measured through internalized values) correlate with sympathy for and the disposition to protest. Discourse-oriented or reconstructive designs also come into question, investigating changes in movement discourse in the way that Boltanski and Chiapello (2001) have examined modes of critique in management literature. It has to be investigated whether social critique is losing ground compared with individualized artistic critique, as was shown for specific social movements (cf. Neumann 2008 for an account of the alternative economy movement). Elements of neo-social governmentality (and resistance to it) can be traced within movement discourse, while the timing and conditions of their appearance need to be scrutinized. Another approach would be to organize interviews or group discussions with activists to reconstruct changes in their activist lives that reflect governmental subjectivities and the changing (self-)perception of protest legitimacy. New fields of research or at least different perspectives on existing ones come into focus. Of special interest seem to be subjectification processes in confrontation with surveillance, taming, delegitimization, and repression (see for example Boyle 2010; Leach and Haunss 2010; Ullrich and Wollinger 2011). New control technologies, such as video surveillance of demonstrations, bureaucratization of the right of assembly, spatial policing strategies, data retention, mobile phone tracking, anti-terror lists, and many more have to be explored in this fashion. With Foucault and his disciples, society can be brought back into social movement research, and this can be achieved in a manner

---

[20]The same applies for Tullney's (2010) analysis of the individualizing and protest-hindering effects of workplace surveillance.

[21]Such a hypothesis turns our attention to a possible counter-development to Rucht's and Neidhardt's (2002) analysis of the "movement society." While they have strong conceptual and empirical evidence that social movement activities are structurally stabilized on a high level, tendencies that may weaken movements must be taken into consideration, too.

that links macro phenomena with subjects on the micro level and addresses the effects on the meso (movement) level.

3   Conclusion

Social movement research and especially discursive opportunity structure approaches can profit from reading Foucault. Foucault's concepts help to specify the context of framing processes and remind us to analyze social movement outcomes in a more long-term perspective. Foucault should be interpreted as a warning to not rely too heavily on the idea of a rational actor with a high degree of freedom to act. Besides strategically influencing discourse, contentious subjects are always influenced by governmental rationalities and the discourses themselves. Thus they cannot freely use discourse as a toolkit. As outlined in this text, Foucault observed that knowledge is always structured by power relations and that the scope of what can be imagined is limited. Social movement actors are embedded in these structures, which enable but also restrict their claims. We can think about such processes of restriction/enablement within the rational paradigm: movement actors shape their claims with an eye on discursive mechanisms: for example placing the right claim in the right arena and trying to positively influence the movement actors' speaker position. But Foucault particularly points to processes that cannot be explained by a rational actor model. Discourse also restricts/enables a movement's possible claims and frames: claims and frames outside the room for maneuver are not thought about at all by movement actors. These claims and frames may have been excluded by the movement's internal communicative practices or by the discursive structures in which the movement is embedded.

Governmentality studies are especially helpful in investigating the relation between discourse/societal practices and the formation of subjects and thus the very conditions for the possibility of protest. Currently, society can be conceptualized as being shaped by an economic rationality producing "enterprising selves." Depending on the specific context, these new ways of governing the self can either prevent the subject from mobilizing or cause changing protest behavior.

There is indeed much more to say about Foucault, social movements and protest than the scope of this article allows. This is partly because Foucault was not only a theorist but also an upright political activist. And although he did indeed spend much more time writing about power, resistance in various forms was always among his concerns. Even more, it was an object of his embrace (Pickett 1996). The various forms of resistance he contemplated (spirituality, contestation, transgression, revolution, resistance, counter-conduct, etc.) have been inspiring for movements themselves and political philosophy. This has led some scholars to analyze the "boundaries of power" (Hechler and Philipps 2008) on the basis of Foucauldian concepts, as well as the more subtle forms of contestation or "counter-conduct" they enable on the fringes, despite the mutually constitutive relationship of power and resistance (Death 2010). Our examples have permitted us to show that, by drawing on Foucault, research on social movements can gain new perspectives worth exploring, while certain approaches to social movements need to be reassessed and more Foucauldian perspectives for social movement research can be developed in the future.

References

Baumgarten, Britta. 2010. *Interessenvertretung aus dem Abseits. Erwerbsloseninitiativen im Diskurs über Arbeitslosigkeit*. Frankfurt/New York: Campus.

Baumgarten, Britta. 2014. Culture and activism across borders. In *Conceptualising culture in social movement research*, ed. Britta Baumgarten, Priska Daphi, and Peter Ullrich, 91–112. Basingstoke: Palgrave Macmillan.

Benford, Robert D. 1997. An insider's critique of the social movement framing perspective. *Sociological Inquiry* 67(4): 409–430.

Benford, Robert D., and David A. Snow. 2000. Framing processes and social movements: An overview and assessment. *Annual Review of Sociology* 26(1): 611–639.

Boltanski, Luc, and Eve Chiapello. 2001. Die Rolle der Kritik in der Dynamik des Kapitalismus und der normative Wandel. *Berliner Journal für Soziologie* 11(4): 459–477.

Boyle, M.S. 2010. The criminalization of dissent. Protest violence, activist performance, and the curious case of the VolxTheaterKarawane in Genoa. In *Prevent and tame. Protest under (self-)control*, ed. Florian Heßdörfer, Andrea Pabst, and Peter Ullrich, 55–72. Berlin: Dietz.

Bröckling, Ulrich. 2003. Das demokratisierte Panopticon. Subjektivierung und Kontrolle im 360°-Feedback. In *Michel Foucault. Zwischenbilanz einer Rezeption. Frankfurter Foucault-Konferenz 2001*, ed. Axel Honneth, and Martin Saar, 77–93. Frankfurt/New York: Campus.

Bröckling, Ulrich. 2005. Gendering the enterprising self. Subjectification programs and gender Differences in guides to success. *Distinktion. Scandinavian Journal for Social Theory* 11(2): 7–25.

Buechler, Steven M. 1999. *Social movements in advanced capitalism*. The Political Economy and Cultural Construction of Social Activism. Oxford: Oxford University Press.

Buechler, Steven M. 2004. The strange career of strain and breakdown theories of collective action. In *The Blackwell Companion to social movements*, ed. D.A. Snow, Sarah Anne Soule, and Hanspeter Kriesi, 47–66. Malden: Blackwell.

Butler, Judith. 1993. *Bodies that matter: On the discursive limits of "sex"*. London: Routledge.

Crossley, Nick. 2002. *Making sense of social movements*. Buckingham: Open University Press.

d'Anjou, Leo, and John van Male. 1998. Between old and new. Social Movements and Cultural Change. *Mobilization* 3(2): 207–226.

Death, Carl. 2010. Counter-conducts. A foucauldian analytics of protest. *Social Movement Studies: Journal of Social, Cultural and Political Protest* 9(3): 235–251.

Donati, Paolo. 1992. Political discourse analysis. In *Studying collective action*, ed. M. Diani, and R. Eyermann, 136–167. London: Sage.

Ellingson, Stephen. 1995. Understanding the dialectic of discourse and collective action— Public debate and rioting in Antebellum Cincinnati. *American Journal of Sociology* 101(1): 100–144.

Ferree, Myra Marx, W.A. Gamson, J. Gerhards, and Dieter Rucht. 2002. *Shaping abortion discourse. Democracy and the public sphere in Germany and the United States*. Cambridge: Cambridge University Press.

Fitzgerald, Kathleen, and Diane Rodgers. 2000. Radical social movement organizations: A theoretical model. *The Sociological Quarterly* 41(4): 573–592.

Foucault, Michel. 1974. *The archaeology of knowledge*. London: Tavistock Publications.

Foucault, Michel. 1979. *Discipline and punish. The birth of the prison*. New York: Vintage Books.

Foucault, Michel. 1980. *Power/Knowledge: Selected interviews and other writings, 1972–1977*. NY: Pantheon.

Foucault, Michel. 1982. The subject and power. *Critical Inquiry* 8(4): 777–795.

Foucault, Michel. 1998. *The history of sexuality Vol. 1: The will to knowledge*. London: Penguin.

Foucault, Michel. 2002. *The order of things. An archaeology of the human sciences*. London: Routledge.

Foucault, Michel. 2008. *The birth of biopolitics. Lectures at the Collège de France, 1978–79*, ed. Michael Sennellart. New York: Palgrave Macmillan.

Gamson, William. 1988. Political discourse and collective action. In *From structure to action: Comparing social movement research across cultures. International social movement research*, ed. Bert Klandermans, Hanspeter Kriesi, and Sidney Tarrow, 219–244. London: JAI Press.

Gerhards, Jürgen. 1992. Dimensionen und Strategien öffentlicher Diskurse. *Journal für Sozialforschung* 32(3/4): 307–318.

Gerhards, Jürgen. 1995. Framing dimensions and framing strategies: Contrasting ideal- and real-type frames. *Social Science Information* 34(2): 225–248.

Goldberg, Chad Allan. 2001. Welfare recipients or workers? Contesting the workfare State in New York City. *Social Theory* 19(2): 187–218.

Gusfield, Joseph. 1981. *The culture of public problems. Drinking-driving and the symbolic order*. Chicago: The University of Chicago Press.

Gusfield, Joseph. 1996. *Contested meanings. The construction of alcohol problems*. Wisconsin: The University of Wisconsin Press.

Hart, Stephen. 1996. The cultural dimension of social movements. A theoretical reassessment and literature review. *Sociology of Religion* 57(1): 87–100.

Hechler, Daniel, Axel Philipps, et al. 2008. *Widerstand denken. Michel Foucault und die Grenzen der Macht.* Bielefeld: transcript.

Heßdörfer, Florian, and Jan Bachmann. 2009. ASBO. Die Gesellschaft existiert. In *Kontrollverluste. Interventionen gegen Überwachung,* ed. Leipziger Kamera, 168–173. Münster: Unrast.

Heßdörfer, Florian, Andrea Pabst, and Peter Ullrich (eds.). 2010. *Prevent and tame. Protest under (self-)control.* Berlin: Dietz.

Kastner, Jens. 2008. Was heißt Gegenverhalten im Neoliberalismus? In *Widerstand denken. Michel Foucault und die Grenzen der Macht,* ed. Daniel Hechler, and Axel Philipps, 39–56. Bielefeld: transcript.

Koopmans, Ruud, and Susan Olzak. 2004. Discursive opportunities and the evolution of Right-Wing violence in Germany. *American Journal of Sociology* 110(2): 198–230.

Lahusen, Christian, and Britta Baumgarten. 2010. *Das Ende des sozialen Friedens? Politik und Protest in Zeiten der Hartz-Reformen.* Frankfurt/New York: Campus.

Leach, Darcy K., and Sebastian Haunss. 2010. "Wichtig ist der Widerstand". Rituals of taming and tolerance in movement responses to the violence question. In *Prevent and tame. Protest under (self-)control,* ed. Florian Heßdörfer, Andrea Pabst, and Peter Ullrich, 73–98. Berlin: Dietz.

Lembke, Robert. 2005. Der Mensch als Untertan. Zum Begriff der Subjektivierung bei Michel Foucault. Tabula Rasa. *Jenenser Zeitschrift für kritisches Denken,* No. 23, Oktober 2005. http://www.tabvlarasa.de/23/lembke.php. Accessed 5 Oct 2015.

Lemke, Thomas. 2000. Die Regierung der Risiken. Von der Eugenik zur genetischen Gouvernementalität. In *Gouvernementalität der Gegenwart. Studien zur Ökonomisierung des Sozialen,* ed. Ulrich Bröckling, Susanne Krasmann, and Thomas Lemke, 227–264. Frankfurt: Suhrkamp.

Lessenich, Stephan. 2008. *Die Neuerfindung des Sozialen.* Bielefeld: transcript.

Lorey, Isabell. 2006. Gouvernementalität und Selbst-Prekarisierung. http://transform.eipcp.net/transversal/1106/lorey/de#redir. Accessed 5 Oct 2015.

Marullo, Sam, Ron Pagnucco, and Jackie Smith. 1996. Frame changes and social movement contradiction. U.S. Peace movement framing after the Cold War. *Sociological Inquiry* 66(1): 1–28.

McAdam, Doug. 1994. Culture and social movements. In *New social movements. From ideology to identity,* ed. Enrique Laraña, Hank Johnston, and John Gusfield, 36–57. Philadelphia: Temple University Press.

McCammon, Holly, Courtney S. Muse, Harmony Newman, and Teresa Terrell. 2007. Movement framing and discourse opportunity structures. The political successes of the U.S. women's jury movements. *American Sociological Review* 72(5): 725–749.

Miller, Peter, and Nikolas Rose. 1990. Governing economic life. *Economy and Society* 19(1): 1–31. doi:10.1080/03085149000000001.

Mooney, Patrick H., and Scott A. Hunt. 1996. A repertoire of interpretations: Master frames and ideological continuity in US agrarian mobilization. *The Sociological Quarterly* 37(1): 177–197.

Neidhardt, Friedhelm (ed.). 1994. *Öffentlichkeit, öffentliche Meinung, soziale Bewegungen, Sonderheft 34 der Kölner Zeitschrift für Soziologie und Sozialpsychologie.* Opladen: Westdeutscher Verlag.

Neumann, Arndt. 2008. *Kleine geile Firmen. Alternativprojekte zwischen Revolte und Management.* Hamburg: Edition Nautilus.

Offen, Karen. 2000. *European feminisms 1700–1950.* Stanford: Stanford University Press.

Oliver, Pamela, and Hank Johnston. 2005. What a good Idea! Ideologies and frames in social movement research. In *Frames of protest. Social movements and the framing perspective*, ed. Hank Johnston, and J.A. Noakes, 185–204. Boston, Lanham: Rowman and Littlefield.

Paulus, Markus. 2009. Die Stellung des Subjekts bei Foucault und Habermas. *Tabula Rasa. Jenenser Zeitschrift für kritisches Denken*, 38, Oktober 2009. http://www.tabvlarasa.de/38/Paulus.php. Accessed 29 Dec 2009.

Pettenkofer, Andreas. 2010. *Radikaler Protest Zur soziologischen Theorie politischer Bewegungen.* Frankfurt/New York: Campus.

Philipps, Axel. 2008. Proteste und Resitenzen der Erwerbslosen. In *Widerstand denken. Michel Foucault und die Grenzen der Macht*, ed. Daniel Hechler, and Axel Philipps, 261–275. Bielefeld: transcript.

Pickett, Brent L. 1996. Foucault and the politics of resistance. *Polity* 28(4): 445–466.

Raschke, Joachim. 1991. Zum Begriff der sozialen Bewegung. In *Neue soziale Bewegungen in der Bundesrepublik Deutschland*, ed. Roland Roth, and Dieter Rucht, 31–39. Frankfurt: Campus.

Roose, Jochen. 2014. Culture and movement strength from a quantitative perspective. A partial theory. In *Conceptualizing culture in social movement research*, ed. Britta Baumgarten, Priska Daphi, and Peter Ullrich, 140–161. London: Palgrave/Macmillan.

Rose, Nikolas. 1996. Governing "advanced" liberal democracies. In *Foucault and political reason*, ed. Andrew Barry, Thomas Osborne, and Nikolas Rose, 37–64. Chicago/London: UCL Press.

Rose, Nikolas, Pat O'Malley, and Mariana Valverde. 2006. Governmentality. *Annual Review of Law and Social Science* 2(1): 83–104. doi:10.1146/annurev.lawsocsci.2.081805.105900.

Roth, Roland, and Dieter Rucht (eds.). 1987. *Neue Soziale Bewegungen in der Bundesrepublik Deutschland.* Frankfurt: Campus.

Rucht, Dieter, and Friedhelm Neidhardt. 2002. Towards a 'movement society'? On the possibilities of institutionalizing social movements. *Social Movement Studies* 1(1): 7–30.

Sandberg, Sveinung. 2006. Fighting Neo-liberalism with Neo-liberal discourse: ATTAC. *Social Movement Studies* 5(3): 209–228.

Snow, David A. 2004. Framing processes, ideology and discursive fields. In *The Blackwell Companion to social movements*, ed. David A. Snow, Sarah A. Soule, and Hanspeter Kriesi, 380–412. Malden: Blackwell.

Snow, David A. 2008. Elaborating the discursive contexts of framing. Discursive fields and spaces. *Studies in Symbolic Interaction* 30: 3–28.

Snow, David A., and Robert Benford. 1988. Ideology, frame resonance, and participant mobilization. In *From structure to action: Comparing social movement research across cultures. International social movement research*, ed. Bert Klandermans, Hanspeter Kriesi, and Sidney Tarrow, 197–217. London: JAI Press.

Snow, David A., Peter B. Owens, and Anna E. Tan. 2014. Libraries, social movements, and cultural change. Toward an alternative conceptualization of culture. *Social Currents* 1(1): 35–43.

Spillmann, Lynn. 1995. Culture, social structures, and discursive fields. *Current Perspectives in Social Theory* 15(1): 129–154.

Steinberg, Marc. 1999. The talk and back talk of collective action: A dialogic analysis of repertoires of discourse among nineteenth-century English cotton spinners. *American Journal of Sociology* 105(3): 736–780.

Swart, William J. 1995. The league of nations and the Irish question. Master frames, cycles of protest, and 'master frame alignment'. *Sociological Quarterly* 36(3): 465–481.

Swidler, Ann. 1986. Culture in action: Symbols and strategies. *American Sociological Review* 51(2): 273–286.

Thompson, Edward P. 1968. *The making of the English working class*. Toronto: Pelican Books.

Tullney, Marco. 2010. Organizing employees under surveillance. My Boss is spying on me, so I better keep my mouth shut. In *Prevent and tame. Protest under (self-)control, RLS Manuskripte*, ed. Florian Heßdörfer, Andrea Pabst, and Peter Ullrich, 35–48. Berlin: Dietz.

Ullrich, Peter. 2008. *Die Linke, Israel und Palästina. Nahostdiskurse in Großbritannien und Deutschland*. Berlin: Dietz.

Ullrich, Peter. 2010. Preventionism and obstacles for protest in Neoliberalism. Linking governmentality studies and protest research. In *Prevent and tame. Protest under (self-)control*, ed. Florian Heßdörfer, Andrea Pabst, and Peter Ullrich, 14–23. Berlin: Dietz.

Ullrich, Peter. 2013. Kulturvergleich, diskursive Gelegenheitsstrukturen und linke Nahostdiskurse. Entwurf einer wissenssoziologischen und diskurstheoretischen Perspektive für die Protestforschung. In *Wissenssoziologische Diskursanalyse: Exemplarische Anwendungen Band. 1*, ed. Reiner Keller, and Inga Truschkat, 315–337. Wiesbaden: VS Verlag.

Ullrich, Peter, and Gina R. Wollinger. 2011. A Surveillance Studies Perspective on Protest Policing. The case of video surveillance of demonstrations in Germany. *Interface. A journal for and about social movements* 3(1): 12–38.

Ullrich, Peter, Priska Daphi, and Britta Baumgarten. 2014. Protest and culture: Concepts and approaches in social movement research. An introduction. In *Conceptualizing culture in social movement research*, ed. Britta Baumgarten, Priska Daphi, and Peter Ullrich, 1–20. Basingstoke: Palgrave Macmillan.

Ullrich, Peter, and Reiner Keller. 2014. Comparing discourse between cultures. A discursive approach to movement knowledge. In *Conceptualizing culture in social movement research*, ed. Britta Baumgarten, Priska Daphi, and Peter Ullrich, 113–139. Basingstoke: Palgrave Macmillan.

Walsh, James. 2008. Community, surveillance and border control. The case of the Minuteman project. In *Surveillance and Governance: Crime control and beyond*, ed. Mathieu Deflem, and J.T. Ulmer, 11–34. Bingley: Emerald Group.

Wuthnow, Robert. 1989. *Communities of discourse. Ideology and social structure in the reformation, the enlightenment, and European socialism*. Cambridge, Mass: Harvard University Press.

Zimmermann, Bénédicte. 2006. *Arbeitslosigkeit in Deutschland. Zur Entstehung einer sozialen Kategorie*. Frankfurt/New York: Campus.

Author Biographies

Dr. Britta Baumgarten is contracted researcher at the Centre for Research and Studies in Sociology (CIES-IUL) and invited lecturer at the School of Sociology and Public Policy (ESPP), Lisbon. Her research interests are social movements in Portugal and in Brazil, with a focus on processes of transnationalization and on participation of marginalized people. Recent publications are "Conceptualizing Culture in Social Movement Research" (edited with P. Daphi and P. Ullrich, Palgrave 2014), "Geração à Rasca and Beyond" (Current Sociology 2013), "Time to Get Re-Organized!" (Research in Social Movements, Conflicts and Change, Vol. 40 2016).

Peter Ullrich, Dr. phil. Dr. rer. med. is a sociologist and head of the research unit "Social Movements, Technology, Conflicts" at the Centre for Technology and Society, fellow at the Centre for Research on Antisemitism (both at Technische Universität Berlin) and research associate at the Institute for Protest and Social Movement Studies. His current research focuses on social movements, gouvernmentality, surveillance and the police. He is author of „The Left, Israel and Palestine" (Dietz 2008) and „Germans, Leftists and the Middle East Conflict" (Wallstein 2013). He edited various books, among them „Conceptualizing Culture in Social Movement Research" (with B. Baumgarten and P. Daphi, Palgrave 2014) and „Prevent and Tame. Protest Under (self-)control" (with F. Heßdörfer and A. Pabst, Dietz 2010).

Social Movements and the Rationality of Choice

Annette Schnabel

Most people would agree that a healthy environment is desirable, that women's rights still need realization all over the world, and that torture should be abandoned. Besides these more general objectives, most people face constraints that they see as highly unsatisfying and that they want to be changed. But although such deprivation is ubiquitous, most people do not take (political) joint action for change. Why is that?

Rational choice theories (RC theories) provide an answer to this question and, at the same time, are challenged by every collective action that takes place. Social movements therefore are of particular concern for rational choice theorists, giving rise to a broad debate about the additional conditions under which social movements are likely to emerge.

Within the theoretical framework of RC theories, social movements are discussed as a particular form of "collective action." The debate about supporting or hindering factors of collective action had its peak during the 1990s. It developed out of the quest for the minimal conditions of cooperative action among egoistic, rational actors. Social movements are seen as a more advanced and complex form of cooperation. RC theories tie in with economic theories and game theory but also with resource mobilization theory and it always focuses on individual action as the key to all collective phenomena. Collective action comprises all kinds of action that is set up in order to jointly realize a goal. It does not only comprise social movement activities but all forms of coordinated and cooperative action by a larger

A. Schnabel (✉)
Heinrich-Heine-Universität, Düsseldorf, Germany
e-mail: annette.schnabel@uni-duesseldorf.de

© Springer Fachmedien Wiesbaden 2016
J. Roose and H. Dietz (eds.), *Social Theory and Social Movements,*
DOI 10.1007/978-3-658-13381-8_3

number of people like riots, revolts, demonstrations, strikes, spontaneous flash
mobs, and all kinds of antagonistic cooperation (which can be part of movements
but do not need to be).[1]

1   Grounds for Rational Choice Theories

RC theories comprise quite a heterogeneous group of theories that share some
common core characteristics but differ with regard to their assumptions (a) about
the knowledge that rational actors are supposed to have, (b) about the process of
choosing, and (c) about which aspects should count as individual "costs" and
"benefits". Narrow RC theories are distinguished from wider ones: while the first
group comprises all approaches that concentrate exclusively on egoistic and mostly
pecuniary incentives for action, the latter also takes moral incentives into consideration (Kunz 2004; Diekmann and Voss 2004).

1.1   Economic and Resource Mobilization Theory: Similar
        but Different

Economic theory and resource mobilization theory provided the broader framework
for the development of RC-based social movement analysis: In contrast to earlier
mass psychology suggesting that social movement participants react emotionally
and irrationally, the economic and the resource mobilization perspective both stress
that movement participants have "good reasons" for their actions and must be well
organized in order to rationally achieve their aims. On the one hand, RC theories
follow the tradition of economic theories by focusing on individual action and
searching for those conditions that are necessary in order to stimulate collective
action. Hypotheses on individual action are derived from an axiomatic cost–benefit
model as it is employed in microeconomics (for exemplary application of such a
theoretical framework to other than strictly economic behavior see (Becker 1976,
1982) or Frey 1997). The general considerations are developed on the basis of
thought experiments and theoretical derivations or computer simulations (e.g. by
Marwell and Oliver 1993); empirical research on social movements is rare (ex-
ception: e.g. Opp 2009). Following economic research on market failure, Olson
(1965) called attention to one of the main obstacles of RC-related social movement

---

[1]See Lichbach (1994).

research, namely that larger groups face disadvantages when it comes to collectively joining forces. Although his group-size argument is highly contested (e.g. Marwell and Oliver 1993; Opp 2009) it emphasized that the sameness of interests is not sufficient to mobilize joint action—a problem that all movements face in practice and all social scientists in theory when explaining social movements.

Resource mobilization theory, on the other hand, provided the perspective of organized action. Similar to economic-based theories, it shares a critical view on theories of relative deprivation and structural strains (e.g. Davis 1969; Gurr 1972; or focusing on structural strains: Brand et al. 1986; Kriesi 1987) by stressing that dissatisfaction with structural conditions is necessary but not sufficient for movement action. Resource mobilization theory assumes that people are guided by cost–benefit calculations in their political actions; they develop movement goals according to societal cleavages but need organization of resources and an opportunity structure in order to realize these goals. Because dissatisfaction is ubiquitous, the emergence of social movements depends on additional conditions which are provided by movement entrepreneurs who gather resources and organize the opportunities for social action (McCarthy and Zald 1977, p. 1221; Jenkins 1983, p. 528). However, the relationship between individually felt deprivation and the supply of mobilization resources is less straightforward than suggested (for critiques see: Pollack 2000, p. 44; Hellmann 1999, p. 96; Jenkins 1983, p. 532): Resource mobilization theory tends to underspecify the relationship between additional resources and the degree of mobilization, the allocation of resources, and the consequences of the unequal distribution of power as well as the framing of dissatisfaction. While approaches of relative deprivation and structural strains see dissatisfaction as key to social movement activities, resource mobilization focuses on the movement resources and the movement entrepreneurs as central factors. However, movement evolvement seems to be more complex and the existence of organizations is also not sufficient to explain how dissatisfaction is shared and transformed into joint action.

1.2 Basic Assumptions: Of Situations, Actors, and Aggregated Choices

RC theories suggest a different way to approach social movements. They do not as much start with the question of "why men rebel" (Gurr 1972) but rather why they do not. For RC theorists, the mere conviction that a goal can be realized more easily in cooperation is not sufficient to explain why actors are willing to join collective action or social movements.

This conclusion arises from the basic assumptions of the theories: Based on the research program of methodological individualism, RC theories try to explain macro-phenomena such as rebellions, demonstrations, strikes, or the development of movement organizations out of individual courses of action. The program suggests three analytical steps (Coleman 1990, p. 8; Hechter and Kanazawa 1997, p. 193):

(a) Actions take place in situations that provide the conditions under which rational actors choose their actions. Situations offer resources and constraints but also the "window of opportunity" for what can possibly be achieved. RC theories aim to use assumptions about this situational frame that are as economic as possible in order to predict individual action most correctly (Lindenberg 1992). With regard to movement mobilization, dissatisfying conditions, already existing political and opportunity structures, available ideologies but also the embeddedness into social networks may be part of the situational framework (Schnabel 2003).

(b) Accordingly, the theory assumes that rational actors identify the situation and its possibilities for action (A_1, A_2, ..., A_m) and that they choose a course of action that offers them an expected maximum of utilities ($U_1 < U_2 < \cdots < U_n$). In choosing a particular course of action, rational actors try to maximize their own individual utility, which may comprise different dimensions: Taking part in a demonstration may provide the possibility to support the political aim but also to have fun in joint actions, the feeling of "doing the right thing," or meeting friends ($\Sigma U_{(i)}$). According to some theorists, the utility of beloved others can be part of the individual utility function as well (e.g. Andreoni and Miller 2008). The model of rational action is a teleological one: RC theories assume that people make choices about a future state of affairs that basically is insecure. Rational actors do not know if their actions will be successful in achieving the actor's goals—they make assumptions about the likelihood ($p_{(i)}$) and in this way they are just able to maximize their *expected* (subjective) utility ((S)$EU_{(Ai)} = \Sigma p_{(i)} * U_{(i)}$).[2] But actions do not come without costs. They have to be subtracted from the expected utilities. Costs may lie in the time that is

---

[2]There are differences between RC theories according to the assumption whether rational actors try to maximize their expected utility or their subjective expected utility (basic considerations by Savage 1954).

needed to organize political actions, the effort of reaching a compromise about aims and strategies, the costs of printing leaflets or buying and organizing weapons, or in being punished by authorities but also by friends and neighbors. It is assumed that action $A_{(1)}$ is preferred over action $A_{(2)}$ if: (S) $EU_{(A1)} > (S)EU_{(A2)}$. This general formula provides the model from which more concrete hypotheses can be derived. For example, Coleman (1990, p. 492) suggests that protest activities become rational if $qU > r(1 - p)C$: If the utility of protest (U) multiplied by the probability that Ego's action contributes to its success (q) exceeds the costs (C) that originated in the probability of punishment in the event that the protest fails (r) multiplied by the counter-probability that the revolution's success is related to Ego's action.

(c) However, to fully understand collective action it is not sufficient to just model individual choices. They have to be aggregated in order to explain the collective macro-phenomena. This is because the individual attempts to realize a goal may end in "unintended aggregated consequences of individually intentional action" (Boudon 1979). The logic of aggregation may comprise either simple summarization of individual action, but also voting rules (e.g. Buchanan and Tullock 1962), models of diffusion (e.g. Schelling 1978), or game theory (e.g. Rasmusen 1989). For social movements, especially models of diffusion are of interest because they show how attitudes, evaluations, and actions "infect" larger populations (Schelling 1978, pp. 93ff.).

2   Why Do People not Rebel?

RC theories suggest that the combination of particular characteristics of movement aims and the logic of rational decision-making prevents joint action even if rational actors are convinced that they can reach a goal only by cooperation. Olson was the first who argued that joint goals are not enough to provide incentives for collective action (Olson 1965). But why is it that social movements are rare events and that additional conditions must be fulfilled until they can start off?

2.1   The Problem: Collective Goods, Common Goods, and Their Challenge

Olson argued that the challenges of collective action and social movements are brought on by the special characteristics of the goals collective action and social movements are initiated for. These special characteristics are those of collective goods: *jointness of supply* and *nonexcludability*. If a good is in joint supply, its costs do not depend on how many people benefit. The expenses of getting equal rights for men and women, for example, do not increase when additional women benefit from them. Nonexcludability means that there is no realistic way (either for practical or political reasons) to exclude anyone from benefiting once these goods are provided even if this person has not contributed to the joint effort. If, for example, carbon monoxide concentration in the air is reduced there are no (politically, economically, or technically) justifiable means to charge users for breathing or to forbid breathing in the event that they do not pay. Furthermore, many collective goods can not be produced by a single person—they require the pooling of resources of several actors. Social movements are one kind of collective action, particularly initiated to produce collective goods that require such joint efforts. These characteristics of collective goods provide incentives for rational actors to withhold their contribution and wait for others "to do the job," especially in larger groups: The results of any individual person's actions are uncertain, because they depend on the willingness of others to contribute as well. Furthermore, as argued above, no individual can be excluded from benefiting if the collective good is produced successfully and, above all, punishment for withholding is unlikely, because in large groups a missing contribution often remains unnoticed (Olson 1965, p. 12).

While collective goods tend to get stuck in their early production phases and are not produced in a sufficient amount, common goods suffer from being protected because of the same reasons. Common goods are goods that already exist but tend to be exploited. This is because exclusion of users is (technically, economically, or socially) not feasible but preservation of these goods requires that the users do not benefit from them to a maximum extent. Environmental goods like the red tuna or smog-free air are most often common goods. Hardin (1968) discussed their exploitation under the headline of the "Tragedy of the Commons"; Ostrom (1998, 2000) suggested conditions under which this tragedy can be prevented. Social movements sometimes are initiated in order to protect common goods like fishing resources, biodiversity, or other kinds of natural resources. However, movements concerned with common goods face similar problems as social movements trying to initiate rights or collective goods: Rational actors wait until others reach a commitment or regulation and bare the costs of negotiation, control of compliance, and sanctions (and just continue to exploit the common good).

While the rationale behind both the collective goods problem and the tragedy of the commons lies in the individual rational choice (not) to act, the problem itself emerges from strategic action. Individuals choose their action according to

Table 1 Pay-off matrix of the prisoner's dilemma

| | | Actor B | |
		Contribution	Retention
Actor A	Contribution	2/2	−3/0
	Retention	0/−3	0/0

expected decisions of others, either by waiting for others to perform or by joining them in their efforts. In this case, the probability of success or failure (p) depends on the actions of others. Game theorists suggest modeling this particular strategic interaction between individual decisions with regard to collective or common goods as the so-called "prisoner's dilemma." They propose that in such situations the dominant strategy of all actors typically leads to a result that is suboptimal for all partners. Individual rationality and social rationality fall apart in this case.

Without going into much detail, the prisoner's dilemma for collective goods looks as follows (Hardin 1982, p. 25) (Table 1).

This decision model is developed for two persons but can be transferred to more persons as well; the logic does not change if A faces more than one interaction partner. However, there are authors who suggest that under particular circumstances the collective goods problem may be better modeled as a chicken's or assurance game (e.g. Sandler 1992).

All in all, these considerations give rise to the question of why a rational actor should contribute to a social movement or any kind of collective action if the actor's benefit does not noticeably depend on his or her efforts.

2.2 Theory-Immanent Solutions: Iteration, Reputation, Selected Incentives, and a Critical Mass

Nevertheless, there are social movements in the real world and they are in fact not unexplained by RC theories. Several writers suggest theoretical explanations which specify additional, necessary conditions under which even rational actors may join collective action. Although most suggestions derive their conclusions on the basis of the rational-actor model as described above, the necessary conditions always refer to strategic action in relations to others. Three different lines of arguments can be distinguished within the comprising and rich debate about theory-immanent solutions.

For two-person games, game theorists argue that the likely iteration of the prisoner's dilemma may help players to overcome the logic of the game even without external incentives. Iteration supports cooperation if the expected future benefits of working together outweigh the benefits of "defecting" in the current game (Axelrod 1984). This requires that the "player" must be able to remember the last decision of their interaction partners (memory) and they must be able to react accordingly (conditionality of the decision) (Raub and Voss 1986, p. 315). However, the players should not know when they are meeting for the last time because this initiates a backward induction. If these conditions are met the potential one-sided withdrawal of future cooperation benefits can work as internal sanctions and force strategic actors to contribute. If a third party is involved, reputation effects towards this third party can provide such internal sanctions as well because actors do not want to lose the possibility of cooperation benefits just because they developed a reputation as untrustworthy (Raub and Weesie 1990). However, for social movements iteration and reputation seem to be an explanation that is too weak to explain commitment: In most cases more than two or three actors are involved and the actor's investments in terms of time, money, and cognitive and emotional capacity appear to be higher than rewards which realistically could be expected from direct cooperation with other movement members. However, iteration and reputation effects may help to detect the mechanism behind opportunity structures: They not only provide the possibility to meet other like-minded people but to meet them regularly and to develop familiarity, predictability, and trust. Trust, again, is one of the key factors of consciousness rising and of adopting alternative interpretations and ideologies (Snow and Benford 1988; Oliver and Johnston 2000) or to "cognitive liberation" (McAdam 1988, p. 135).

Incentives additional to the benefits from collective goods provide the second group of additional conditions that help to overcome the collective goods problem. They are considered more helpful in explaining social movement commitment. The production of collective goods (as the maintenance of common goods) are often combined with additional benefits or costs that are "private" in the sense that they are not in joint supply and that they are excludable. Such "selective incentives" (Olson 1965, p. 63) are immediately connected to the individual contribution and thereby provide motivation to act. Such selective incentives can consist of material advantages. But most often, social movements offer moral or social incentives (Opp 1996, p. 357). Moral incentives pledge morally to contribute and are often connected to the good consciousness "to do what's right." Social incentives consist of the fun one has while performing a group activity, the social identity that social movements can provide, but also of organizing against "hate speech" and physical attacks that movement involvement provokes. Oliver (1980) showed that while positive selective incentives are more efficient in motivating small groups of activists to start collective action, negative selective incentives help in larger groups to maintain a certain level of involvement. Selective incentives, however, are demanding: Keller (1988) argued that within social movements the supply of selective incentives most often is rather the result than the cause of organization. Selective incentives seem to be a "second-order collective goods problem." Hechter (1990) suggested that the "second-order problem" can be solved if actors join forces to produce "joint goods" which only need the pooling of resources but provide benefits that are individually accountable. Such goods offer incentives to solitarily establish rules and sanctions and form a group that later will be able to produce pure collective goods by using already established structures. Hechter, by that, suggests that the collective goods problem can be solved if group structures including decision rules and rules of sanctions are previously established on other grounds than the production of collective goods. Heckathorn (1988, 1989, 1993) similarly argues that rules of control are vital for the production of collective goods. He argues that rational actors are confronted with the decision either to actively support a system of sanctions or not. If a larger group of people vote for negative sanctions without enforcing them the system will eliminate itself by "hypocritical cooperation." If the sanctions are too harshly executed however, the likelihood of revolts will increase.

The third kind of explanation is offered by Oliver and Marwell (1993): They propose to start with the analysis of the collective good's production function. They provide a detailed analysis of different kinds of collective goods showing that the collective goods problem emerges to different degrees depending on the particular features of the production process. That is that some production functions (those with increasing returns to scale) enable a small group of highly interested and resourceful actors to produce the collective good or initiate the social movement necessary for its production. Marwell et al. (1985, p. 522) called this a "critical mass." They state: "A pool of highly interested and resourceful individuals willing to contribute in the initial region [of the production function, A.S.] of low returns may therefore become a 'critical mass' creating the conditions for more widespread contributions" (Marwell et al. 1985, p. 543). By that, they show that Olson's initial conjecture that larger groups are disadvantaged is wrong: Larger groups have a higher probability of containing highly interested and/or highly resourceful people that are able to start a critical mass. McCarthy and Zald suggested already in (1977) that mobilization entrepreneurs are necessary to pool resources and organize collective action. In contrast to resource mobilization theory, Marwell and Oliver, however, provide the exact conditions under which such highly motivated actors are able to effectively start a protest. That is, in order for a critical mass to work, the production function must show increasing returns, actors must have time to observe others in their action (sequential strategic action), and resources and interests must not be correlated negatively within the group that form the critical mass. It is only then that the first contribution increases the likelihood of the second and so on until the collective action roles.

All these approaches indicate that within the framework of RC theories, several types of "additional conditions" are discussed. They are necessary to overcome the individual incentives for rational actors to withhold their contribution. Iteration of contact may lead to enduring cooperation and to the development of socially shared conventions, norms of fairness and reciprocity, and of trust. They facilitate the highly demanding investments into movement involvement. In this way, iteration enables the merging of individual and collective rationality. The heterogeneous distribution of interests and resources within the collective of those who may benefit from the movement's success enables the development of a critical mass which can initiate the formation of movement organizations. Selective incentives change the individual cost–benefit structure so that contributions become individually increasingly attractive. Movement participation under these conditions can be explained as a strategically and individually rational choice.

3   Remaining Questions

Some of the considerations that are presented here are part of other movement theories as well. One of the huge advantages of RC explanations of social movement activity emerges from the fact that RC theories are a group of axiomatic theories that deduce their hypotheses logically out of a set of explicit presumptions. That makes it possible to derive and adopt a comprising set of hypotheses for several kinds of collective action, to distinguish between core assumption (about individual and strategic action) and additional bridging hypotheses, and to provide a full explanation that does not focus on a particular set of variables but on structural and situational factors, on the logic of the selection of a particular course of action, and on the aggregation of individual actions.

Critics have argued that especially the core assumptions of RC theories are questionable: In their everyday life people do not act according to rational cost–benefit calculations. Several studies about the perceptions of risk and about ambiguity have shown that this objection is empirically valid. RC theorists argue that they do not perceive actors as acting *in fact* according to the assumptions of rationality. They are just modeled "as if" they would do. This provides the possibility to start with an economic set of assumptions and to develop more demanding hypotheses about minimal, necessary conditions which can then be tested empirically.[3]

Besides these epistemological critiques there are some topics that have rarely been covered in RC explanations of social movement participation. Among them is firstly the question of how people agree upon movement aims. Secondly, the question of emotions as motivators for movement activities is still open. In my view, it is however possible and productive to address both questions within the framework of RC theories.

3.1 Movement Aims as Contested Grounds

While RC theories provide several answers to the question of why people *start* "collective action" (despite the fact that it would seem rational to leave it to others to do so), RC theories rarely pose the question of how actors come to the conclusion that a particular issue is worth fighting for. For some issues this is fairly obvious—water in the desert is beneficial for individuals and groups alike but a group might be more successful in digging a well. From a scientist's view, merely looking at the "objective" side effects of a good or bad cause does not seem to answer satisfactorily the question of why some issues receive the status of a "collective good" or a "collective bad" in people's perception while others do not. This is because many external effects remain unnoticed or seem to be rather unimportant unless some political actors discover the "real" degree of these effects and evaluate them.

Framing approaches have sufficiently stressed the point that issues and events have to be interpreted and "framed" in order to become politicized and that small groups help to cognitively liberate people and to raise activists' self-efficacy (McAdam 1988; Gamson and Modigliani 1989; Snow et al. 1986; Snow and Benford 1988). RC theories tie in with these considerations in stressing the context dependency of individual choices and their conditionality. Esser (1993) and Kroneberg (2005) have shown that by enlarging the RC framework, it is possible to model the "choice" of a situational frame (or the definition of the situation) as a rational choice. Although these considerations are not precisely within the narrow concept of RC theories, they provide the backbone for considerations about the conditions under which rational actors "decide" for a particular frame of events.

---

[3]For an extended debate about the epistemological grounds of RC theories see MacDonald (2003).

While in everyday life, we have a set of standardized frames at our disposal that we apply to typified situations. We start to re-think a definition of a situation when disturbing situational elements pop up that give rise to the suspicion that "something different is going on." We then try to find a more fitting interpretation. One may argue that movement ideologies provide a set of alternative ideas about how to frame a situation (e.g. Oliver and Johnston 2000, p. 7; Denzau and North 2000, p. 24; Schnabel 2008, p. 84). They offer a set of situational frames under a particular "Leitthema" like sustainable consumption or equality. Their adaptation always goes with a change of this set.

But why do ideologies become attractive? The attractiveness—and thereby the likelihood of adaptation—is highly conditional: They become individually attractive if the benefits of the former set of standardized frames are considered to be decreasing and/or if its maintenance costs are considered to be increasing (for example because of social change and changed expectations by the self and others) *and* if the costs of searching and adopting the alternative ideology are considered small and/or they can surely be found because of still existing alternative ideas and a "critical mass" that already promotes them and helps to adopt them (Schnabel 2006, 2008). While classical frame approaches only state *that and how* ideologies are important, such a list of conditions provide the answer to the question of *why* people may be attracted to some but not to other ideologies (out of a pool of different available alternatives).

Once actors accept the interpretation the movement offers, they become interested in the ideology persisting because the adaptation meets demanding conditions—actors now try to avoid the devaluation of their newly achieved investments (or production functions as Lindenberg 1989 argues). To avoid devaluation actors may feel incentives to mobilize new members or they might feel the need to fight for changes within the movement if the movement's ideology, its goals, strategies, and tactics do not provide enough selective incentives anymore. Actors therefore are driven to negotiate permanently about the movement's ideology and as long as payoffs are expected, negotiating, to some extent, is more benefiting than leaving the movement.[4] In the logic of RC theories, this will happen until the marginal costs of negotiating exceed the marginal utility obtained by attending a group meeting of the movement. Indeed, leaving the organizational context of the movement does not necessarily imply that actors will replace their set of selection and interpretation rules automatically.

---

[4]See the according argumentation by Hirschman (1970) on "exit, voice, and loyalty."

3.2   Emotions and Rational Choice—A Complicated Relationship

The recent boom of emotions in social theory and research leaves no field of study untouched, including the study of social movements (e.g. Goodwin et al. 2001; Goodwin and Jasper 2004), and has led to a rethinking of the relation between emotions and rationality. Emotions in social movement research matter in (at least) three regards. First, the framing—and *interpretation*—of circumstances and events provided by social movements entail emotion management. Social movements not only provide cognitive frames but also link events to emotions that should be felt, to cognitive explanations, and to arguments that provide legitimacy for action. Emotional experiences of anger or rage about injustice, unfairness, and inequality which are supported by social movements thereby help participants to evaluate events and to give meaning to such events. Within the context of mobilization, emotions can be seen as a particular "way of knowing" as suggested by Jaggar (1989). Second, emotions *motivate* action through feelings generated by partici- pating in collective activities. Mobilization takes place in social networks[5] which provide the conditions for collective action. Networks are stabilized emotionally by feelings of solidarity and bonds of love, loyalty, and attachment fostered in the formation of a collective identity. They provide satisfaction and comfort as well as obligations. Third, social movements have the power to *change* and reinterpret emotions. Mobilization requires that people feel able or empowered to influence social and political change. By emotional reframing, social movements change more "passive" feelings such as grief, shame, or fear of failure into more "active" ones such as anger or pride. In sum, emotions help people to understand their environment and living conditions, thereby motivating them to take action; emo- tions sustain people's action through affective networks cultivated within move- ment organizations; and emotions constitute an integral dimension of the outcomes sought by social movements, including by challenging established "feeling rules."

It will be one of the future challenges to combine these considerations with RC theories on social movements. Up till now, in RC-related literature emotions are perceived as important for explaining how preferences emerge through the emo- tional evaluation of outcomes, how emotions help to bridge information deficits in interaction, and how they can coordinate individual and social rationality (e.g. Frank 1988; Elster 1999; Bolle 2006). They are no longer seen as merely dis- turbing aspects. On the contrary, perceiving emotions as important costs, benefits,

---

[5]McAdam (1988: 134) calls those "micromobilization contexts."

or aspects of information, RC theories not only adopt neuroscience research (e.g. Damasio 2000), but also gain the possibility to endogenize the development of preferences into the RC model. The bridge to social movement research here, however, is yet to develop.

RC theories have their strength in explaining why social movements do not appear more often and which are the necessary conditions that mobilize people in order to take matters into their own—joint—hands. It is one of the merits of RC theories to stress that it is a long and demanding way for similar interests to become common concerns and for common concerns to turn into collective action. The simulation studies by Marwell and Oliver (1993) provide an encompassing summary of the factors necessary and how they work. RC theories offer a comprising model of collective action derived from a set of economic assumptions that help to develop complex hypotheses within the field of social movements. RC theories fall short, however, when science-of-knowledge-related issues are involved like the social construction of common aims, how ideologies are adopted, or how preferences develop socially. Although there are attempts to close this gap, a systematic argumentation or model is still missing.

References

Andreoni, James, and John Miller. 2008. Analyzing choice with revealed preferences: Is altruism rational? *Handbook of Experimental Economics Results* 1(4): 481–487.
Axelrod, Robert. 1984. *The Evolution of Cooperation*. New York: Basic Books.
Becker, Gary S. 1976. Altruism, Egoism, and Genetic Fitness: Economics and sociobiology. *Journal of Economic Literature*, 14(3), 817–826.
Becker, Gary S. 1982. *Der ökonomische Ansatz zur Erklärung menschlichen Verhaltens*. Tübingen: Mohr.
Bolle, Friedel. 2006. Gefühle in der ökonomischen Theorie. In *Emotionen und Sozialtheorie*, ed. Rainer Schützeichel, 48–66. Frankfurt/M., New York: Campus.
Boudon, Raymond. 1979. *Widersprüche sozialen Handelns*. Darmstadt: Luchterhand.
Brand, Karl-Werner, Büsser Detlef, and Rucht Dieter. 1986. *Aufbruch in eine andere Gesellschaft. Neue soziale Bewegungen in der Bundesrepublik*. Frankfurt/M., New York: Campus.
Buchanan, James, and Gordon Tullock. 1962. *The calculus of consent: Logical foundations of constitutional democracy*. Ann Arbor: University of Michigan Press.
Coleman, James S. 1990. *Foundations of social theory*. Cambridge: Harvard University Press.
Damasio, Antonio R. 2000. *Descartes' error*. New York: Harper Collins Books.
Davis, James C. 1969. The J-curve of rising and declining satisfactions as a cause of some great revolutions and a contained rebellion. In *Violence in America: Historical and*

comparative perspectives, ed. Hugh D. Graham, and Gurr Ted, 547–576. Washington D. C: Government Printing Office.

Denzau, Arthur T., and Douglas C. North. 2000. Shared mental models: Ideologies and institutions. In *Elements of reason*, ed. Arthur Lupia, Mathew Daniel McCubbins, and Samuel L. Popkin, 23–67. Cambridge: Cambridge University Press.

Diekmann, Andreas, and Thomas Voss. 2004. Die Theorie rationalen Handelns. Stand und Perspektiven. In *Rational-Choice-Theorie in den Sozialwissenschaften. Anwendungen und Probleme*, ed. Andreas Diekmann, and Thomas Voss, 13–29. München: Oldenbourg.

Elster, Jon. 1999. *The Alchemies of the mind*. Cambridge: Cambridge University Press.

Esser, Hartmut. 1993. The rationality of everyday behavior: A rational choice reconstruction of the theory of action by Alfred Schütz. *Rationality and Society* 5(1): 32–46.

Frank, Robert. 1988. *Passion within reason: The strategic role of emotions*. New York: Norton.

Frey, Bruno. 1997. *Not Just for the money: An economic theory of personal motivation*. Cheltenham, UK: Edward Elgar.

Gamson, William, and Andre Modigliani. 1989. Media discourse and public opinion on nuclear power: A constructionist approach. *American Journal of Sociology* 95(1): 1–37.

Goodwin, Jeff, James M. Jasper, and Francesca Polletta. 2001. Why emotions matter. In *Passionate politics. Emotions and social movements*, ed. Goodwin Jeff, James M. Jasper, and Francesca Polletta, 1–24. Chicago: The University of Chicago Press.

Goodwin, Jeff and James M. Jasper. 2004. *Rethinking Social Movements: Structure, Meaning, and Emotion*. Lanham, Boulder, New York: Rowman & Littlefield Publishers.

Gurr, Ted. 1972. *Why men rebel*. Princeton: Princeton University Press.

Hardin, Garrett. 1968. The tragedy of the commons. *Science* 162(3859): 1243–1248.

Hardin, Russell. 1982. *Collective action*. Baltimore, Maryland: The John Hopkins University Press.

Hechter, Michael. 1990. The emergence of cooperative social institutions. In *Social institutions*, ed. Michael Hechter, Karl-Dieter Opp, and Reinhard Wippler, 13–35. Berlin: de Gruyter.

Hechter, Michael, and Satoshi Kanazawa. 1997. Sociological rational choice theory. *Annual Review of Sociology* 23(1): 191–214.

Heckathorn, Douglas. 1988. Collective sanctions and the creation of prisoner's dilemma norms. *American Journal of Sociology* 94(3): 535–562.

Heckathorn, Douglas. 1989. Collective action and the second-order free-rider problem. *Rationality and Society* 1(1): 78–100.

Heckathorn, Douglas. 1993. Collective action and group heterogeneity: Voluntary provision versus selective incentives. *American Sociological Review* 58(3): 329–350.

Hellmann, Kai-Uwe. 1999. Paradigmen der Bewegungsforschung. In *Neue soziale Bewegungen*, ed. Ansgar Klein, Hans-Josef Legrand, and Thomas Leif, 91–113. Opladen: Westdeutscher Verlag.

Hirschman, Albert O. 1970. *Exit, Voice, and Loyalty: Responses to Decline in Firms, Organizations, and States*. Cambridge: Harvard University Press.

Jaggar, Alison. 1989. Love and knowledge: Emotion in feminist epistemology. In *Gender/body/knowledge*, ed. Alison Jaggar, and Susan R. Bordo, 145–172. Rutgers: The State University Press.

Jenkins, Craig J. 1983. Resource mobilization theory and the study of social movements. *Annual Review of Sociology* 9(1): 427–453.

Keller, Berndt. 1988. Olsons „Logik des kollektiven Handelns". Entwicklung, Kritik–und eine Alternative. *Politische Vierteljahresschrift*, 23(3): 388–406.

Kriesi, Hanspeter. 1987. Neue soziale Bewegungen: Auf der Suche nach ihrem gemeinsamen Nenner. *Politische Vierteljahresschrift* 28(3): 315–334.

Kroneberg, Clemens. 2005. Die Definition der Situation und die variable Rationalität der Akteure. Ein allgemeines Modell des Handelns. *Zeitschrift für Soziologie* 34(5): 344–363.

Kunz, Volker. 2004. *Rational choice*. Frankfurt/M., New York: Campus.

Lichbach, Mark I. 1994. Rethinking rationality and rebellion. *Rationality and Society* 6(1): 8–39.

Lindenberg, Siegwart. 1989. Social production functions, deficits, and social revolutions. *Rationality and Society* 1(1): 51–77.

Lindenberg, Siegwart. 1992. The method of decreasing abstraction. In *Rational choice theory. Advocacy and critique*, ed. James S. Coleman, and Thomas J. Fararo, 3–20. Newbury Park: Sage.

MacDonald, Paul K. 2003. Useful fiction or miracle maker: The competing epistemological foundations of rational choice theory. *American Political Science Review* 97(4): 551–565.

Marwell, Gerald, and Pamela Oliver. 1993. *The critical mass in collective action*. Cambridge: University Press.

Marwell, Gerald, Pamela Oliver, and Ruy A. Teixeira. 1985. A theory of the critical mass I: Interdependence, group heterogeneity, and the production of collective action. *American Journal of Sociology* 91(3): 522–556.

McAdam, Doug. 1988. Micromobilization contexts and recruitment to activism. In *From structure to action: Comparing social movement research across cultures*, ed. Klandermans Bert, Hanspeter Kriesi, and Sidney Tarrow, 125–154. Greenwich: JAI Press.

McCarthy, John D., and Mayer N. Zald. 1977. Resource mobilisation and social movements. *American Journal of Sociology* 82(6): 1212–1241.

Oliver, Pamela. 1980. Rewards and Punishments as Selective Incentives for Collective Action: Theoretical Investigations. *American Journal of Sociology*, 85(6): 1356–1375.

Oliver, Pamela, and Hank Johnston. 2000. What a good idea! frames and ideologies in social movement research. http://www.ssc.wisc.edu/ ~ oliver/PROTESTS/ArticleCopies/Frames.2.29.00.pdf. Accessed 5 Oct 2015.

Olson, Mancur. 1965. *The logic of collective action*. Cambridge: Harvard University Press.

Opp, Karl-Dieter. 1996. Aufstieg und Niedergang der ökologischen Bewegung in der Bundesrepublik. In *Umweltsoziologie. Sonderheft der Kölner Zeitschrift für Soziologie und Sozialpsychologie, Band 36*, ed. Diekmann Andreas, and Carlo C. Jaeger, 350–379. Opladen: Westdeutscher Verlag.

Opp, Karl-Dieter. 2009. *Theories of political protest and social movements*. New York: Routledge.

Ostrom, Elinor. 1998. A Behavioral approach to the rational choice theory of collective action. *American Political Science Review* 92(1): 1–22.

Ostrom, Elinor. 2000. Reformulating the commons. *Swiss Science Review* 6(1): 29–52.

Pollack, Detlef. 2000. *Politischer Protest: Politisch alternative Gruppen in der DDR.* Opladen: Leske & Budrich.

Rasmusen, Eric. 1989. *Games and information.* Cambridge, Oxford: Blackwell.

Raub, Werner, and Jeroen Weesie. 1990. Reputation and efficiency in social interactions: An example of network effects. *American Journal of Sociology* 96(3): 626–654.

Raub, Werner, and Thomas Voss. 1986. Die Sozialstruktur der Kooperation rationaler Egoisten. Zur „utilitaristischen" Erklärung sozialer Ordnung. *Zeitschrift für Soziologie* 15 (5): 309–323.

Sandler, Todd. 1992. *Collective action. Theory and applications.* New York: Harvester Wheatsheaf.

Savage, Leonard J. 1954. *The Foundations of Statistics.* New York: Wiley.

Schelling, Thomas C. 1978. *Micromotives and macrobehavior.* New York, London: Norton & Company.

Schnabel, Annette. 2003. *Die Rationalität der Emotionen.* Wiesbaden: Westdeutscher Verlag.

Schnabel, Annette. 2006. What Makes Collective Goods a Shared Concern? Re-constructing the Construction of the Collectiveness of Goods. *Rationality and Society*, 18(1), 5–34.

Schnabel, Annette. 2008. Wo kämen wir hin, wenn wir Ideologien reduzierten? Ideologien in methodologisch-individualistischer Perspektive. In *Das Mikro-Makro-Modell der soziologischen Erklärung. Zur Ontologie, Methodologie und Metatheorie eines Forschungsprogramms,* ed. Greve Jens, Annette Schnabel, and Rainer Schützeichel, 79–108. Wiesbaden: VS Verlag für Sozialwissenschaften.

Snow, David A., and Robert D. Benford. 1988. Ideology, frame resonance, and participant mobilisation. In *From structure to action: Comparing social movement research across cultures,* ed. Klandermans Bert, Hanspeter Kriesi, and Sidney Tarrow, 197–217. Greenwich: JAI Press.

Snow, David A., E. Burke Rochford, Steven K. Worden, and Robert D. Benford. 1986. Frame alignment processes, micromobilization, and movement participation. *American Sociological Review* 51(4): 464–481.

Author Biography

Dr. Annette Schnabel is Professor for Sociology and Sociological Theory at the Heinrich-Heine-University Düsseldorf. Her main research areas are: National identities and religion in Europe and social movements and civil society and the sociology of emotions. She is interested in further developing rational-choice-theories by application and linking them to other theories. She works as well comparatively with attitude data for Europe. Recent publications are: "Religion and Value Orientations in Europe" (with F. Grötsch in Journal of Religion in Europe 2015); "How Religious Cleavages of Civil Society Shape National Identity" (with M. Hjerm in SAGE Open 2014), "Emotionen, Sozialstruktur und Moderne" (edited with R. Schützeichel, VS Verlag 2012).

Bourdieu Meets Social Movement

Lars Schmitt

It follows that the construction of a unified, Europe-wide social movement, capable of gathering together the various movements that are presently divided, both nationally and internationally, presents itself as a reasoned objective for all those who intend to effectively resist the dominant forces (Bourdieu 2003/2001, p. 39).

The general stands high up there, on a hill; he has the overview, he can see everything – that's the philosopher, the social philosopher. He dreams up battles, he describes the class struggle and, of course, does not appear in Waterloo. In contrast, my perspective is the one of Fabrizio, the protagonist of Stendhal's "The Charter-house of Parma," who doesn't see anything, understand anything, while the bullets are flying around his ears. One only needs to position oneself in the frontlines and the view of the social world becomes a fundamentally different one. The view of the generals is of course useful; it would be ideal if one could combine both: the over-view of the general and the isolated perception of the soldier in turmoil (Bourdieu 1993b, pp. 42f.; translation L.S.).

1 Introduction—Why and How to Arrange a Meeting Between Bourdieu and Social Movements?

There are at least three links between the person and work of Pierre Bourdieu (1930–2002) on the one hand and social movement activities on the other. These links may somewhat correspond to what critical observers of Bourdieu may call his pathway from a tough empiricist to a smooth story teller and finally to a political polemic. As we will see this critique is not tenable because his whole work from

L. Schmitt (✉)
Hochschule Düsseldorf, Düsseldorf, Germany
e-mail: lars.schmitt@hs-duesseldorf.de

© Springer Fachmedien Wiesbaden 2016
J. Roose and H. Dietz (eds.), *Social Theory and Social Movements,*
DOI 10.1007/978-3-658-13381-8_4

the beginning is inspired by his socio-epistemological framework and by his "project of enlightenment" that is scientifically unmasking the concealed mechanisms of power (Bourdieu 1992b). Bourdieu (1998) himself counters the objection of ruptures in his oeuvre, namely that his *The Weight of the World* (1999/1993) brings social relations on stage and to life that have been conceptualized and analyzed much earlier in *Distinction* (1984/1979). Nevertheless the vice versa corresponding links between Bourdieu and social movements are Bourdieu as an *activist*, Bourdieu as a *movement researcher*, and Bourdieu's *framework as a toolbox* for movement research.

Bourdieu as a Movement Activist
The first quotation suggests that the work of Pierre Bourdieu can easily be linked to activities of protest or contention. And a first glance at his oeuvre especially of his last ten years seems to confirm this impression: In 1995/96, Bourdieu participated in protest against the dismantling of the welfare state, giving a speech to striking railroaders. In 1998 he published his first *firing back* against the neoliberal invasion and in 1999 he initiated the call for a European social movement (raison d'agir).[1] Nevertheless Pierre Bourdieu has never felt comfortable in political activities, not only because of his own habitus, but knowing well the ambivalent effects of symbolic violence that such an engagement may entail, as we will see…

Bourdieu as a Movement Analyst
In addition to his own protest activities, there is another obvious link between Pierre Bourdieu and social movements: His attempts to analyze the events of May 1968 in Paris. From the perspective of movement research this analysis is rather sub-complex and unsatisfying because of its surprising simplicity referring to the crises and grievances of the academic field during that time (cf. Bourdieu 1988/1984 and critically Crossley 2002, pp. 168ff.).[2]

Bourdieu's Theory as an Analytical Framework
The third way to combine Bourdieu with protest and social movements seems to be the less evident but in our context the most interesting: It's the way his sociological epistemology and his theoretical vocabulary can be used as a critical sociological framework for the analysis of protest and social movements. It is this latter point

---

[1]The French original has two meanings: "reasons to interfere" and "acting reasonably."

[2]Concerning May 1968 in Paris, there exists a better analysis that uses Bourdieu's concepts than his own remarks (cf. Gilcher-Holtey 1995).

that this article is focusing on. Although not referring to the well-known "Bourdieu termini" of habitus, field, social space, different forms of capital, etc. directly, the second quotation above shows that Bourdieu's way of conceptualizing the social world is torn by the relationships of structure and agency or, alternatively, between theory and praxis. And we could easily add many more binaries to that list like the opposition of structure and culture, strategy/rationality and the irrational/emotional, mind and body, and so on. Although there is no doubt that this opposition building is epistemologically at least questionable if not senseless (except the "sense" to create the field of sociology and to entail its typical struggles), one cannot ignore that those juxtapositions have always been and still are decisive for the sociological construction of its objects and above all for the "making sense of social movements" (Crossley 2002) by different approaches of movement research.

But why in general arrange a meeting between a theory of society—or, better, a socio-epistemological framework—and research on social protest and social movements? At first glance it is hardly debatable that collective protest has to do with the social conditions in which it arises and to which it is—in whatever form and to whatever extent—referring to. Thereby it is irrelevant whether those social relations are considered at the level of the nation state with protests for example against welfare state cuts or at the level of world society with protests against the economic globalization or the Iraq war. All the more surprising is that there are hardly any efforts to consider protest in "good company with the society" in a common analytical framework. Indeed, currently the European strand of social movement research is strongly influenced by the Marxist philosophy of history and for that it is based on the structural analysis of society (cf. Hellmann and Koopmans 1998; Hellmann 1999; Crossley 2002, pp. 149ff.). And so these "macro approaches" differentiate between "protest as a result, expression and processing of social crises" (Bonacker and Schmitt 2004, p. 202, translation LS). The two components "protest" and "crisis" remain considered separately and are simply combined: Protest arises from a crisis, indicates a crisis, or claims to process the crisis. Even all three elements taken together remain a combination of analytical elements taken separately. The analytical focus of those so-called "crises approaches" is on the crises and therefore on the structure rather than on the agency side. Crisis/structure in this case can have a triple meaning: Firstly as a general crisis of (post-) modern society, secondly as focusing on a triggering crisis or event, e.g. Chernobyl or the deployment of Pershing II in Germany (cf. Wasmuht 1989, p. 171), and thirdly as the social structure of the protesters themselves or as their milieu anchorage in the wider society (cf. Eder 1985; Vester 1989; Crossley 2002).

In particular, the paradigm of the new social movements (NSM) tries to take into account all elements of this structural "trinity".

It is obvious that these approaches lack the agency side, but they even lack a structural analysis of protest: On the one side of the bridge between latent and manifest conflicts there are structures and crisis and on the other side there is protest (agency). The concepts remain separated. It is far more obvious that the more agency-oriented approaches of the US strand also lack a consideration of society and an adequate concept of agency because they are referring to simplifying rational actor theories (cf. Crossley 2002, pp. 56ff.; Bonacker and Schmitt 2004; Pettenkofer 2010). In these approaches, society and its structures are neglected in a triple sense or vice versa. Structures are at least at three levels important concerning the constitution of protest—they provide reasons for protest and they are an embodied as well as a surrounding part of agency.

Even a combination of the classical approaches would lack the two objectives, i.e. to "get in touch with society" and to overcome the constructed dualities in movement research. One would consider both sides: Structure and agency, rationality/strategy and identity, or emotionality, structure, and culture, but not the structure within the agent, rationality/strategy within the identity, the structure of culture, the visibility of structure by culture, and so on.

Hence the aim of this article is threefold. First, I would like to present Bourdieu's concepts as a whole, that is as a consistent analytical framework capable of overcoming not only the problematic dualities outlined above but additionally some classic problems of movement research. The following part (2) will present the basic notions of Bourdieu in their interconnectedness, thereby carving out possible implications for movement analysis as the second aim. The third aim (3) is to provide my analytical framework of habitus-structure conflicts based on Bourdieu's thoughts on symbolic violence. This heuristic tries to make sense of different kinds of struggles in a (post)modern society with social protest included. In other words: It aims to think research on society and protest under one and the same roof.

2   A Tour Around Bourdieu's Core Concepts and Their Implications for Movement Research

Excellent work has been done by applying Bourdieu in the context of movement research. Vester (1989, 2007) argues for a praxeological movement analysis neither exclusively materialist nor idealist. Klaus Eder tries to locate the new social movements socio-structurally within "Bourdieu's" social space (Eder 1985) and discusses the relationship of the symbolic dimension of protest and the collective identity of protesters (Eder 1998, 2000). Crossley (1999; Crossley and Crossley 2001) has applied Bourdieu's concepts for his own empirical work on the mental health movements in Britain and has above all not only created a fabulous overview of different approaches of movement analysis but also addresses their problems revolving around the structure/agency opposition as well as around the dichotomy of the rational and the irrational or emotional, respectively (Crossley 2002). He shows how Bourdieu's concepts can be used to overcome these problems. He suggests a framework for movement analysis taking Smelser's value added model as the basic framework (cf. Smelser 1962), locating the other classical approaches (political opportunity structures, frames, resource mobilization) in this framework and overcoming their problems using Bourdieu. Since one cannot better discuss the movement approaches and their deficits with Bourdieu than Crossley has already done, my main concern here is rather to provide a perspective based on the overall context of Bourdieu's concepts that one can draw on societal struggles and on social movements.

Actors in Turmoil
Like the metaphor of the battlefield suggests the actors have their own contexts and realities of action. It would be of little use for the soldier if he had the generals' overview because he has to duck each single bullet. In other words, he himself has the most relevant view regarding his specific reality. Bourdieu teaches us that an adequate analysis of social reality, including protest and social movements, has to take this into consideration (Schmitt 2006). This is a methodological rule of thumb, not a substantive one.

   Both sides of the range of social movement approaches, the structure-oriented crises theories as well as those operating with the rational actor (e.g. resource mobilization, political opportunity structures) may have the actors in mind. But it is a theoretical conception of the actor. On such a theoretical level one may call Habermas' concepts for example of the colonization of the lifeworld following systemic imperatives as intermediate (Habermas 1987/1981), bridging the structure/agency dichotomy, but methodologically they all are standing on the hill and so are even the rational actor conceptions.[3]

---

[3]The agency-focused approaches can be separated analytically into three strands, that I call *objectivist or theoretical subjectivism* (e.g. Sartre, the philosophy of the subject), *methodological or empirical subjectivism* (e.g. symbolic interactionism, ethnomethodology), and *methodological individualism* (rational actor theories). Only the methodological subjectivism shares the perspectives of actors in turmoil (Schmitt 2010, p. 35).

Although Bourdieu invites movement research to take the protesters' reality as one important part of the construction of reality, this emphasis on taking the individual context of action into account does not suggest that actors can live their lives freely and autonomously. Firstly, actors are subjected to external "reality barriers" as their *social space* is marked by social inequality and power asymmetries. Secondly, actors internalize this social reality, transmitted through symbols. Pierre Bourdieu calls these internalized social realities *habitus*. The habitus of an actor is an internalized system of boundaries and possibilities, which enables an actor to order and select perceiving, thinking, acting, and judging. Lastly, actors are subjected to the boundaries of the situations or *fields* in which they act. The soldiers on the battlefield have only partially contributed to the battle that is being fought by themselves and observed by the general.

Social Space—Social Inequality and Power Relationships
Modern democracies are structured hierarchically as opportunities for attaining a certain standard of living are unequally distributed. This unequal "probability space" can be understood as a social space in Bourdieu's sense. Yet this social inequality only becomes visible through symbols such as language, hobbies, clothing, body poses, tastes, etc. Those symbols are structured hierarchically and more or less all actors are familiar with the hierarchy. We realize that this or that type of clothing represents "something better." We usually also acknowledge this as normal, natural, just, earned by the person wearing the clothes—and fail to recognize the hierarchy's socially constructed nature. Part of the reason for this failure is that the possibilities of symbolization have expanded enormously. A greater menu of lifestyle choices is available to a greater number of people, which results in a seemingly more egalitarian social space.

This concept is probabilistic, not mechanistic. It is obvious that if for example an unskilled worker wins three million euros in a lottery, he will not start listening to classical music the next day (if he has not already done so before), like his new position in social space would suggest with a certain probability (cf. Schmitt 2006, p. 16, 2010, p. 29). It is his internalized cultural patterns, the hysteresis of his habitus, which leads us to the next station.

The concept of the social space has been used to locate social movements or even a whole movement sector within the social structure of a society at the level of the classical analysis of social structure (income, education, profession) as well as at the level of the probabilistically correspondent symbols, the so-called lifestyle (cf. Vester 1989, 2007; Eder 1985). It is relatively obvious that social movements and their members at least in the "Western world" possess above all cultural capital, are relatively well educated, and located between the upper and the working class. Eder (1985) calls the fight of the new social movements partially a moral crusade that is torn by their position in social space and their struggle for recognition of their cultural identities as legitimate (in sum by their specific class habitus).

Habitus—The Embodiment of Social Relations Mediated Through Symbols

The social space does not remain external to the actor. During their socialization process, actors internalize and embody the social structures, which are expressed through symbols. The structures thereby become part of the actor's identity. This is what Bourdieu calls habitus—internalized patterns of perceiving, thinking, feeling, acting, and judging (Bourdieu 1967, 1984/1979, 1990/1980; Krais and Gebauer 2002). Eager to avoid dissonances, an actor tends to choose other actors, situations, and symbols according to their fit with the habitus, i.e. with the already internalized patterns. This is what is meant by the saying "cobbler, stick to your last"—or you will get a habitus-structure conflict, I could add. The individual habitus functions as the hinge between objective social indicators (income, education, profession) and subjective/collective lifestyles—yet the habitus itself is a social product that is reliant on the structures and symbols which created it.

One can imagine the habitus as a dog leash that belongs to you from birth to the grave. This leash allows any path to be taken, but some of them are much easier to follow than others. We can meet with other "dogs" started from a totally different point in the social space, but we are still connected with our starting point by the leash. That is why persons who nearly have the same positions in the social space, e.g. the same profession, can be totally different, because they differ in the way they got there (which is not probable but possible), in their leashes, that is their habitus. By moving, the leashes are modified themselves. New experiences are integrated into what had already been integrated, so the habitus is something like an always changing stability, allowing infinite possibilities within its borders and always widening these borders by new experiences (Schmitt 2006, pp. 14ff., 2010, pp. 25ff.).

Generally, this concept does not only overcome the structure/agency dichotomy. It also gets over the mind/body duality because social structures and its symbols become embodied and shape our expression, our postures. Moreover, the juxtapositions of strategy and rationality on the one hand and identity and emotionality on the other become dispensable. The way the habitus concept is constructed allows for the idea of a habitual, pre-conscious strategy. It is a rather pre-conscious strategy for example to avoid discrepancies between the habitus and surrounding symbols (persons, professions, locations, lifestyles, behaviors, etc. that do not fit with our habitus), to avoid what I call habitus-structure conflicts (see below; cf. Schmitt 2006, 2007b, 2010). This does not deny the idea of rational action. Behavior and acting are "habitus-rational." Nevertheless, there is a strand above all in the German Bourdieu reception (e.g. Krais 1989; Barlösius 2006, pp. 30ff.) which interprets the habitus as "being in charge of" the automatic, non-reflexive way of acting and that the concept has had its day when reflexivity comes into the game, when things do not happen automatically, e.g. when a person is confronted with a situation and field that does not fit with the habitus, that is a situation of rupture. I have to admit that Bourdieu himself has somewhat supported this interpretation by his own, not always consistent definitions and explanations above all concerning the notion of habitus. But I am quite sure that a hermeneutic analysis of Bourdieu's descriptions leads to the assumption that there cannot be a reasoning, acting, etc. beyond the habitus (c.f. Schmitt 2010, pp. 147ff.). The habitus is an analytical agency concept that neither ignores acts of interpretation by the respective agents, nor their rationalities, nor their emotions, nor the structures of its development. On the contrary, all these are core aspects of habitus formation. "The concept of the habitus thus allows us to preserve what is useful about the RAT [rational actor theory; L.S.] model but also to eject those aspects of it which constitute an obstacle to a useful model of agency and to embrace other useful insights which it precludes" (Crossley 2002, p. 176).

This leads to some implications for movement research. Firstly, wherever a protester comes from socially and sociologically, his or her habitus is shaped by the protest, not least in a bodily sense. The notion of habitus allows biographical impacts of protest to be conceptualized in a more systematic way than McAdam (1988) does in his *Freedom Summer*. This is what Crossley (1999; Crossley and Crossley 2001) calls a *resistance habitus*. At the same time, this does not mean vice versa that habitus is nothing but a product. It is above all a producer of public protest or movements. Secondly, with the habitus concept it becomes easier to understand why some persons are able and willing to express their discontent with whatever conditions in public while others—even those that are more disadvantaged—do not. Some people who have grown up in conditions of disadvantage for example maybe do not know anything about the possibility of protest, do not feel legitimate to name the disadvantages publicly, or even would hurt their "brave" or "honest" habitus by protesting against it (Schmitt 2006, pp. 14ff., 2007a, 2010, pp. 25ff.).

Thirdly, one can focus on what is called a movement entrepreneur in a not too rationalist way by considering the embodied history (habitus) and the location in the social space. In addition to that Bourdieu's own descriptions of the principle of delegation may be helpful in that case. Here, he delineates how the advocate who speaks for the group only exists through the act of delegation by the group and how the group becomes the group because someone is speaking on its behalf (Bourdieu 1984, 1992a, pp. 203ff.). "It is in what I would call the *oracle effect*, thanks to which the spokesperson gives voice to the group in whose name he speaks, thereby speaking with all the authority of that elusive, absent phenomenon, that the function of priestly humility can best be seen: it is in abolishing himself completely in favour of God or the People that the priest turns himself into God or the People. It is when I become Nothing—and because I am capable of becoming Nothing, of abolishing myself, of forgetting myself, of sacrificing myself, of dedicating myself —that I become Everything. I am nothing but the delegate of God or the People, but that in whose name I speak is everything, and on this account I am everything" (ibid. p. 211, original emphasis).

This leads to a fourth point, to the question of creating or applying convenient *frames* (Snow et al. 1986; Snow and Benford 1992) by activists and to the development of a certain *repertoire of contention* (Tilly 1977, 1995). These two approaches of movement research could be systematized and put on sociological feet by discussing what range of collective habitus has to be addressed by the applied frames and symbols or, respectively, how a praxis becomes habitualized. "Having noted the similarity of this observation to that of the framing theorists, however, we should note that Bourdieu's account surpasses theirs in at least three respects. First, Bourdieu explicitly links habitus and the frames they entail to specific social groups and classes, thus extending the social psychological insights of movement theory in a more sociological direction. Second [...] he raises the question of the material and social circumstances which lead different social groups to have different habitus and frames in the first place. [...] Third [...] Bourdieu advances a strong theory of symbolic power which examines the manner in which certain 'frames' (not his term) are elevated and politically backed, at the expense of others" (Crossley 2002, p. 174).

Fields—The Location of Competitive Struggles
So far, I have argued that social inequality is mediated by and accepted through symbols which lead to a failure to see the social genesis of these structures. This has a pacifying effect enabling the relatively smooth reproduction of social prac- tices. Social inequality is widely accepted, partly because it is being veiled by symbols, partly because subaltern actors have internalized these hierarchies. It is

therefore unlikely that actors rebel as this might clash with one's own (disadvantaged) habitus, one's identity. Instead of engaging in "class struggle"—which Bourdieu defines as the collective unveiling of power structures (cf. Schwingel 1993, pp. 140ff.; Schmitt 2006, pp. 20ff.), rendering symbolic violence visible—actors will tend to try and climb up the symbolic ladder themselves. Potentially collective class struggles are thereby transformed in competitive struggles between individuals (Bourdieu 1984, pp. 244ff.; Schwingel 1993, pp. 85ff.; Schmitt 2006, pp. 20ff.).

However, we do not fight for economic, cultural, or other forms of capital[4] and their corresponding symbolic values (i.e. recognition) in some abstract social space, but in specific fields of action. Fields are relatively autonomous entities. They have their own rules, their own rewards, and distribution logics for these rewards. Actors usually engage in fields that fit their habitus. This connection renders society relatively stable as all actors, even the marginalized ones, accept the rules and the meaning of the field. Fighting takes place within the field in the form of individual competitive struggle, but neither the game as such, nor the unequal distribution of opportunities is questioned—the latter would be Bourdieu's "class struggle." The rules governing the fields always favor those with the more fitting habitus. The rules veil power asymmetries as the unequal distribution of opportunities seems to be in conformity with the rules of the game and not socially constructed. Dominating groups, i.e. dominating habitus, can always refer to "facts", i.e. institutionalized interpretations of the past and present, while dominated groups are forced to break the rules of reproductions, thereby creating habitus-structure conflicts. Thus, the field concept is not only a way of visualizing the horizontal differentiation of society but also allows the vertical dimension, a social hierarchy, to be considered.

For movement analysis this concept of field can contribute in multiple ways (cf. Crossley 2002, pp. 178ff.). First of all we can consider and analyze the movement sector as such a field of struggle with its own rules, own benefits and rewards (probably others than economic ones), own habitus constellations, with habitus that

---

[4]Although Bourdieu's notion of capital is in the reception not less important than the other termini, it is in my opinion the most problematic one (cf. Krais 2005) and the one that is least helpful in our context here and in the context of movement research in general. Therefore I forego explaining it right here (cf. Bourdieu 1983; Fröhlich 1994). For movement research aspects that are discussed within the resource mobilization approach like the different forms of capital (economic and cultural as well as social) as a resource may be of interest but provide no further analysis potential.

can arrange better with the field than others are able to. So this field can be analyzed like other fields in view of dominating and dominated persons—regardless of whether all actors—even the dominated ones—believe in the game, believe in the rules and in the benefits, and do not question the game as such. This is what Bourdieu calls *illusio*. Even in cases when disadvantaged habitus realize their position, they possibly would not unmask the game, because they would thereby deconstruct themselves. Instead of evoking a collective protest they struggle for a better position within the field. I do not want to suppose that this is what happens within social movements but it is at least one perspective one can certainly build on. Secondly, applying the concept of social fields one can differentiate between protests taking place in different fields (e.g. the academic field, the field of economic relations, etc.) with different rules. "Specific fields will often have their own forms of control, their own structures of opportunity and their specific types of resource, and thus the possibility of movement formation, development and success within them may be quite specific to them" (Crossley 2002, p. 180).

Thirdly, one can observe what happens when protests cross over into another field or when different fields get in crises synchronically: we can consider when and how fields get in crises so that a certain range of habitus does not fit any more to the field conditions. That is how Bourdieu analyzes—in a somewhat simplifying manner—the events of May 1968. The expectations of students and young scientists created by a growing number of universities led them to protest as it became obvious that these expectations could not be met by the objective conditions. So above all middle-class students that had been good pupils but had not gotten access to the elite universities as well as their upper-class peers who were too bad at school to get access to the same elite institutions could express their disappointment that the academic field could not live up to its promise (Bourdieu 1988; Gilcher-Holtey 1995). Interesting concerning that example is how different fields could synchronize their histories by critical incidents like the "night of the barricades" in Paris on 10 May 1968, when the academic field and the field of labor conflicts temporarily got a common history; something that has never happened for example with the student protest movement in Germany.

Fourthly the field concept allows us to conceptualize not only a hierarchy within the fields, but also a possible relationship of domination between different fields within the whole social space. Although fields are relatively autonomous, they are not closed universes. Protests may arise from the fact that imperatives of the economic field are imposed on other fields. This is reminiscent of Habermas' idea of the colonization of lifeworld (Habermas 1987/1981).

A fifth and last contribution of Bourdieu to movement research can be seen in his work on the *political field* (Bourdieu 1984, 1992a, p. 171). Of course one can analyze social movements as a part of that field. "The 'political field' entails all that we may wish to discuss under the rubric of 'movement industries', 'sectors'. etc., but it theorizes these aspects of movement activism in a more sensitive and instructive way than the overly economistic models of RM [resource mobilization, L.S.] provide for" (Crossley 2002, p. 182).

Movement research does not need to adopt the problems of Bourdieu's field concept. That is above all that he provides different definitions. Often the fields resemble functionally differentiated systems with respective professions. Within this definition it is to be questioned whether for example persons who work in the administration of a university belong to the academic field or not.[5] In another case Bourdieu takes the whole upper part of the social space as his own "field of power," which crosses several "professional fields" and where the economic side dominates the cultural (Bourdieu 1994/1988). Having introduced Bourdieu's essential concepts such as social space, habitus, and field as well as their diverse contributions to movement research, we can now proceed to elaborate the heuristic of symbolic violence and habitus-structure conflicts and to reflect on the impacts of this frame for analyzing protests and movements.

3 Symbolic Violence and Habitus-Structure Conflicts

This heuristic is an application of Bourdieu's framework that goes beyond the way Crossley discusses Bourdieu because it allows a view on movements located in the "totality" of struggles of social inequality on the one hand and it offers a perspective on how movements themselves tend to (re-)produce symbolic violence on the other hand.

Symbolic violence can be understood as a functional principle of modern societies. It keeps conflicts associated with the unequal distribution of opportunities for groups latent by directing them into competitive struggles within fields or within individual actors. Bourdieu's conception of symbolic violence can be seen as an elaboration and extension of Galtung's (1990) concept of "cultural violence." Bourdieu identifies pillars on which symbolic violence rests and demonstrates how

---

[5]An excellent example of whether one belongs to a field or not is the "scene at an exalted restaurant" brilliantly analyzed by Neckel (1993). The waiter is thrown back on his social status by a working-class family dining in this restaurant. Having been part of the upper milieu before, this family reduced him to his function by pragmatically piling the plates in a helping intention to facilitate the waiter's work. In doing so the waiter is reduced to the function of working and is banned from the upper milieu. In addition to this the waiter is ashamed of the family referring back to his cultural "deficiency".

"victims" of symbolic violence participate in their own subjugation. This makes "oppression a cooperative game," as proponents of social dominance theory have aptly put it (Sidanius and Pratto 1999).

One of the pillars is the objective fact of the symbolic. As argued above, social hierarchies are always mediated through symbols. It is via symbols that actors identify them and accept them as natural, freely chosen, earned, etc. Symbols transform socially constructed ("unjust") hierarchies into quasi-natural ("just") hierarchies that are being taken for granted.

Another pillar is the complicity of habitus and structure/field. There is a chance that actors who have been socialized into a deprived environment do not even perceive subsequent instances of discrimination as problematic. They may come to see it as something that fits their habitus, which is another factor leading to the relatively smooth reproduction of social power structures.

Bourdieu sees the phenomenon of symbolic violence as constitutive of all fields, which means that the rules of the field always favor the ruling elite while at the same time representing the "doxa", i.e. something that is unquestioned, taken for granted, and which represents the limits of that which is thinkable. Failing to see collective discrimination, actors are likely to believe in their individual "shortcomings". Even if they are aware of the socially constructed nature of their situation, their lack of power and the resulting fear of dropping out of the game acts as a strong disincentive to challenging the rules. This is one form of what I term a habitus-structure conflict, a form of competitive struggle within the fields (Bourdieu 1984, pp. 244ff.; Schwingel 1993, pp. 85ff.; Schmitt 2006, pp. 20ff.).

The above mentioned type of habitus-structure conflicts does not challenge the function of symbolic violence because actors do not relate the conflicts to power structures and social inequality. But what about those cases in which, as a result of struggles within a field, the rules become the object of contestation? As mentioned above, Bourdieu describes these struggles as "class struggles" and distinguishes them from competitive struggles within the fields (Schwingel 1993, pp. 140ff.). I label them "habitus-structure conflicts within the social space" because they go beyond the field by challenging the rules governing it. In doing so, they leave the path of "legitimate struggle" (legitimated by the rules within a field) by referring to the wider realm of the social space and contesting the ordering criteria of the entire society. Such a move is usually judged as unduly aggressive and unreasonable because it does not conform to the doxa.

All these types of conflicts can be understood as "struggles for recognition" as conceptualized by Honneth (1995/1992; see also Reinmuth in this volume). Honneth, however, focuses on actors who expect to be recognized and the ensuing conflicts once this expectation is not met. Yet this hardly covers all types of potential recognition conflicts. For example, it is possible that an actor within a certain field cannot even conceive of the possibility to be worthy or eligible for potential recognition. In the case of individual human actors, such a conflict is likely to remain entirely internal and will not even spill over into the realm of interpersonal conflicts. I term this an intrapersonal habitus-structure conflict. Honneth's argument is based on the normative assumption that people are able to sense and name their problems as a lack of recognition. This argument is referring to Habermas' "ideal speech situation," which is not based on empirical findings. This is an advantage of Bourdieu's framework and the elaboration of the habitus-structure conflict heuristic. It allows the view from a hill to be broken down to the empirical level of interaction. One can consider empirically who is habitually able to constitute the "ideal speech situation,"[6] to question the lifeworld of which habitus becomes colonized by which structures, to reflect upon which habitus struggles for recognition in which field, and how governance becomes subjectivized (Foucault) by which habitus-structure constellations. "The Moral Grammar of Social Conflicts" (Honneth) can be empirically kept as "The Social Grammar of Social Conflicts" and that is why Bauer and Bittlingmayer (2000; translation L.S.) call Bourdieu's oeuvre "a continuation of the Critical Theory with other means."[7]

Beyond applying Bourdieu's concepts separately to movement research, with the elaboration of the heuristic of habitus-structure conflicts it becomes possible to consider protest and social movements under the roof of societal struggles that are framed by the conditions of symbolic violence. Thus, protest on the one hand can be analyzed under the aspect of how it reacts to symbolic violence; that is, how it tries to reveal the concealed mechanisms of power. On the other hand social movements can be questioned on which role they play in the reproduction of social inequality by their own social structure (with their habitus) and by the symbols applied, suggesting a representation of "all people" or of "marginalized groups," but in doing so probably concealing habitual and symbolical distances to those on whose behalf they are speaking, suggesting participation where exclusion is to be found (cf. Schmitt 2004, 2007a, 2010). This may be Bourdieu's strongest

---

[6]Bourdieu states that to have an opinion and the "ability" to speak are not at all distributed equally, but are a luxury reserved to a certain range of habitus (cf. Bourdieu 1993a/1980, pp. 60ff., 194ff.).

[7]Of course the habitus concept itself is to be bridged to the level of interaction. This is a task beyond the range of this chapter. Wittpoth (1994) has shown how to use Bourdieu to differentiate George Herbert Mead's ideas on the interactional level, for example of the "generalized other" with Bourdieu's habitus concept. I have made use of this for my empirical work on habitus-structure conflicts in the field of academic education (Schmitt 2010).

contribution to movement research and above all to social movements: not to delegitimate protest, but to provide a socio-analysis, i.e. the possibility to see habitual, structural, and field-specific boundaries as well as symbolic exclusions. This insight is a prerequisite for a symbolic revolution which he estimates as the basis for real change (Bourdieu 1996).

> By forcing one to discover externality at the heart of internality, banality in the illusion of rarity, the common in the pursuit of the unique, sociology does more than denounce all the impostures of egoistic narcissism; it offers perhaps the only means of contributing, if only through awareness of determinations, to the construction, otherwise abandoned to the forces of the world, of something like a subject (Bourdieu 1990, p. 21).

References

Barlösius, Eva. 2006. *Pierre Bourdieu*. Frankfurt: Campus.

Bauer, Ullrich, and Uwe H. Bittlingmayer. 2000. Pierre Bourdieu und die Frankfurter Schule. Eine Fortsetzung der Kritischen Theorie mit anderen Mitteln? In *Verstehen und Kritik. Soziologische Suchbewegungen nach dem Ende der Gewissheiten*, ed. Claudia Rademacher, and Peter Wiechens, 241–298. Wiesbaden: Westdeutscher Verlag.

Bonacker, Thorsten, and Lars Schmitt. 2004. Politischer Protest zwischen latenten Strukturen und manifesten Konflikten. Perspektiven soziologischer Protestforschung am Beispiel der neuen Friedensbewegung. *Mitteilung des Instituts für soziale Bewegungen* 32: 193–213.

Bourdieu, Pierre. 1967. Postface (Nachwort) zu: Erwin Panofsky: *Architecture gothique et pensée scolastique. Precédé de l'Abbé Suger de Saint-Denis,* edited and translated by Pierre Bourdieu. Paris: Les Editions de Minuit.

Bourdieu, Pierre. 1983 Ökonomisches Kapital, kulturelles Kapital, soziales Kapital. In: *Soziale Ungleichheiten.* Soziale Welt, Sonderband 2, ed. Ronald Kreckel, 183–198. Göttingen: Schwartz.

Bourdieu, Pierre. 1984/1979. *Distinction. A social critique of the judgement of taste.* Cambridge: Harvard University Press.

Bourdieu, Pierre. 1988/1984. *Homo academicus.* Cambridge: Polity Press.

Bourdieu, Pierre. 1990/1980. *The logic of practice.* Stanford: Stanford University Press.

Bourdieu, Pierre. 1992a/1984. *Language and symbolic power.* Cambridge, Malden: Polity Press.

Bourdieu, Pierre. 1992b. *Die verborgenen Mechanismen der Macht. Schriften zu Politik und Kultur 1.* Hamburg: VSA.

Bourdieu, Pierre. 1993a/1980. *Sociology in question.* London: Sage.

Bourdieu, Pierre. 1993b. *Satz und Gegensatz. Über die Verantwortung des Intellektuellen.* Frankfurt: Fischer.

Bourdieu, Pierre. 1994/1989. *State nobility. Elite schools in the field of power.* Oxford: University Press.

Bourdieu, Pierre. 1996. Masculine domination revisited. *The Berkeley journal of sociology* 41: 189–201. (The Goffman Prize Lecture, University of Berkeley, April 4, 1996).

Bourdieu, Pierre. 1998. *Interview with J. Kneihs*. Transcript of a talk at the Collège de France, Paris, the 19.06.1998. www.iwp.jku.at/lxe/wt2k/div/bourdieu.htm. Accessed 9 Jan 2016.

Bourdieu, Pierre et al. 1999/1993. *The weight of the world. Social suffering and impoverishment in contemporary society*. Cambridge: Polity Press.

Bourdieu, Pierre. 2003/2001. *Firing back. Against the tyranny of the market 2*. New York, London: The New Press.

Crossley, Nick. 1999. Fish, field, habitus and madness. On the first wave mental health users in Britain. *British Journal of Sociology* 50(4): 647–670.

Crossley, Nick. 2002. *Making sense of social movements*. Buckingham, Philadelphia: Open University Press.

Crossley, Michele L., and Nick Crossley. 2001. Patient voices, social movements and the habitus. How psychiatric survivors speak out. *Social Science and Medicine* 52(10): 1477–1489.

Eder, Klaus. 1985. The new social movements. Moral crusades, political pressure groups, or social movements. *Social Research* 52(4): 869–890.

Eder, Klaus. 1998. Protest und symbolische Gewalt. Zur Logik der Mobilisierung kollektiver Identitäten. *Forschungsjournal Neue Soziale Bewegungen* 11(4): 29–40.

Eder, Klaus. 2000. *Kulturelle Identität zwischen Tradition und Utopie. Soziale Bewegungen als Ort gesellschaftlicher Lernprozesse*. Frankfurt, New York: Campus.

Fröhlich, Gerhard. 1994. Kapital, Habitus, Feld, Symbol. Grundlage der Kulturtheorie bei Pierre Bourdieu. In *Das symbolische Kapital der Lebensstile. Zur Kultursoziologie der Moderne nach Pierre Bourdieu*, ed. Ingo Mörth, and Gerhard Fröhlich, 31–54. Frankfurt: Campus.

Galtung, Johan. 1990. Cultural violence. *Journal of Peace Research* 27(3): 291–305.

Gilcher-Holtey, Ingrid. 1995. *Die Phantasie an die Macht. Mai 68 in Frankreich*. Frankfurt: Suhrkamp.

Habermas, Jürgen. 1987/1981. *Theory of Communicative Action, Volume Two: Lifeworld and System: A Critique of Functionalist Reason*. Boston: Beacon Press.

Hellmann, Kai-Uwe. 1999. Paradigmen der Bewegungsforschung. Eine Fachdisziplin auf dem Weg zur normalen Wissenschaft. In *Neue soziale Bewegungen. Impulse, Bilanzen, Perspektiven*, ed. Ansgar Klein, Hans-Josef Legrand, and Thomas Leif, 91–113. Opladen: Westdeutscher Verlag.

Hellmann, Kai-Uwe, and Ruud Koopmans (eds.). 1998. *Paradigmen der Bewegungsforschung. Entstehung und Entwicklung von Neuen Sozialen Bewegungen und Rechtsextremismus*. Opladen: Westdeutscher Verlag.

Honneth, Axel. 1995/1992. *The struggle for recognition. The moral grammar of social conflicts*. Cambridge: Polity Press.

Krais, Beate. 1989. Soziales Feld, Macht und kulturelle Praxis. Die Untersuchungen Bourdieus über die verschiedenen Fraktionen der "herrschenden Klasse" in Frankreich. In *Klassenlage, Lebensstil und kulturelle Praxis. Theoretische und empirische Beiträge zur Auseinandersetzung mit Pierre Bourdieus Klassentheorie*, ed. Klaus Eder, 47–70. Frankfurt: Suhrkamp.

Krais, Beate. 2005. Die moderne Gesellschaft und ihre Klassen. Bourdieus Konstrukt des sozialen Raumes. In *Pierre Bourdieu. Deutsch-französische Perspektiven*, ed. Catherine Colliot-Thélène, Etienne François, and Gunter Gebauer, 79–105. Frankfurt: Suhrkamp.

Krais, Beate, and Gunter Gebauer. 2002. *Habitus*. Bielefeld: transcript.

McAdam, Doug. 1988. *Freedom summer*. New York: Oxford University Press.

Neckel, Sighard. 1993. Soziale Scham. Unterlegenheitsgefühle in der Konkurrenz von Lebensstilen. In *Praxis und Ästhetik. Neue Perspektiven im Denken Pierre Bourdieus*, ed. Gunter Gebauer, and Wulf Christoph, 270–291. Frankfurt: Suhrkamp.

Pettenkofer, Andreas. 2010. *Radikaler Protest. Zur soziologischen Theorie politischer Bewegungen*. Frankfurt, New York: Campus.

Schmitt, Lars. 2004. Kritische Wissenschaft und Friedensbewegung. Soziologische Selbstreflexion zur Stärkung der Bewegung. *Wissenschaft und Frieden* 22(3): 49–52.

Schmitt, Lars. 2006. *Symbolische Gewalt und Habitus-Struktur-Konflikte. Entwurf einer Heuristik zur Analyse und Bearbeitung von Konflikten*. CCS Working Papers 2/2006. Marburg: Zentrum für Konfliktforschung.

Schmitt, Lars. 2007a. Soziale Ungleichheit und Protest. Waschen und rasieren im Spiegel von ,Symbolischer Gewalt' *Forschungsjournal Neue Soziale Bewegungen* 20 (1): 34–45.

Schmitt, Lars. 2007b. Symbolische Gewalt und Habitus-Struktur-Konflikte. Mit Bourdieu Konflikte analysieren und bearbeiten? In *Bourdieu und die Linke. Politik – Ökonomie – Kultur*, ed. Effi Böhlker, and Rainer Rilling, 166–192. Berlin: Dietz.

Schmitt, Lars. 2010. *Bestellt und nicht abgeholt. Soziale Ungleichheit und Habitus-Struktur-Konflikte im Studium*. Wiesbaden: VS Verlag für Sozialwissenschaften.

Schwingel, Markus. 1993. *Analytik der Kämpfe. Macht und Herrschaft in der Soziologie Bourdieus*. Hamburg: Argument.

Sidanius, Jim, and Felicia Pratto. 1999. *Social dominance, an intergroup theory of social hierarchy and oppression*. Cambridge: Cambridge University Press.

Smelser, Neil. 1962. *Theory of collective behaviour*. London: Routledge and Kegan Paul.

Snow, David, and Robert Benford. 1992. Master frames and cycles of protest. In *Frontiers in social movement theory*, ed. Aldous Morris, and Carol McClurg Mueller, 133–155. New Haven: Yale University Press.

Snow, David, et al. 1986. Frame alignment processes, micromobilization and movement participation. *American Sociological Review* 51(4): 464–481.

Tilly, Charles. 1977. Getting it together in Burgundy. *Theory and Society* 4(4): 479–504.

Tilly, Charles. 1995. Contentious repertoires in Great Britain, 1758–1834. In *Repertoires and cycles of contention*, ed. Mark Traugott, 15–42. Durham: Duke University Press.

Vester, Michael. 1989. Neue soziale Bewegungen und soziale Schichten. In *Alternativen zur alten Politik? Neue soziale Bewegung in der Diskussion*, ed. Ulrike C. Wasmuth, 38–63. Darmstadt: Wissenschaftliche Buchgesellschaft.

Vester, Michael. 2007. Weder materialistisch noch idealistisch. *Für eine praxeologische Bewegungsanalyse Forschungsjournal Neue Soziale Bewegungen* 20(1): 22–33.

Wasmuht, Ulrike C. 1989. Zur Untersuchung der Entstehung und Entwicklung sozialer Bewegungen. Ein analytischer Deskriptionsrahmen. In *Alternativen zur alten Politik? Neue soziale Bewegung in der Diskussion*, ed. Ulrike C. Wasmuth, 159–176. Darmstadt: Wissenschaftliche Buchgesellschaft.

Wittpoth, Jürgen. 1994. *Rahmungen und Spielräume des Selbst. Ein Beitrag zur Theorie der Erwachsenensozialisation im Anschluss an George H. Mead und Pierre Bourdieu.* Frankfurt: Diesterweg.

Author Biography

Dr. Lars Schmitt is Professor for Political Sociology at the University of Applied Sciences in Düsseldorf. His research interests are Social Inequality, Conflicts and Participation above all in contexts of Higher Education and Social Movements. He developed the methodology of Habitus-Structure-Reflexivity. Recent publications are „Konflikte vermitteln?" (edited with M. Bös and K. Zimmer, Springer VS 2015), „Herausforderungen hochschulischer Diversity-Politik" (with V. Eickhoff, in: Fereidooni/Zeoli: Die diversitätsbewusste Ausrichtung des Bildungs- und Kulturwesens, der Wirtschaft und Verwaltung, Springer VS 2016), „Studentische Sozioanalysen und Habitus-Struktur-Reflexivität" (in: Rheinländer: Ungleichheitssensible Hochschullehre, Springer VS 2015), „Habitus-Struktur-Reflexivität im Spiegel sozialer Ungleichheitsbeschreibungen" (in: Sander: Habitussensibilität, Springer VS 2014).

Social Movements and Sociological Systems Theory

Isabel Kusche

The Luhmannian strand of systems theory encountered the topic of social movements more or less unexpectedly; that is, not due to its centrality for the theoretical approach but as a reaction to the proliferation of new social movements in the 1980s. An attempt at a synthesis of a theory of communication systems, a theory of societal differentiation, and a theory of long-term social change, the theory had by that time developed a description of modern society that emphasized its functional differentiation on the one hand, and the relevance of interactions and organizations as particular types of systems below the level of societal differentiation on the other. Whereas older social movements might have been regarded as a transitional phenomenon, pointing to the historical intricacies of the change from a primarily stratified society to one based on functional subsystems, new social movements obviously had to be related to the existence of the latter. In the course of doing this, systems theory did not so much develop a consistent theory of social movements as a number of theoretical ideas that primarily concern the relevance of social movements for modern society and the particularities of their form of communication.

1 Theorizing Social Movements—Challenges to and of Systems Theory

Proposing a theory of communication systems, systems theory understands communication not as the transmission of information but as a selection from a horizon of possible references. Communication is conceived as a synthesis of three

I. Kusche (✉)
Aarhus University, Aarhus, Denmark
e-mail: isabelkusche@aias.au.dk

© Springer Fachmedien Wiesbaden 2016
J. Roose and H. Dietz (eds.), *Social Theory and Social Movements*,
DOI 10.1007/978-3-658-13381-8_5

selections: information, utterance, and understanding (Luhmann 1995, pp. 139ff). As the latter manifests itself only in a subsequent utterance, communication is always constituted in retrospect (cf. Stichweh 2000, p. 10). Communication is thus a continuous flow of immensely short communicative events, each of which uses the distinction between information and utterance in order to attribute a specific meaning to a previous communicative event, and to each of which a specific meaning is attributed by a subsequent communicative event. Thus, it is the understanding that constitutes the communicative event, but this understanding is relative to other communicative events and does not represent a more or less correct understanding of intentions. Moreover, due to the backwards direction in which communication is constituted, communications are never singular events but concatenate into systems which consist of a continuous stream of communications referring to other such communications, thereby producing a difference between the system and its environment.

Since the attribution of communicative meaning is an effect of the ongoing process of communication, each communicative event is a contingent operation that could select differently. This basic contingency of communication often does not become a manifest problem as it has always already been reduced by expectations that constrain the range of likely further communicative events (cf. Luhmann 1995, p. 292). These expectations operate as structures of communication. They do not preclude deviation and surprises but introduce an orientation towards what has happened in the past of a social system. The structures of expectations within a society consequently make all the difference with regard to what is considered likely or unlikely, rational or irrational, desirable or undesirable.

Against this background, as a theory of societal differentiation systems theory takes up and modifies Parsons' structural functionalism in order to understand the characteristics of modern society. Whereas Parsons analytically distinguishes four basic functions, which are fulfilled by societal subsystems as prerequisites of a stable social order, Luhmann assumes that such subsystems actually constitute themselves on the basis of specialized expectations that orient communications. The major structural feature of modern society is the fact that it comprises a number of societal subsystems that specialize in one basic societal function and operate with communications, the form of which corresponds to this function (Luhmann 1984, pp. 63ff). In the same way that the continuous concatenation of, for example, specialized economic communications constitutes the economic subsystem of society, other subsystems, such as politics, law, or science, constantly reproduce themselves by processing their own specialized communications. As a result, they combine autonomy concerning the fulfillment of their function with indifference to anything that does not register as relevant for such communications. Although not all communications in society belong to such a functional subsystem, they are a pervasive feature of modern society, which can therefore be considered a functionally differentiated society.

In line with these theoretical interests, systems theory has often focused on the analysis of functional subsystems, the structures (e.g. symbolical generalized media of communication, binary distinctions) that affect their constant reproduction, and the overarching change from a primarily stratified society to a functionally differentiated society instantiated by them. As the changes include a distancing between the scope of face-to-face interactions and the horizon of all societal communication, as well as the advent of formalized, decision-making organizations, dealing with the contingent options functionally specialized structures produce, the theory has also analyzed interactions and organizations as particular forms of social systems and discussed their relation to function systems.

Against this background, social movements are a phenomenon that challenges central concepts of systems theory. They comprise more than a mass of face-to-face interactions, they differ from organizations due to the informal character of communication and the consequent lack of decision-making capacity, and their relationship to the function systems of society is highly ambivalent (Luhmann 1997, p. 850). On the one hand, they address problems and grievances an observer could attribute to the working of function systems. For example, the feminist movement may protest against inequalities of gender as manifested in the job market or the legal regulation of divorce, and the environmental movement may raise its voice against the construction of new nuclear power plants, which scientists claim to be safer than any previous generation of this technology, and which politicians support as part of an energy policy that attempts to reduce the dependence on oil. On the other hand, the communication in social movements itself does not frame the problem in such terms. It rather criticizes the state of society in general and identifies opponents flexibly according to current topics that resonate with its overarching concern. The protest is framed in moral terms, thus appealing to opponents to abandon their incorrect path of action and decision-making in favor of what is perceived as right. It usually does not take into account the communicative logic of function systems, which entails specialized structures of expectation, e.g. expectations of return on investment in the economic system or expectations of legally consistent decision-making in the realm of law, that are not receptive to moral evaluations.

Taking the functional differentiation of society as its point of departure, systems theory is consequently skeptical as to whether the perspective of actors involved in or affected by social movements renders an adequate conception of their workings and effects. In contrast to other theories in the field, it therefore does not depart from the perspective of actors who might form a social movement, provided they manage to act collectively in spite of individual rationality (Hardin 1982) or they frame a grievance in such a way that it attracts supporters (Snow et al. 1986; Snow and Benford 1988). Systems theory regards interests and preferences as an effect of attributions in the process of communication and not as causes of action. Consequently, it is the concatenation of communications claiming to speak for certain, generalized interests or concerns and the concomitant identification of opponents who ignore these interests or concerns that produces the possibility of collective action (Japp 1986a, b, p. 178). Instead of focusing on actors, systems theory proposes analyzing social movements in terms of the problems of a modern society that is differentiated into functional realms, i.e. shaped by different communicative rationalities (economic, legal, scientific, political, etc.), none of which is superior to the others.

2 The Communication of Social Movements

2.1 'Systemness'

Concatenating communications, oriented by specific structures of expectation, form social systems within an environment in which other such systems, based on other structures of expectation, are constituted in the same way. In this sense, a social system exists based on an identity that is the result of distinguishing its own operations from all that happens outside the system. Consequently, it is in such terms that systems theory poses the question of collective identity so prominent in the social movement literature (e.g. Melucci 1989; Friedman and McAdam 1992). To the extent that the respective authors emphasize the process-based character of collective identity, it is communications that ascribe, reproduce, and alter it. Therefore, systems theory reframes the question of collective identity as a question about the systemic character of social movements. They can be regarded as social systems if it is possible to demonstrate that there are communicative operations constituting them and in what way they differ from other communications, thus creating a self-referential network of communications that distinguishes itself from its societal environment and concomitantly establishes an identity of its own.

In this regard, we have to distinguish between the specificity of social movement communication in general and the specificity of particular social movements. A social movement is neither identical to a single or a number of organizations—even if the contributions of resource mobilization theory (cf. McCarthy and Zald 1977) have focused on social movement organizations, which undoubtedly play an important but also varying role within social movements—nor is it simply a sum of face-to-face interactions. Systems theory therefore tends to regard social movements as a systems type of its own.[1]

What distinguishes them from other types of social systems must be a specific kind of observation embedded in their communications. Observation, in a systems theoretical context, does not refer to the cognitive act of a conscious being but is the application of a distinction with two sides. Communication always uses one such a distinction, namely the one between information and utterance. But the expectations that orient the concatenation of operations based on this distinction add further distinctions in the way of filtering schemas. This is particularly obvious in the case of function systems, the communications of which are oriented by a binary code, such as government/opposition in the case of the political system (Luhmann 1989, pp. 84ff) or payment/non-payment in the case of the economic system (Luhmann 1989, pp. 51ff). These distinctions limit what is considered relevant information within a system. Thus, for example, only those communications pertaining to potential or actual changes in liquidity differentials are operations of the economic function system. The distinctions thereby establish the difference to communications with other relevance and, consequently, the system in contrast to its societal environment.

Looking at social movements, a preliminary characterization of their mode of communication may reveal several aspects: it seems to be about mobilizing people for protest against certain lamentable states or decisions, and the protest itself is a major means for this mobilization. Ahlemeyer (1995, pp. 88ff) therefore suggests understanding social movement communication as mobilizing communication, i.e. communication that combines the selection of information with an expectation to act as a consequence of this information (Ahlemeyer 1995, pp. 88ff). The

---

[1]While it is certainly feasible to nominally define social movements in a way that equates them with social movement organizations, a focus on communication systems implies the attempt to identify a form of communication that is particular to social movements. This includes the possibility that organizations use this form of communication and thus become part of a social movement in this regard.

expectation is a demand addressed to others, but based on the binding effect it has on those communicating it. In other words, the demand has the potential to convince others only insofar as it implies that those calling for it already act accordingly and will do so in the future. Thus, the demand to protest against nuclear power plants functions as a mobilizing communication only because those demanding to protest protest themselves. More precisely, it is the protest itself that functions as mobilizing communication since it insinuates that anything provoking protest must be problematic to such a degree that those still passive can no longer plausibly abstain from protesting (Luhmann 1997, p. 854f.). But even when the effort to mobilize others is not (yet) successful, mobilizing communications further the movement through their self-binding effects, as long as other such communications follow subsequently.

Although mobilization communications occur in face-to-face interaction and formal organizations may be used in order to intensify such communications, social movements are neither identical with a series of interactions nor with organizations. Whereas situations of co-presence make it more likely that a mobilization communication is followed by a consenting communication, formal organization can increase the visibility of mobilization communication; for example, by aiming for mass media coverage. However, the social movement itself is produced and reproduced as long as mobilization communications concatenate with other such communications.

2.2   Distinctive Attributions

Protest functions as mobilizing communication by establishing and reproducing a specific distinction, namely the one between protest and protesters on the one hand and the issue and opponents against which they protest on the other (Luhmann 1997, p. 854f.). Whereas social movements protest against different things, the communication of protest always has the form of a distinction between friends on the one hand and enemies on the other, which entails the expectation, addressed to bystanders, to choose a side. The distinction between protesters and opponents thus posits a conflict with societal relevance without limiting the occasions for invoking such a conflict. But why is it able to bind commitments to such a degree that a social movement can reproduce itself by finding ever new occasions for protest? Instead of describing the basis of such a reproduction as collective identity (Melucci 1989; Friedman and McAdam 1992), systems theory points to a fundamental difference at the heart of any attempt to form the identity of a movement. It is a difference that owes its relevance to neither the creation of powerful symbols nor a convincing interpretation of the commonalities within the movement, but to the structure of modern society, namely its dependence on decision-making.

Since function systems cannot refer to a superior guiding authority, their communications concatenate in relation to expectations, which are themselves a result of past operations of the respective systems.[2] This self-reference of social systems produces the necessity of selection and, consequently, of decision-making. All decision-making is contingent, as each decision could be taken differently and thus leads to other consequences. But whereas these consequences are often relevant to many people, and just how many is usually not even clear, the decisions are often attributed to a few decision-makers—no matter how many constraints they faced when making the decision, which could theoretically be traced back to an infinite number of other decisions and their respective decision-makers, and regardless of whether there was any clearly identifiable decision.

Modern society thus constantly produces a difference between decision-makers and those affected by the respective decisions (Luhmann 1993, pp. 101ff). This difference provides the grounds for rejecting decisions simply because they were taken by others (cf. Japp and Kusche 2008, pp. 90ff). They are then observed as risky decisions endangering those not involved in their making. Especially in cases in which decisions appear to risk catastrophic damage, no matter how unlikely its actual occurrence may be (Halfmann and Japp 1993, p. 439), the difference between decision-makers and those affected can be the basis for mobilizing communications of the latter against the former.

Due to its fundamental character, the difference cannot be overcome by giving 'reasonable arguments' for a decision. It is the result of divergent attributions: Whereas the decision is attributed to someone else, its (negative) consequences are attributed to oneself, triggering a rejection on principle. The two fundamentally different ways of observing decisions consistently provide occasions for protest. Moreover, the protest is relatively immune to the often elaborate attempts of decision-makers to explain the rationality of their decisions. Neither the authority of experts nor an appeal to trust is able to bridge this divide (cf. Douglas 1985; Fowlkes and Miller 1987; Japp 2000) since it is possible to attribute hidden motives to anything decision-makers may attempt in order to convince those affected by a decision of its plausibility (Otway and Wynne 1989).

In social movement research, framing approaches (Snow et al. 1986; Snow and Benford 1988) have pointed to the fact that social movements rely on schemata of

---

[2]This includes the possibility that communications depart from the expected course and thus produce variation. However, this variation can only be observed by referring to an expectation it did not fulfil.

interpretation in order to identify issues, causes, and solutions. Systems theory also emphasizes the importance of schemata, but integrates this aspect into its theory of communication. Since the meaning of a communication is not determined by a previous intention but by a retrospective attribution in the course of another communicative event, schemata orient all communications by providing typical meanings that attract further communications (Luhmann 1997, p. 110). Causal schemata are especially prominent in this regard as they are involved in all kinds of communication, both mundane and specialized. Whenever we talk about causes, they are attributed causes since each event is in principle the result of a plethora of causes that brought it about and is itself a cause for a plethora of effects. Any reference to causality picks out only a few causes, and systems theory is primarily interested in this selectivity that follows different logics in different social systems.

Thus, in the political system, the selection of causes is oriented by the binary code of this system, i.e. the distinction between government and opposition or, more generally, the logic of power differentials. This concerns both the setting of the political agenda and the suggestion of political solutions. The more complex such causal stories are, the less practicable political interventions appear in order to ameliorate or even solve a problem. Consequently, problems tend to be attributed to a complex mix of causes whenever blame is to be avoided, they tend to be attributed to one or two clearly identifiable causes whenever political actors wish to present a credible political program, and typically government and opposition will use different attributions (Stone 1989). According to a different logic of selectivity, mass media attribute causes and effects of the events they cover, focusing on conflict and debate, moderated, for example, by a balance norm (Gamson and Modigliani 1989, pp. 7ff).

In the same way, the framing practices described for social movements follow the logic of mobilization of protesters against problems and opponents, and select in a manner that is appropriate for its specific kind of communication. Whereas framing approaches in social movement research assume that the framing problem is one of matching individual interpretive frames with the frames social movements or social movement organizations respectively offer (Snow et al. 1986), systems theory argues that all frames derive from the basic problem of highlighting the difference between decision-makers and their decisions on the one hand, and those affected by these decisions and the negativity of the effects on the other, which is the precondition for the specific form of social movement communication. This implies an emphasis on causes that are unlikely to disappear anytime soon, on actors who are visible enough to be addressed without much effort to identify them, and on the inevitability and absoluteness of being affected.

2.3 Values and Morality

To be affected by decisions without being involved in the decision-making process opens up the potential to criticize the effects of such decisions on moral grounds. Systems theory does not wish to judge whether the actions of social movements are good or bad, but it notes that this distinction, which is at the basis of morality, plays an important role in the communication of social movements. Any morality denotes conditions under which another person is respected or disrespected. These conditions vary historically, but with the advent of functional differentiation there is no overarching hierarchy of values from which conditions for personal respect or disrespect could be deduced in a way that is binding for all (Luhmann 1997, pp. 244ff; Luhmann and Fuchs 1988, p. 32). However, this does not lead to the abandonment of morality. Quite the contrary, moralizing communications prosper because conflicts can be communicated not only in terms of factual arguments but also by pitting values against each other. Whenever such a value is treated as absolute, the observation that the other side does not act according to this value is prone to provoke a reference to morality.

Social movements refer to values as absolute, although one characteristic of modern society is the relativity of all values. As there is no consented hierarchy of values, a communication may refer to a certain value in order to justify a demand or judgment, only to be countered by a reference to another, in principle equally important value. Within the function systems, the non-existence of a hierarchy of values permits flexibility with regard to decision-making, in the sense that a decision at one point in time may be justified by the value of freedom, and at a later point in time it may be modified or corrected by another decision, pointing to the value of equality. In contrast, social movements are fundamentalist in that they insist on the absolute priority of one value. But they are modern nonetheless since the values on which they insist are points of reference in the function systems as well (Krohn 1999). However, social movements make them absolute by linking them to something unquestionable.

Luhmann (1989, pp. 127ff) stresses the communication of anxiety as the basis on which modern social movements demand absolute respect for certain values and attribute respect and disrespect accordingly. Anxiety cannot be denied and a reference to it therefore blocks attempts to argue about the justification of demands. However, the moral implications of the communications of anxiety are not necessarily linked with the mobilizing communications of social movements; instead, anxiety may take the form of moral panic amplified by mass media coverage and thus come to be regarded as a broad public concern to which decision-makers promptly attend (Ungar 2001; Hier 2003). In contrast, Ahlemeyer (1995, p. 218) regards the reference to life as a value above all others as the ultimate basis for moral distinctions within social movements. Since various problems can be framed as a threat to the value of a self-determined, unharmed life, social movements can take up many occasions and link them with mobilizing communications. They implicitly make this connection when they relate information about a lamentable state or situation with the expectation to do something about it (Ahlemeyer 1995, p. 227). Whereas those who remain passive may be convinced to act with the help of further mobilizing communications, the identified opponents find themselves on the other side of the moral divide, because as decision-makers they would be able to do something but clearly do not.

Consequently, a reference to morality does not foster agreement or compromise. However, it binds at least those referring to a value by linking it with the question of respect versus disrespect, thus making the continuation of social movement communication likely even though the fundamental difference between decision-makers and those affected by their decisions severely limits the hopes for an understanding.

With regard to the question of how fundamentalist the reference to the value of life is, systems-theoretical views differ. Whereas Luhmann emphasizes the moralizing dimension of social movement communication and the way it tends to reduce the complexity of modern society to a distinction between supporters and opponents of a social movement, Ahlemeyer (1995, p. 269) points out that social movements can indeed consider the logic of function systems and, as a consequence, may formulate demands that seem less radical and more concerned with the potential for change within function systems. The way in which parts of the anti-globalization movement promoted the Tobin tax as a way to tame the financial markets and consequently globalization (Ruggiero 2002, p. 49) is an example of how social movements can take into consideration the specific logic of function systems, in this case the economic system.

3   Functional Differentiation and Social Movements

Social movements rely on protest as a form with the two sides of protesters and opponents. This form of communication differs from that of function systems, each of which also uses a binary distinction. The government of today can be the opposition of tomorrow due to election results, the truth of certain scientific facts can be found to be false as a result of new research, and financing one investment may result in the inability to finance others. In contrast, the distinction on which social movements base their communications cannot be crossed. Pointing to the difference between decision-makers and those affected by decisions, the distinction is nonetheless related to the functional differentiation of society (Hellmann 1996, pp. 65ff).

In the course of differentiation, roles with complementary expectations develop around functions—on the one hand, roles for providing services within the framework of the function system (professional roles or performance roles), and on the other hand, specialized audience roles for receiving these services (Luhmann 1977, p. 35). It is critical to understand that each function system has its own audience, which plays its role in reference to the expectations attached to the leading roles within the respective system. In principle, the same persons can switch between a professional role and audience role. This is a common feature of the scientific system, in which scientists produce research results and publish them but are themselves the main audience for reading such publications. In other systems the role differentiation is much more pronounced, for example in the case of the economic system with producers and consumers or the political system with politicians and voters. Although consumers or voters make decisions, they are observable only in the aggregate form of public opinion or the market (Stichweh 1988). In contrast, the decisions of producers and politicians can be attributed to distinct persons or organizations and thus can be observed as consequential for others. Here, the differentiation of roles implies, therefore, that the decision-making capacity is unequally distributed. Moreover, the role set that a system-specific audience entails provides very limited channels to influence these decision-makers.

Consequently, a difference between decision-makers and those affected by decisions is continuously produced within function systems, especially politics and the economy, as a result of role differentiation. For the communications of function systems this does not—and even cannot—pose a problem due to the complementarity of role expectations. However, this does not rule out the possibility of communications that categorically refuse to accept the decisions of politicians or producers. The overwhelming majority of such communications are without much consequence as they occur casually in everyday life. They may take the form of a general complaint about the ignorance of all politicians or the greed of all capitalist producers and may be provoked by all kinds of troubles. The function of social movements only becomes clear against this background. By protesting, they reject decisions in a way that does not conform to the role expectations of a function system. To the degree that the protest is visible, it renders problems observable that escape the binary logic of function systems.

Obvious problems created by the operation of function systems regard their coordination, which is not guaranteed when each is driven by its own communicative logic. That also means that a function system may produce effects neither itself nor any other function system observes as relevant for its own operations (Hellmann 1996, pp. 61ff). The unique combination of autonomy and indifference that function systems realize creates a dynamic within each such system, the societal consequences of which cannot be controlled. Oriented towards their respective function, they treat it as their priority. As a consequence, problems that function systems do not treat as such are difficult to observe on a scale that outreaches ephemeral interactions.

A glance at the older social movement of socialism illustrates (Luhmann 1993, pp. 133ff) that mobilizing communication can be closely related to one particular function system. It focused on matters of scarcity and the functioning of an increasingly autonomous economic system, the communications of which used the medium of money exclusively, without consideration for the distributive effects, at a time when this autonomy also meant that ensuing inequalities could no longer be justified by referring to divine will or other sources of legitimacy. Both companies and the state were clear focus points for demands to extend social rights, which were compatible with the economic and political logic in so far as they were expected to contribute to the calming down of conflicts (Japp 1986a, p. 327). From an economic point of view, demands for higher wages made sense with regard to the extension of markets and the role of the consumer. From a political point of view the formation of socialist parties had the potential to transform what was seen as a societal conflict into a purely political one. With broadened access to roles within the function systems, the socialist movement thus crystallized into a number of organizations (unions, parties) that make their decisions according to criteria the function systems provide.

Issues and addressees of conflict are less clear in the case of the so-called new social movements. In spite of their diversity, a common denominator appears to be that their protest is centered less on the effects of one particular function system and more on the effects of their ensemble, i.e. of the modern, functionally differentiated society that the function systems themselves have ignored so far (Luhmann 1997, p. 859; Luhmann and Fuchs 1988, p. 36). Although new social movements flexibly identify fitting opponents for the continuation of mobilizing communications, protest directed at political entities remains especially prominent. This reflects the importance that continues to be attributed to politics in terms of fostering or stalling social change. Systems theory emphasizes that a concept of society that still sees politics at its center does not adequately describe modern society, as it ignores the implications of functional differentiation, namely the autonomous operation and, accordingly, autonomous changes of each function system (Luhmann 1989, p. 84). Social movements, in contrast, invoke a general perspective of the alternative, insisting that it is always possible to completely change seemingly inevitable societal developments. In this way, they negate society as it is, refuse to consider the constraints functional differentiation implies for all kinds of decision-makers and thus provide an observation of modern society against itself (Luhmann 1993, p. 142, 1997, p. 864). This does not preclude resonance within the function systems, which a look at the political system and, additionally, the economic system can illustrate.

Protest addressed to political actors, typically the acting government, posits itself as an opposition to the government, but one that is not the outcome of regular elections. As a fundamental opposition, it claims the right to reject decisions in spite of the formal legitimacy to decide, which the government has. When the parliamentary opposition rejects a decision, it merely points out that another decision would have been possible and thus marks the contingency of all political decision-making. In the case of social movements, the rejection does not only concern the content of a decision but also its collectively binding character. In the interest of a value that is treated as absolute, the decision is categorically refused (Schneider and Kusche 2011, pp. 197ff).

Although the communications of a social movement obviously do not conform to the binary logic of the political system, the latter may nevertheless apply this logic in order to react to the movement. Their protest is then treated as an unconventional form of political participation that raises a potentially important issue; this potential corresponds to the probability that it may influence the outcome of an election. Observing social movements as comprised of potential voters, certain parties may modify their political programs in order to attract these votes. In other words, aspects of the protest themes can be transformed into political issues within the framework of party competition (Luhmann 1993, p. 128). This resonance within the political system undermines the fundamentalist opposition of social movements against the existing order. It may trigger the development of programmatic proposals within the movement, for which protest is then no longer an adequate form of communication. Protest may flare up again whenever the programmatic approach appears to lead into a political dead-end. Still, success in terms of resonance in a function system weakens a social movement (Luhmann 1997, p. 858). Alternatively, it may insist on the fundamental character of its protest and also protest against its political exploitation (Schneider and Kusche 2011, p. 199). However, the more open a political system is for unconventional forms of participation, the more resonance it will allow and the more difficult it is to insist on protest.[3]

Protest is often also directed against economic actors. Quite similar to the case of politics, a rather categorical rejection of consumption in favor of local subsistence projects and experiments with barter exchange in this case has opened the way for so-called political consumerism. The binary logic of the economic system may observe the refusal to consume as a demand for alternative, e.g. 'green', products. To the extent that such products become available, the rejection of consumerism tends to be transformed into political consumerism. The latter owes its attribute 'political' to the fact that it nevertheless eludes established expectations of the consumer role, as it is not based on individual consumption choices but on collective signaling that relies on mobilizing communication in favor of certain products and against others (cf. Holzer 2006).

4   Conclusion

In contrast to many strands of social movement research, systems theory decidedly does not offer concepts that could inform the practice of social movements. Whereas the latter bases its communications on the mobilization against threats to absolute values and against those held responsible for these threats, systems theory argues that functional differentiation does away with any authoritative order of preferences and inevitably creates a difference between decision-makers and those affected by decisions. Although this amounts to the diagnosis that social movements actually protest against effects of functional differentiation, and that these effects at the same time render the success of social movements impossible, systems theory accords them an important function. They provide modern society with an alternative mode of self-observation, which can create resonance within function systems, such as the political and the economic system, albeit only according to the communicative logic of the respective function system, and thus may contribute to incremental changes within them.

Due to its focus on functional differentiation, the theory is most interested in modern social movements in democratic contexts. Due to its concept of communication systems, it can conceive of social movements only in terms of

---

[3]Violence may then become an alternative form of communication, as it rejects the exclusive right of the state and government in this regard, turning a social movement into a terrorist one (Schneider and Kusche 2011, pp. 200ff).

concatenating operations and thus leaves open the question of phases of latency. Recent efforts to integrate a concept of networks into the theory (Bommes and Tacke 2011) may, however, open up a new theoretical perspective in both regards. In any case, and in contrast to new social movement theories, the scope of the approach is not restricted to progressive movements, but encompasses conservative or fundamentalist social movements within the same theoretical framework. This framework establishes a focus that is markedly different from those of typical social movement research. Whereas for the latter, the beginning and the ending of social movements are crucial theoretical problems, systems theory concentrates on the communicative logic that reproduces social movements. Instead of causal explanation, it thus aims at an evolutionary perspective on the development of social movements and the possible resonances they can have in the function systems of society.

References

Ahlemeyer, Heinrich W. 1995. *Soziale Bewegungen als Kommunikationssystem. Einheit, Umweltverhältnis und Funktion eines sozialen Phänomens.* Opladen: Leske + Budrich.

Bommes, Michael, and Veronika Tacke (eds.). 2011. *Netzwerke in der funktional differenzierten Gesellschaft.* Wiesbaden: VS Verlag.

Douglas, Mary. 1985. *Risk acceptability according to the social sciences.* London: Routledge & Kegan Paul.

Fowlkes, Martha R., and Patricia Y. Miller. 1987. Chemicals and Community at Love Canal. In *The Social and Cultural Construction of Risk. Essays on Risk Selection and Perception,* ed. Johnson, Branden B., and Vincent T. Covello, pp. 55–78. Dordrecht: Reidel.

Friedman, Debra, and Doug McAdam. 1992. Collective identity and activism. In *Frontiers in social movement theory,* ed. Aldon D. Morris, and Carol McClurg Mueller, 156–173. New Haven: Yale University Press.

Gamson, William A., and Andre Modigliani. 1989. Media discourse and public opinion on nuclear power: A constructionist approach. *American Journal of Sociology* 95(1): 1–37.

Halfmann, Jost, and Klaus P. Japp. 1993. Modern social movements as active risk observers: A systems-theoretical approach to collective action. *Social Science Information* 32(3): 427–446.

Hardin, Russell. 1982. *Collective action.* Baltimore, Maryland: The John Hopkins University Press.

Hellmann, Kai-Uwe. 1996. *Systemtheorie und neue soziale Bewegungen.* Identitätsprobleme in der Risikogesellschaft. Opladen: Westdeutscher Verlag.

Hier, Sean P. 2003. Risk and panic in late modernity: Implications of the converging sites of social anxiety. *British Journal of Sociology* 54(1): 3–20.

Holzer, Boris. 2006. Political consumerism between individual choice and collective action. Social movements, role mobilization and signalling. *International Journal of Consumer Studies* 30(5): 405–415.

Japp, Klaus P. 1986a. Neue soziale Bewegungen und die Kontinuität der Moderne. In *Die Moderne – Kontinuitäten und Zäsuren. Soziale Welt, Sonderband 4*, ed. Berger, Johannes, 311–334. Göttingen: Schwartz.

Japp, Klaus P. 1986b. Kollektive Akteure als soziale Systeme? In *System und Selbstreproduktion. Zur Erschließung eines neuen Paradigmas in den Sozialwissenschaften*, ed. Unverferth, Hans-Jürgen, 166–191. Frankfurt: Peter Lang.

Japp, Klaus P. 2000. *Risiko*. Bielefeld: transcript.

Japp, Klaus P., and Isabel Kusche 2008. Risk and Systems Theory. In *Social Theories of Risk and Uncertainty: An Introduction*, ed. Zinn, Jens, 76–105. Malden, Massachusetts: Blackwell.

Krohn, Wolfgang. 1999. Funktionen der Moralkommunikation. *Soziale Systeme* 5(2): 313–338.

Luhmann, Niklas. 1977. Differentiation of society. *Canadian Journal of Sociology* 2(1): 29–53.

Luhmann, Niklas. 1984. The Self-description of society. crisis fashion and sociological theory. *International Journal of Comparative Sociology* 25(1): 59–72.

Luhmann, Niklas. 1989. *Ecological communication*. Cambridge: Polity Press.

Luhmann, Niklas. 1993. *Risk: A sociological theory*. Berlin/New York: de Gruyter.

Luhmann, Niklas. 1995. *Social systems*. Stanford: Stanford University Press.

Luhmann, Niklas. 1997. *Die Gesellschaft der Gesellschaft*. Frankfurt/M.: Suhrkamp.

Luhmann, Niklas, and Stephen Fuchs. 1988. Tautology and paradox in the self-descriptions of modern society. *Sociological Theory* 6(1): 21–37.

McCarthy, John D., and Mayer N. Zald. 1977. Resource mobilization and social movements: a partial theory. *American Journal of Sociology* 82(6): 1212–1241.

Melucci, Alberto. 1989. *Nomads of the present*. Philadelphia: Temple University Press.

Otway, Harry, and Brian Wynne. 1989. Risk communication: Paradigm and paradox. *Risk Analysis* 9(2): 141–145.

Ruggiero, Vincenzo. 2002. Attac: A Global social movement? *Social Justice* 29(1–2): 48–60.

Schneider, Wolfgang Ludwig, and Isabel Kusche. 2011. Parasitäre Netzwerke in Wissenschaft und Politik. In *Netzwerke in der funktional differenzierten Gesellschaft*, ed. Michael Bommes, and Veronika Tacke, 173–210. Wiesbaden: VS Verlag.

Snow, David A., and Robert D. Benford. 1988. Ideology, frame resonance, and participant mobilisation. In *From Structure to Action: Comparing Social Movement Research Across Cultures*, ed. Klandermans, Bert, Hanspeter Kriesi, and Sidney Tarrow, 197–217. Greenwich, Connecticut: JAI Press.

Snow, David A., E. Burke Rochford, Steven K. Worden, and Robert D. Benford. 1986. Frame alignment processes, micromobilization, and movement participation. *American Sociological Review* 51(4): 464–481.

Stichweh, Rudolf. 1988. Inklusion in Funktionssysteme der modernen Gesellschaft. In *Differenzierung und Verselbständigung. Zur Entwicklung gesellschaftlicher Teilsysteme*, eds. Mayntz, Renate, Bernd Rosewitz, Uwe Schimank, and Rudolf Stichweh, 261–293. Frankfurt/M., New York.

Stichweh, Rudolf. 2000. Systems theory as an alternative to action theory? The Rise of 'communication' as a theoretical option. *Acta Sociologica* 43(1): 5–13.

Stone, Deborah A. 1989. Causal stories and the formation of policy agendas. *Political Science Quarterly* 104(2): 281–300.

Ungar, Sheldon. 2001. Moral panic versus the risk society: The implications of the changing sites of social anxiety. *British Journal of Sociology* 52(2): 271–291.

Author Biography

Dr. Isabel Kusche is Associate Professor and Research Fellow at the Aarhus Institute of Advanced Studies in Denmark. Her research focuses on political communication and the (re-)production of political power in contemporary democracies. Recent publications are „Politischer Klientelismus: Informelle Macht in Griechenland und Irland" (Campus 2016), „Europäische versus postkoloniale Staatsbildung im Kontext funktionaler Differenzierung" (in: Goeke et al., Konstruktion und Kontrolle, Springer VS 2015), „Political Clientelism and Democracy" (Acta Sociologica 2014), „Konstruktivismus und funktionale Analyse" (in: Martinsen, Spurensuche, Springer VS 2014).

Inequality, Inclusion, and Protest. Jeffrey Alexander's Theory of the Civil Sphere

Thomas Kern

Macro-sociological theory is currently dominated by two great traditions that address social conflicts and protest movements in completely different ways (Schimank 2005, pp. 237–253). While theories of social inequality regard distributional conflicts over money, power, and recognition as the primary source of social change, theories of social differentiation consider social strain a product of the division of labor and rationalization.

For the most part, the study of protest has been closely associated with theories of social inequality: Since the mid-1970s, the so-called "European" paradigm of protest research conceived—in the tradition of the Old and New Left—the "new" (environmental, women's rights, peace, civil rights, etc.) social movements as representatives of a rising new middle class and as key actors in struggles against economic, political, and cultural inequalities (Kriesi 1989; Melucci 1985; Touraine 1981). Likewise, the so-called "American" paradigm of protest research—in particular, resource mobilization and political process theory (McAdam 1982; Tilly 1978; Zald and McCarthy 1977)—also rested on the assumption "that wealth and power are concentrated [...] in the hands of a few groups, thus depriving most people of any real influence over the major decisions that affect their lives. Accordingly, social movements are seen [...] as rational attempts by excluded groups to mobilize sufficient political leverage to advance collective interests through institutionalized means" (McAdam 1982, pp. 36–37).[1]

---

[1]Concerning the distinction between the "European" and "American" paradigms of protest research, see Edelman (2001) and Cohen (1985).

T. Kern (✉)
Universität Bamberg, Bamberg, Germany
e-mail: thomas.kern@uni-bamberg.de

© Springer Fachmedien Wiesbaden 2016
J. Roose and H. Dietz (eds.), *Social Theory and Social Movements*,
DOI 10.1007/978-3-658-13381-8_6

In contrast to this intellectual position, theories of differentiation have shown only weak interest in the development of social movements and conflicts (see also Kusche in this volume). For many years, problems of social inequality have not been at the top of the agenda. Under the hegemony of structural functionalism, the rise of social movements was usually associated with rapid social change, economic crises, and deficits of social integration. From this point of view, revolutions, unrest, and protests indicate a breakdown of social control (Davies 1962; Gurr 1974). Researchers have conceived of protest movements not as purposeful collectivities, but as unorganized masses of frustrated, alienated, and uprooted "losers" to modernization. Supposedly spontaneous and irrational outbreaks of collective violence have been regarded as a psychological response to social anomie and strains. Therefore, many students have considered social movements as a part of the problem rather than a part of the solution (Smelser 1962).

However, in the 1980s, the so-called neofunctionalist movement developed a great interest in the relationship between social movements and structural differentiation (Pettenkofer 2010, pp. 107–127; Alexander 1985; Alexander and Colomy 1990). The neofunctionalists conceived of structural differentiation as a contentious process driven by economic, political, and cultural interests. Subsequently, the concept of social movement shifted to the center of neofunctional analysis. This discourse was strongly shaped by a young intellectual named Jeffrey Alexander. In the 1990s, he took the discussion further and developed a comprehensive theory of the civil sphere that puts great emphasis on social movements and attempts to build bridges between the two great traditions of sociological theory. He conceives of the civil sphere, on the one hand, as an analytically differentiated social realm beside the so-called "non-civil" spheres such as economy, politics, law, science, and religion. The discursive structure of this civil sphere is, on the other hand, shaped by the "ideal of a horizontal relationship, of a broad and universalizing solidarity [...] that makes every form of domination fundamentally unstable and every unequal distribution contestable" (Alexander 2007b, pp. 25–26). The civil sphere constitutes a relatively independent realm of discourse and contention about economic, political, and cultural inequality.[2] In this way, Alexander provides a

---

[2]At first glance, this approach closely resembles Habermas' distinction between system and lifeworld (Habermas 1987, 1996; Cohen and Arato 1992). However, Alexander strongly objects to the notion that "civil society is a world of rationality and consensus." He demands the recognition of "the unconscious and nonrational elements [...] that structure civil societies to be placed within the meaning-making process of civil discourse itself rather than forcing them into residual categories that are projected onto the noninterpretative domains outside it" (Alexander 1993, p. 801).

comprehensive macro-sociological framework for the analysis of social movements.

This article aims to highlight the central elements of Alexander's theory of the civil sphere with special emphasis on the relationship between structural differentiation and social movements. In the first part, I will focus on the transition from functionalism to neofunctionalism in differentiation theory. In the second part, I will examine the institutional framework and the cultural codes of the civil sphere. In the third part, I will shift my attention to the boundary relations of the civil sphere and the role of social movements.

1   From Functionalism to Neofunctionalism

In the 1950s and 1960s, the sociological debate was largely dominated by the structural functionalist theory of Talcott Parsons. Parsons understood history as an evolutionary process in which the societal capacities of solving problems are continually enhanced. From his point of view, the social system is continuously affected by random variations, leading to more efficient solutions in coping with the environment of a society. As a consequence, the adaptive capacities of the social system continuously increase and enable it to realize higher levels of structural complexity. Parsons conceived of functional differentiation as the key to increasing the complexity of society: Every time a given social system fails to solve a specific problem, the pressures toward structural differentiation grow. Consequently, the more society advances on this developmental path, the greater its capacity to solve problems.

Considering that limits of performance stimulate the development of new ("superior") institutions, the concept of structural differentiation is in this stage inextricably linked to the idea of social progress. However, Parsons largely ignored the existence of permanent tensions between normative ideals and institutional reality. He also remained silent about the unequal distribution of benefits and costs in the process of differentiation (Rueschemeyer 1977). His optimistic conclusion was diametrically opposed to the history of violence in the 20th century. Likewise, his idealization of the United States as an "almost perfect blend of social integration and social justice" (Alexander 2005, p. 98)—despite the continual social exclusion of many U.S. ethnic groups—not only met with the resistance of his opponents, but it also stimulated criticism among his sympathizers.

At this point, the neofunctionalists—including Alexander—began to reconstruct and reinterpret the work of Parsons. The neofunctionalists constituted a group of sociologists who sought "to broaden functionalism's intellectual scope while retaining its theoretical core" (Alexander and Colomy 1985, p. 11). However, as some critical observers have pointed out, the heterogeneity of this group was so great that it sometimes appeared difficult to identify a common denominator (Joas 1988). Despite this problem, at least for the inner circle around Alexander, the concept of neofunctionalism is characterized by focusing on social phenomena in analytical levels (culture, structure, and personality); social systems and subsystems, as well as their interchanges; normative processes; differentiation dynamics; and differentiated substructures (Turner and Maryanski 1988, p. 118). Although the neofunctionalists preserved the substance of the Parsonian action scheme, they refused to explain social change in functional terms of need states and social requisites. Instead, their attention shifted from the (functional) consequences to the (historical) *causes* of structural differentiation.[3] They distanced themselves from Parsons' linear concept of social progress and conceived institutional change as a contingent outcome of conflicts between strategic groups and social movements.

Thus, the relationship between social differentiation and integration shifted to the center of the discussion. In contrast to Parsons' idea of exhaustive social integration through shared cultural values, Shils (1975, 1982b) and Eisenstadt (1982) introduced the distinction between the cultural center and the periphery. According to them, the cultural value system is neither consistent nor exhaustive. In a pluralistic society, many sets of cultural values and beliefs—for example, the cultural orientations of ethnic or religious minorities—exist side by side. The cultural center includes only the values of the social elites. Accordingly, the cultural integration of a society will never reach the degree of perfection suggested by Parsons. Therefore, the legitimacy of social order is always incomplete and disputed. Considering that there are always individuals and groups—as primary carriers of structural differentiation—who attempt to expand their access to the cultural center of society, structural differentiation turns out to be inherently contentious.

At this point, Alexander and Colomy (1985) established a systematic link between structural differentiation and social movements by shifting the attention to the cultural center. First, they theorized, functional deficits of social structures are

---

[3]The neo-functionalists underscored that structural differentiation is the result of a complex negotiation process between individual and collective actors. Consequently, structural differentiation must be linked to cultural ideas and distributions of interests and resources (Alexander 1990a; Eisenstadt 1990; Colomy 1985, 1990; Smelser 1985; Rüschemeyer 1977; Alexander and Colomy 1985).

not effective by themselves. They must be perceived and defined before they become objects of change-seeking, collective action. The result of this process depends not only on the distribution of power and interests; it is also shaped by cultural patterns of meaning. As social movements produce public awareness of social deficits and provide alternative definitions and interpretations of social reality, they exert a great influence on the institutional outcomes of social conflicts. Second, in the process of institutionalization, individual and collective actors articulate and substantiate the cultural values of society. By doing so, they get in touch with the cultural center and produce "charisma" (Shils 1982a; Eisenstadt 1968). Therefore, structural differentiation is always linked to the symbolic activities of individuals, groups, and social movements.

To conclude, neofunctionalism shed light on the independent role of the cultural center in the process of structural differentiation. In the 1990s, Alexander increasingly distanced himself from the neofunctionalist movement. This decision does not mean that he moved away from earlier insights concerning the reconstruction of Parsons. Rather, he declared the project of neofunctionalism to be concluded and called, at the same time, for an "urgent necessity to go beyond it" (Alexander 1998a, pp. 221–228). In the following years, he systematically pursued his theoretical interest in the relationship between the cultural center and society by promoting a strong program of cultural sociology and developing a comprehensive theory of the civil sphere (Alexander and Smith 2002).

2   Structures of Civil Sphere

Alexander's theory of the civil sphere centers on the concept of inclusion as a unique feature of modern societies. He defines inclusion as "the process by which previously excluded groups gain solidarity in the terminal community[4] of society" (Alexander 1990b, p. 268). Parsons originally introduced this concept in order to describe the solidary relationship between the individual and society: On the one hand, inclusion concerns membership in a collectivity (citizenship) and shapes collective identities; on the other hand, it defines the capacities and opportunities for individual participation in the functional spheres of society (i.e., politics, economy, law, education, and health) (Parsons 1965, 1971). Thus, inclusion "refers

---

[4]The concept of "terminal community" refers "to those feelings that, extending beyond family and friends, create the boundaries of acknowledged society" (Alexander 1990b, p. 269). Accordingly, the concept of the "terminal community" largely corresponds with the collective identity of a society.

to a change in solidarity status" (Alexander 1990b, p. 269) of an individual or group. As mentioned above, Parsons believed that modernization and differentiation strengthen solidarity and lead to more inclusion. He assumed that modern societies are able to develop a broader concept of solidarity by including a greater diversity of groups and individuals than any earlier type of society. This process is accompanied by expanding adaptive capacities, increasing social inclusion, and by value generalization (Parsons 1966).

At this point, Alexander clearly departed from Parsons. He conceived inclusion as a permanent issue of social conflicts. Therefore, the civil sphere—in the sense of a solidarity sphere—constitutes a realm of discourse and contention about the measure of social recognition that makes an individual a legitimate member of the civil community. As an analytically independent social sphere beside the non-civil spheres, such as economy, politics, law, science, and religion, the civil sphere has to be studied in its own right (Alexander 1998b). This section provides an overview of its central components: The institutional fields constituting the regulative and communicative framework of the civil sphere, and the cultural codes that shape its discourses.

3   Regulative and Communicative Institutions

In modern societies, the structure of the civil sphere is shaped by mainly three institutional fields providing regulative and communicative infrastructures for its development: (I) politics, (II) law, and (III) the mass media. The political system translates civil discourses into collectively binding decisions. The legal system protects the independence of the civil sphere against intrusions by state power. The mass media endow citizens with communicative means for public discussions. The following paragraphs discuss the interrelation between these institutional fields and the civil sphere.

3.1   Politics

According to Alexander, the stability of modern *political systems* rests to a large extent on the independent production of a new kind of power, which he describes as "civil power," that restricts particularistic influences on the political process and obligates officeholders to the universal values of the civil sphere. Modern democracies obtain this effect foremost through free and fair elections: "To the degree that there is democracy, voting breaks up the direct translation of social into political power" (Alexander 2006, p. 114). The principle of equality—"one person, one vote"—neutralizes particularistic claims against the state and prevents direct, particular, and personal entanglements between state bureaucracy and specific social groups (Luhmann 1974, p. 178). In this way, political power rests on its own source of legitimacy, relatively independent from economic influences, kinship relations, and religious affiliations.

However, in modern democracies, the influence of the civil sphere on state bureaucracy is not limited to free and fair elections. First, political parties "propose platforms obligating candidates to exercise state power in relation to shared political values" (Alexander 2006, p. 123). Although this commitment is usually limited to its own members, candidates, and programs, the influence of civil power increases with the plurality of the political party landscape. Second, the general public outside and the opposition inside the legislature exert civil control over the use of political power by questioning candidates and programs. Third, in contrast to particularistic forms of political organization, political offices in modern democracies are more or less obligated to the universal values and goals of the civil sphere: The very concept of political office "institutionalizes a universalistic understanding of organizational authority that has emerged only recently in human history, growing gradually with the creation of the civil sphere" (Alexander 2006, pp. 133–134).

3.2   Law

Strong interrelations between the political and civil spheres protect the democratic process of collective decision-making from external intrusions by economic, religious, or other powers: The stronger the civil power, the more independent and democratic is the political process. However, from a differentiation theoretical perspective, it is not enough to protect only the independence of the political sphere and the state. Conversely, the civil sphere must protect itself and other non-civil spheres against intrusions by state power. In democratic societies, this function is usually performed by the *legal system*, particularly through constitutional guarantees of freedom of expression and human rights. The legal boundaries of state power establish a social space where citizens are enabled to articulate their interests and create their cultural identities relatively independent from interference by the state. In this way, the legal system empowers citizens to uphold their claims, even against state bureaucracy (Alexander 2006, p. 153). Although the legal system operates relatively independently of the norms and values of a population, Alexander insists on a close relationship between judicial interpretations and moral judgments. Accordingly, the legal right to file a lawsuit provides citizens with opportunities to restrict state power and to change legal structures in accordance with the moral orientations of the population.

3.3 Mass Media

Despite their importance, Alexander underscores that political and legal processes "by no means exhaust the organizational structures of the solidary sphere. The inclusive and exclusive relationships established by civil society are articulated by communicative institutions as well" (Alexander 2006, p. 70). At this point, the public sphere shifts to the center of his analysis. The concept of public sphere usually refers to an open forum in which a speaker communicates in front of a potentially infinite audience (Habermas 1989). Therefore, the *mass media* considerably affect citizens' opportunities to participate in the discourse of the civil sphere.

Assuming that civil society is "a sphere of commitment and influence, mediated through public opinion, the media is critically important not as a forum for public information but, rather, for public influence, identity, and solidarity" (Alexander and Jacobs 1998, pp. 25–26). Consequently, Alexander does not limit his analysis of the mass media to the "factual" media—such as newspapers, television, radio, etc.—that select and distribute information relevant for the members of society. He also pays attention to the "fictional" media, including popular literature and movies that weave cultural values of the civil sphere "into broad narratives and popular genres" (Alexander 1990c, 2006, p. 75). By creating typified representations and moral evaluations of actors, the mass media exert a great influence on moral judgments about who should be included as legitimate members of society. In this way, the mass media substantiate the solidarity of the civil sphere. Their power depends not only on the selection and diffusion of information, but also on its symbolic representation. Alexander (2006) illustrated this connection in his discussion about the "cultural pragmatics" of the civil sphere. Accordingly, the opportunities of individual citizens, social groups, and movements to win the approval of a broader segment of the population for their ideas and demands are strongly linked to the plurality and diversity of the public discourse: The broader the diversity of opinions and ideas, the better are the opportunities for the members of a population to exert their influence on the public (Gamson 2004; Gamson and

Wolfsfeld 1993). Therefore, the relative autonomy of the mass media turns ot be fundamental to the independence of the civil sphere.

Politics, law, and mass media provide the regulative and communicative infrastructure for the development of the civil sphere. Civic associations use them in order to shift the attention of the broader population to their concerns. As a vast number of studies illustrate, the civil sphere is full of civic associations that affect each other's intentions and action. The scope of these associations includes, on the one hand, social movement organizations (SMOs), NGOs, and NPOs that have established themselves as voices of the "common good" in the public. On the other hand, there are particular interest organizations—such as political parties, trade unions, professional organizations, churches, and congregations—that step out of the functional contexts of the non-civil spheres in order to win approval of the broader public.

4   Cultural Codes and Moral Mobilization

Every notion of solidarity necessarily includes the idea of a boundary (Eisenstadt and Giesen 1995; Eder 2005; Kern et al. 2014). Members have to be made distinguishable from non-members, and internal and external markers have to be drawn. Consequently, the relationship between the cultural system—in the sense of a society's values, ideas, codes, and symbols—and the civil sphere is central to the process of inclusion. Values are usually associated with the "good". However, the constitutive role of the cultural system for the definition of social boundaries implicates that the existence of the "evil" is also necessary for our understanding of a good society. Accordingly, the orientation of actors and institutions toward the good is also linked to social constructions of evil.

This aspect is important to Alexander's understanding of the civil sphere. Most current theories associate the civil sphere with democracy, trust, inclusion, recognition, and social consensus (Habermas 1996; Cohen and Arato 1992; Putnam 2000; Keane 2009). In contrast, Alexander stressed that the moral qualifications for membership in the civil sphere are always *exclusive*. The discourse of "real" civil spheres is divided between universalism and particularism: Individual and collective demands for more inclusion and participation are always countered by restrictive codes that link full inclusion to (quasi)-ascriptive qualities of individuals and collectivities.

Against this backdrop, the discourse of the civil sphere is shaped by a binary structure. The positive side refers to those individuals who deserve full membership in the civil sphere; the negative side refers to those considered unworthy.

Table 1 The discursive structure of social motives, relations, and institutions

Motives		Relationships		Institutions	
+	−	+	−	+	−
Activism	Passivity	Open	Secret	Rule regulated	Arbitrary
Autonomy	Dependence	Trusting	Suspicious	Law	Power
Rationality	Irrationality	Critical	Deferential	Equality	Hierarchy
Reasonableness	Hysteria	Honorable	Self-interested	Inclusive	Exclusive
Calm	Excitability	Conscience	Greed	Impersonal	Personal
Self-control	Passion	Truthful	Deceitful	Contractual	Ascriptive loyalty
Realism	Unreality	Straightforward	Calculating	Groups	Factions
Sanity	Madness	Deliberative	Conspiratorial	Office	Personality

Source Alexander (2001, pp. 164–166)

Civic associations and movements actively shape this cultural structure of the civil sphere by labeling themselves as "good" and their opponents as "evil". Over the past two decades, Alexander systematically elaborated and developed his theory about the cultural codes of the civil sphere in order to describe and explain the dynamics of civil discourse (Alexander 2007b, pp. 644–645). His efforts were supported by a number of empirical studies (Edles 1995; Ku 1998; Smith 1998; Baiocchi 2007; Kern 2009). Accordingly, the binary structure (codes) of the civil discourse is constituted by "sets of homologies, which create likeness between various terms of social description and prescription, and antipathies, which establish antagonisms between these terms and other sets of symbols" (Alexander 1992, p. 291). The legitimate members who are included in the civil community are labeled with positive values. Those who are labeled with negative values are excluded. Thus, the boundaries of the civil community are grounded in this cultural classification system (see Table 1).

The codes and countercodes of civil discourse describe the motives, social relationships, and institutional outcomes of human action in diametrically opposed ways (Alexander 2001, pp. 162–168). For example, in most Western societies,[5] the public often evaluates the degree to which (I) an individual's motives correspond with the idea of an active, rational, realistic, self-controlled, and autonomous actor. Individuals and groups who are labeled as passive, irrational, unrealistic,

---

[5]In non-Western societies, the moral codes of civil discourse are sometimes mapped by other cultural patterns (Kern 2009; Baiocchi 2007).

passionate, and dependent are suspicious. The (II) social relationships between legitimate members of the civil community are expected to be open, trusting, deliberative, and truthful. Those people who deviate from this moral standard are suspected to be secretive, suspicious, conspiratorial, and deceitful. With respect to (III) institutional outcomes, the public discourse links legitimate forms of organization to pro-democratic principles, such as the rule of law, equality, and inclusiveness. Undemocratic institutions are believed to rest on arbitrary power, inequality, and exclusiveness.

The cultural codes of the civil sphere constitute the core of a binary discursive structure that gives rise to widespread public stories and narratives. During political struggles, social actors are continuously redistributed between the two extremes of the moral spectrum (Alexander 2001, p. 168). The positive side of the spectrum refers to ideas of purity, beauty, and goodness. The objects produced by this discourse constitute the cultural center of society. The negative side stands for impurity, ugliness, and badness. Social actors usually attempt to distance themselves from this side of the spectrum. The objects produced by this discourse are usually regarded as a source of pollution and, therefore, as a threat to the cultural center:

> The cause of victory and defeat, imprisonment and freedom, and sometimes even of life and death, is often discursive domination, which depends upon how public narratives about good and evil are extended. [...]. The general discursive structure is used to legitimate friends and delegitimate opponents in the course of real historical time (Alexander 2001, p. 168).

Accordingly, the persuasive power of public narratives or claims depends to a large extent on the degree to which the members of a collectivity are familiar with their underlying meaning. Therefore, civic actors often attempt to increase their influence on public opinion by framing[6] their claims in terms of the (moral) structures that compose the cultural center of society. Alexander (2011) recently

---

[6]Over recent decades, Goffman's (1974) interactionist concept of "frame analysis" has become a central paradigm of social movement research (Snow and Benford 2000; Snow et al. 1986). Although Alexander highly sympathizes with the interactionist tradition of social theory, he criticizes the framing concept for "treating the interpretative strategies of social movement actors as if they were generated in an entirely situational, practical, here-and-now way" (Alexander 1996, p. 212). In other words, the framing concept neglects the institutional frameworks that exercise control over the situation and, therefore, relies on the macro-sociological perspective provided by the (utilitarian) resource mobilization model. Instead of treating the creative dimension of social movements as a means to an end, Alexander stresses that social movements "are meaningful in themselves" (Alexander 1996, p. 212).

introduced the notion of "social performance" in order to describe this ritual-like process "by which actors, individually or in concert, display for others the meaning of their social situation" (Alexander 2004, p. 529). In a social performance, "audiences identify with actors, and cultural scripts achieve verisimilitude through effective *mise-en-scène*" (Alexander 2004, p. 527). If social performances fail, then social action appears to be inauthentic, artificial, and unconvincing. Therefore, the persuasiveness and resonance of civic actors—and, hence, the experience of collective solidarity—greatly depends on successful performances. Alexander (2004) developed a theory of cultural pragmatics that identifies their elements and reveals the mechanisms that determine their persuasiveness. A detailed discussion of this contribution would exceed the scope of this article. Nevertheless, it considerably clarifies the role of civil society as an intermediary sphere between culture and social structure.

5   Facilitation, Intrusion, and Social Repair

Classical modernization theory linked the growing institutionalization of the civil sphere and increasing social inclusion to processes of structural differentiation, urbanization, secularization, and industrialization. From this point of view, social inclusion was conceived as a function of modernization and progress (Parsons 1971). Although Alexander recognizes that "real" civil spheres are inseparably connected with the non-civil spheres in a dense network of mutual interdependencies, he demands "that the construction of a wider and more inclusive sphere of solidarity must be studied in itself" (Alexander 2006, p. 193). In this respect, he shifts attention to the boundary relations between the civil sphere and the non-civil spheres.

Increasing functional specialization and expansion of the non-civil spheres enable modern societies to conduct more and different operations at the same time. As a consequence, problem-solving capacities increase considerably: Modern market economies are able to produce and distribute a greater number of different goods, modern democratic systems politicize more issues, and modern education systems endow more students with more opportunities for individuation than any earlier type of society. In this sense, the growth of the non-civil spheres *facilitates* the development of an independent civil sphere by providing the average individual with unique opportunities for self-determination and self-realization. Simultaneously, the expansion of the non-civil spheres confronts society with difficulties that confine the capacity of the individual to participation in the civil sphere. Economic growth is often accompanied by unemployment, poverty, urbanization, pollution, class conflicts, etc. The increasing concentration of state power and state control intimidates the autonomy of individuals and groups. The "dark sides" of modern education are discipline, conformity, and high education fees excluding the poor.

This is where social movements—and the theoretical accounts of protest research (Della Porta and Diani 2006)—come in. According to Alexander, social movements play a critical role in balancing the tension between productive inputs and *destructive intrusions* at the boundaries between the civil sphere and the non-civil spheres, as, for instance, the case of the *environmental movement* illustrates. Over the past decades, in many countries, the public has increasingly realized that the expansion of the non-civil spheres not only stimulates national welfare, but it also entails a great potential for social self-endangerment and self-destruction (Beck et al. 2003; Beck 1997). In particular, the growing dependence of modern society on science and technology creates irresolvable problems. This trend concerns not only nuclear, biological, chemical, and technological systems, but also the knowledge-based infrastructure of social organizations (Perrow 2007): transport systems, hospitals, nuclear plants, factories, shopping malls, sports stadiums, etc. As a consequence, technological progress accumulates enormous costs for the environment and restricts the citizens' quality of life.

In this sense, environmental pollution has turned into an issue of justice: The mobilization of the environmental movement centers on the insight that neither the costs of pollution nor the benefits of environmental protection are fairly distributed. Environmental activists mobilize their supporters by constructing "apocalyptic imaginaries," creating the impression that "the earth and many of its component parts are in an ecological bind that may short-circuit human and non-human life in the not too distant future if urgent and immediate action to retrofit nature to a more benign equilibrium is postponed for much longer" (Swyngedouw 2010, p. 216). However, environmental activists are not the only voices of civil society: For instance, in the United States, conservative movements massively challenge the environmentalists' approach and attempt to reassert the industrial capitalist social order by "attacking the scientific evidence concerning environmental problems, (mis)labeling their initiatives with terms like 'Clear Skies' and 'Healthy Forests'" (McCright and Riley 2010, p. 108). This way, the civil discourse turns into a moral battleground between environmental and conservative activists attempting to win the approval of a broader segment of the population for their problem definitions and political demands.

This brief example illustrates that the non-civil spheres sometimes produce inequalities, leading to considerable tensions and undermining the solidarity of the civil sphere. However, Alexander emphasized that the non-civil spheres are not the only source of threats: By justifying economic, political, religious, or ethnic inequalities, the civil discourse often legitimates and abets particularistic tendencies and the exclusion of social groups:

> If you are poor or lower class, you are often constructed as irrational, dependent, and lazy, both in the economy and in society as such. In this manner the material asymmetry inherent in economic life becomes translated into projections about civil competence and incompetence. Inside this translated social language, it becomes much more difficult for actors without economic achievement or wealth to communicate effectively in the civil sphere, to receive full respect from its regulatory institutions, and to interact with other, more economically advantaged people in a fully civil way (Alexander 2006, p. 207).

In other words, the civil discourse often constrains and intrudes on the non-civil spheres. For instance, ethnic or fundamentalist movements frequently question the legitimacy of the membership of specific groups, such as women, non-whites, homosexuals, and heretics, in the civil sphere. Sometimes they even deny human rights and freedom of expression to these groups. If they succeed in the public sphere and conquer state power, the autonomy of the non-civil spheres may decline due to the implementation of restrictions in the freedom of communication and democratic will formation. Accordingly, social movements play a key role—as social carriers either of "intrusion" or "repair"—in the process of institutionalization.

6   Conclusions

Alexander's theory of the civil sphere builds a bridge between the two great paradigms of sociology: inequality and differentiation. He understands the civil sphere as an analytically (but not empirically) independent social realm in which struggles over justice, inclusion, and distribution are mediated by cultural structures: "Vis-à-vis the binary codes of civil society, protest movements pollute hegemonic forces and purify subordinate groups in its name" (Alexander 2007a, p. 23). In this sense, the social construction of inequalities and claims for equality is nested inside the discourse of the civil sphere. This discourse defines the limits of solidarity by articulating and translating the symbolic and ideal premises of social order into tangible projects of inclusion (or exclusion). Accordingly, social movements considerably affect the implementation of social norms and, hence, the process of institutionalization in the non-civil spheres.

Alexander introduces the concepts of "facilitation" and "intrusion" in order to describe the interdependencies between the civil sphere and the non-civil spheres. On the one hand, the non-civil spheres facilitate the development of the civil sphere by providing their members with increasing life chances and opportunities for self-determination in a historically unprecedented way. But they also continuously exert strong pressures that undermine the solidarity of the civil community. Thus, the universal ideals of the civil sphere become socially powerful only to the degree that the regulative and communicative institutions of society protect its independence. On the other hand, the civil discourse may strengthen the autonomy of the civil sphere by stimulating processes of solidarity extension and civil repair. At the same time, particularistic movements frequently undermine the solidarity of the civil sphere and endanger the autonomy of the non-civil spheres. The degree to which collective actors are able to make an appeal to the entire civil community and to shape the process of institutionalization depends on the complex boundary relations between the civil sphere and the non-civil spheres.   *e.g. religion*

In sum, social repair is not preordained but contingent. The binary codes of civil discourse always limit the possibilities of social integration and divide the civil sphere. In this respect, Alexander shifts the study of social movements to the center of sociological theory by highlighting the contentiousness of institutionalization and inclusion. He systematically elaborates the links between culture, social structure, and protest mobilization, and he provides a powerful theoretical framework for the analysis of discourses about justice and social movements within the broader context of the civil sphere. Based on this, students of social movements are challenged to step further down this path in order to develop a more comprehensive understanding of how social movements affect and change society.

References

Alexander, Jeffrey C. 1985. *Neofunctionalism*. Newbury Park: Sage.
Alexander, Jeffrey C. 1990a. Differentiation theory: Problems and prospects. In *Differentiation theory and social change. comparative and historical perspectives*, ed. J.C. Alexander, and P. Colomy, 1–15. New York: Columbia University Press.
Alexander, Jeffrey C. 1990b. Core solidarity, ethnic outgroups, and social differentiation. In *Differentiation theory and social change. Comparative and historical perspectives*, ed. J. C. Alexander and P. Colomy, 267–293. New York: Columbia University Press.
Alexander, Jeffrey C. 1990c. The mass news media in systemic, historical, and comparative perspective. In *Differentiation theory and social change. Comparative and historical perspectives*, ed. J. C. Alexander, and P. Colomy, 323–366. New York: Columbia University Press.
Alexander, Jeffrey C. 1992. Citizen and enemy as symbolic classification: On the polarizing discourse of civil society. In *Cultivating differences. Symbolic boundaries and the*

making of inequality, ed. M. Lamont, and M. Fournier, 289–308. Chicago: University of Chicago Press.

Alexander, Jeffrey C. 1993. The return to civil society. *Contemporary Sociology* 22(6): 797–803.

Alexander, Jeffrey C. 1996. Collective action, culture and civil society: Secularizing, updating, inverting and displacing the classical model of social movements. In *Alain touraine*, ed. M. Diani, and J. Clarke, 205–234. London: Falmer Press.

Alexander, Jeffrey C. 1998a. After neofunctionalism: Action, culture, and civil society. In *Neofunctionalism and after*, ed. J.C. Alexander, 210–233. Malden: Blackwell Publishers.

Alexander, Jeffrey C. 1998b. Introduction. Civil society I, II, III: Constructing an empirical concept from normative controversies and historical transformations. In *Real civil societies: Dilemmas of institutionalization*, ed. J. C. Alexander, 1–19. London: Sage.

Alexander, Jeffrey C. 2001. Towards a sociology of evil: Getting beyond modernist common sense about the alternative to the good. In *Rethinking evil: Contemporary perspectives*, ed. M.Pia Lara, 153–172. Los Angeles: University of California Press.

Alexander, Jeffrey C. 2004. Cultural pragmatics: Social performance between ritual and strategy. *Sociological Theory* 22(4): 527–573.

Alexander, Jeffrey C. 2005. Contradictions in the societal community: The promise and disappointment of parson's concept. In *After parsons: A theory of social action for the twenty-first century*, ed. R.C. Fox, V.M. Lidz, and H.J. Bershady, 93–110. New York: Russel Sage Foundation.

Alexander, Jeffrey C. 2006. *The civil sphere*. Oxford: Oxford University Press.

Alexander, Jeffrey C. 2007a. The meaningful construction of inequality and the struggles against it: A strong program approach to how social boundaries change. *Cultural Sociology* 1(1): 23–30.

Alexander, Jeffrey C. 2007b. On the interpretation of the civil sphere: Understanding and contention in contemporary social science. *Sociological Quarterly* 48(4): 641–659.

Alexander, Jeffrey C. 2011. *Performance and power*. Cambridge: Polity Press.

Alexander, Jeffrey C., and Paul Colomy. 1985. Toward neo-functionalism. *Sociological Theory* 3(2): 11–23.

Alexander, Jeffrey C., and Paul Colomy. 1990. *Differentiation theory and social change. Comparative and historical perspectives*. New York: Columbia University Press.

Alexander, Jeffrey C., and Philip Smith. 2002. The strong program in cultural theory. elements of a structural hermeneutics. In *Handbook of sociological theory*, ed. J.H. Turner, 135–150. New York: Springer.

Alexander, Jeffrey C., and Ronald N. Jacobs. 1998. Mass communication, ritual, and civil society. In *Media, ritual and identity*, ed. T. Leibes, and J. Curran, 23–41. New York: Routledge.

Baiocchi, Gianpaolo. 2007. The civilizing force of social movements: Corporate and liberal codes in Brazil's public sphere. *Sociological Theory* 24(4): 285–311.

Beck, Ulrich. 1997. Subpolitics. Ecology and disintegration of institutional power. *Organization and environment* 10(1): 52–65.

Beck, Ulrich, Wolfgang Bonss, and Christoph Lau. 2003. The theory of reflexive modernization: Problematic, hypotheses and research programme. *Theory, Culture and Society* 20(2): 1–33.

Cohen, Jean L., and Andrew Arato. 1992. *Civil society and political theory*. Cambridge: MIT Press.

Colomy, Paul. 1985. Uneven structural differentiation: Toward a comparative approach. In *Neofunctionalism*, ed. J.C. Alexander, 131–156. Newbury Park: Sage.

Colomy, Paul. 1990. Revisions and progress in differentiation theory. In *Differentiation theory and social change. Comparative and historical perspectives*, ed. J.C. Alexander, and P. Colomy, 465–495. New York: Columbia University Press.

Davies, James C. 1962. Toward a theory of revolution. *American Sociological Review* 27(1): 5–19.

Della Porta, Donatella, and Mario Diani. 2006. *Social movements: An introduction*. Malden: Blackwell.

Edelman, Marc. 2001. Social movements: Changing paradigms and forms of politics. *Annual Review of Anthropology* 30(1): 285–317.

Eder, Klaus. 2005. Remembering national memories together: The formation of a transnational identity in Europe. In *Collective memory and European identity. The effects of integration and enlargement*, ed. K. Eder, and W. Spohn, 197–219. Aldershot: Ashgate.

Edles, Laura Desfor. 1995. Rethinking democratic transition: A culturalist critique and the spanish case. *Theory and Society* 24(3): 355–384.

Eisenstadt, Shmuel N. 1968. Introduction. In *Max weber on charisma and institution building: Selected papers*, ed. S.N. Eisenstadt, ix–lvi. Chicago: University of Chicago Press.

Eisenstadt, Shmuel N. 1982. The axial age: The emergence of transcendental visions and the rise of clerics. *European Journal of Sociology* 23(2): 294–314.

Eisenstadt, Shmuel N. 1990. Modes of structural differentiation, elite structure, and cultural visions. In *Differentiation theory and social change. Comparative and historical perspectives*, ed. J.C. Alexander, and P. Colomy, 19–51. New York: Columbia University Press.

Eisenstadt, Shmuel Noah, and Bernhard Giesen. 1995. The construction of collective identity. *European Journal of Sociology* 36(1): 72–102.

Gamson, William A. 2004. Bystanders, public opinion, and the media. In *The blackwell companion to social movements*, ed. D.A. Snow, S.A. Soule, and H. Kriesi, 242–261. Oxford: Blackwell.

Gamson, William A., and Gadi Wolfsfeld. 1993. Movements and media as interacting systems. *Annals of the American Academy of Political and Social Science* 528(1): 114–125.

Goffman, Erving. 1974. *Frame analysis*. New York: Harper Colophon.

Gurr, Ted. 1974. *Why men rebel*. Princeton: Princeton University Press.

Habermas, Jürgen. 1987. *Lifeworld and system: A critique of functionalist reason*. Boston: Beacon Press.

Habermas, Jürgen. 1989. *The structural transformation of the public sphere: An inquiry into a category of bourgeois society*. Cambridge: MIT Press.

Habermas, Jürgen. 1996. *Between facts and norms: Contributions to a discourse theory of law and democracy*. Cambridge: Polity Press.

Joas, Hans. 1988. The antinomies of neofunctionalism. A critical essay on Jeffrey Alexander. *Inquiry* 31(4): 471–494.

Keane, John. 2009. Civil society, definitions and approaches. In *International encyclopedia of civil society*, ed. H.K. Anheier, and S. Toepler, 461–464. Berlin: Springer.

Kern, Thomas. 2009. Cultural performance and political regime change: The democratic transition of South Korea in the 1980s. *Sociological Theory* 27(3): 291–316.

Kern, Thomas, Lotta Mayer, and Sang-hui Nam. 2014. The construction of regional identities in East Asia. In *Social theory and regional studies in the global age*, ed. S.A. Arjomand, 415–435. New York: SUNY Press.

Kriesi, Hanspeter. 1989. New social movements and the new class in the Netherlands. *The American Journal of Sociology* 94(5): 1078–1116.

Ku, Agnes S. 1998. Boundary politics in the public sphere: Openness, secrecy, and leak. *Sociological Theory* 16(2): 172–192.

Luhmann, Niklas. 1974. *Grundrechte als Institution. Ein Beitrag zur politischen Soziologie*. Berlin: Duncker & Humblot.

McAdam, Doug. 1982. *Political process and the development of black insurgency, 1930–1970*. Chicago: University of Chicago Press.

McCright, Aaron M., and Riley E. Dunlap. 2010. Anti-reflexivity. The American conservative movement's success in undermining climate science and policy. *Theory, Culture and Society* 27(2–3): 100–133.

Melucci, Alberto. 1985. The symbolic challenge of contemporary movements. *Social Research* 52(4): 789–816.

Parsons, Talcott. 1965. Full citizenship for the Negro American? *A Sociological Problem. Daedalus* 94(4): 1009–1054.

Parsons, Talcott. 1966. *Societies. Evolutionary and comparative perspectives*. New Jersey: Prentice-Hall.

Parsons, Talcott. 1971. *The system of modern societies*. Englewood Cliffs: Prentice-Hall.

Perrow, Charles. 2007. *The next catastrophe: Reducing our vulnerabilities to natural, industrial, and terrorist disasters*. Princeton, NJ: Princeton University Press.

Pettenkofer, Andreas. 2010. *Radikaler Protest. Zur soziologischen Theorie politischer Bewegungen*. Frankfurt: Campus.

Putnam, Robert D. 2000. *Bowling alone. The collapse and revival of American community*. New York, NY: Simon & Schuster.

Rueschemeyer, Dietrich. 1977. Structural differentiation, efficiency, and power. *The American Journal of Sociology* 83(1): 1–25.

Schimank, Uwe. 2005. *Differenzierung und Integration der modernen Gesellschaft. Beiträge zur Akteurzentrierten Differenzierungstheorie 1*. Wiesbaden: VS Verlag.

Shils, Edward. 1975. *Center and periphery. Essays in macrosociology*. Chicago: University of Chicago Press.

Shils, Edward. 1982a. Charisma. In *The constitution of society*, ed. E. Shils, 110–118. Chicago: University of Chicago Press.

Shils, Edward. 1982b. *The constitution of society*. Chicago: University of Chicago Press.

Smelser, Neil J. 1962. *Theory of collective behavior*. London: Routledge.

Smelser, Neil J. 1985. Evaluating the model of structural differentiation in relation to the educational change in the nineteenth century. In *Neofunctionalism*, ed. J.C. Alexander, 113–130. Beverly Hills: Sage.

Smith, Philip. 1998. Barbarism and civility in the discourses of fascism, communism, and democracy: Variations on a set of themes. In *Real civil societies. Dilemmas of institutionalization*, ed. J.C. Alexander, 115–137. London: Sage.

Snow, David A., and Robert D. Benford. 2000. Framing processes and social movements: An overview and assessment. *Annual Review of Sociology* 26(1): 611–639.

Snow, David A., Steven K. Worden, and Robert D. Benford. 1986. Frame alignment processes, micromobilization and movement participation. *American Sociological Review* 51(4): 464–481.

Swyngedouw, Erik. 2010. Apocalypse forever? Post-political populism and the spectre of climate change. *Theory, Culture and Society* 27(2–3): 213–232.

Tilly, Charles. 1978. *From mobilization to revolution*. Reading: Addison-Wesley.

Touraine, Alain. 1981. *The voice and the eye. An analysis of social movements*. Cambridge: Cambridge University Press.

Turner, Jonathan H., and Alexandra R. Maryanski. 1988. Is 'neofunctionalism' really functional? *Sociological Theory* 6(1): 110–121.

Zald, Mayer N., and John D. McCarthy. 1977. Resource mobilization and social Movements: A partial theory. *The American Journal of Sociology* 82(6): 1212–1241.

Author Biography

Dr. Thomas Kern is Professor of Sociology at the University of Bamberg in Germany. His major research interests are related to the fields of political sociology, sociology of religion, and economic sociology. Recent Publications are „Die Umweltbewegung und der Wandel der institutionellen Logik auf dem Strommarkt" (Zeitschrift für Soziologie 2014), „The Construction of Regional Identities in East Asia" (with Sang-hui Nam and Lotta Mayer, in: S. A. Arjomand (Ed.): Social Theory and Regional Studies in the Global Age, SUNY Press, 2014), „From 'Corruption' to 'Democracy': Cultural Values, Mobilization and the Collective Identity of the Occupy Movement" (with Sang-hui Nam, Journal of Civil Society 2013), „Megakirchen als religiöse Organisationen: Ein dritter Gemeindetyp jenseits von Kirche und Sekte?" (with Uwe Schimank, Kölner Zeitschrift für Soziologie und Sozialpsychologie 2013).

Social Movements and Neo-Institutionalism: A Fruitful Merger?

Jochen Roose

For years social movement research has focused on social movement organizations. To a large extent movement research has been research on the size, structure, and activities of movement organizations (McCarthy and Zald 1977; Edwards and McCarthy 2007). Taking this into account, it is surprising that the research has been reluctant to use theoretical approaches and insights from the sociology of organizations, and vice versa. The sociology of organizations has dealt with a wide array of different organizations, but social movement organizations have rarely been regarded as a type of organization worth studying.[1]

This missing link between the sociology of organizations and social movement research cannot be fully established in this article. Rather, I want to focus on one influential tradition in organization research: neo-institutionalism.

Neo-institutionalism has gained considerable prominence beyond the realm of organization theory (Scott 2008b), and is claimed to be "one of the most broad-ranging 'theoretical research programs' (...) in contemporary sociology and

This paper has profited much more than usual from a thorough discussion in the research group and from the comments of the two fellow editors. I am very grateful for these improvements.

[1] As often, there are exceptions to this general rule. Some ideas of organization research have been integrated into studies of movement organizations (e.g., Roose 2003). A broader review of the opportunities for social movement research and organization research to inform each other was made by Davis et al. (2005).

J. Roose (✉)
Willy Brandt Center for German and European Studies,
University of Wrocław, Wrocław, Poland
e-mail: roose@wbz.uni.wroc.pl

© Springer Fachmedien Wiesbaden 2016
J. Roose and H. Dietz (eds.), *Social Theory and Social Movements,*
DOI 10.1007/978-3-658-13381-8_7

113

one of the most empirically developed forms of institutional analysis" (Jepperson 2002, p. 229; with reference to Berger and Zelditch 1998).

In the following section, I will first present the basic ideas of neo-institutionalism relevant for the analysis of social movements. In Sect. 2, I will show briefly that the core arguments of the approach are as applicable to social movement organizations as they are to others, and argue that concepts from neo-institutionalism are also helpful to refine the analysis of how social movement actors choose their strategies. In Sect. 3, I show what neo-institutionalism and social movement research can learn from one another.

1   Neo-Institutionalism

It is not my intention to present another general introduction to neo-institutionalism (see, for instance, Jepperson 2002; Scott 2008a, b; Scott and Meyer 1994). Rather, I want to point out central arguments of the approach that are particularly applicable to social movements.

The starting point for neo-institutionalism is the observation of isomorphism. Organizations of a similar kind or, in the diction of the approach, in a particular organizational field (DiMaggio 1983) tend to have very similar structures and apply similar strategies. For Weber (1968) this phenomenon was by no means surprising. Rationalization as a general process of modernity was his answer. Organizations apply the most rational structure, the most rational technology, and the most rational strategies to achieve their goals. In this perspective, isomorphism is simply the empirical evidence of rationalization, e.g., the most rational procedure evolves, as all organizations or other kinds of actors adopt the one best way to maximize their respective output.

In their classical article Meyer and Rowan (1977) question whether such output oriented rationalism is an adequate explanation. They argue that in some cases it is by no means evident what the most rational procedure or action is in order to maximize organizational output. It may even be unclear what the optimal output in terms of volume and/or quality is and whether or not this has been actually achieved, possibly because the envisaged output is undefined or the degree of goal achievement is impossible to measure. Even in these cases where the concept of rationalization is difficult to apply isomorphism can be observed. As an alternative, Meyer and Rowan suggest institutions in the sense of generalized beliefs and culturally established rules to explain isomorphism. Common practices are not common because they are most efficient but because it is commonly believed that they are adequate, normal, or in some way "modern." In this sense, common practices are regarded as "rational." However, their "rationality" is not derived from their contribution to successful outcome production. These common practices are the result of a social process of institutionalization that led to their being labeled as "rational." The efficiency of such "norms of rationality" (Meyer and Rowan 1977, p. 343) in terms of output production is only loosely related, and possibly even unrelated, to their dissemination.

Institutionalized norms or, more generally, rules are thus of central importance for neo-institutionalism. But what institutionalized rules are has been spelled out in varying ways. Scott (2008b, pp. 50ff) distinguishes three types of institutionalized rules: regulative, normative, and cultural-cognitive rules. These kinds of rules are enforced in different ways. Regulative institutions are enforced by legal regulations, by coercion. A violation of these regulative institutions is usually an offense for which punishment is applied (if detected). Normative institutions are binding expectations which are enforced by the normative expectations of significant others. Social sanctions can be expected as the reaction to a violation of these rules. Cultural-cognitive rules are not enforced in a direct sense. They refer to constitutive schemata of what is taken for granted. They are institutions in the sense in which Berger and Luckmann (1967) introduced them. Cultural-cognitive rules are regarded as self-evident and as such they need no further enforcement. They can be institutionalized to varying degrees, ranging from rules which are commonly accepted and which people do not bother to reconsider up to rules which are so deeply embedded in common thinking that people are not even able to consider alternatives.[2] These three types are located on a continuum "from the conscious to the unconscious, from the legally enforced to the taken for granted" (Hoffmann 1997, p. 36; see similarly Giddens 1986, pp. 41ff). Obviously, these three kinds of rules do not exist in isolation from one another. Rather, rules in social reality are almost always a mixture of these different types, with some elements being more pronounced than others.

The rules in these three forms could in principle suffice to explain isomorphism. However, the explanation would only be sufficient if either coercion is strong and guarantees compliance, or if the rules are deeply internalized and unquestioned. These are the two extremes in a continuum between (strongly) legally enforced and fully taken for granted. But these extremes cannot account for the existing extent of isomorphism. Meyer and Rowan (1977) were most interested in the realm between

---

[2]The Foucauldian tradition analyzes the latter aspect in more detail (see Baumgarten and Ullrich in this volume).

these extremes. They argue that institutionalized rules are powerful in structuring the social world even if they are neither strongly enforced legally nor so deeply accepted that alternatives are unthinkable. And they look for reasons why we find isomorphism within one organizational field while in other fields similar tasks are solved quite differently.

Meyer and Rowan thus develop their argument to explain isomorphism for practices that fulfill three conditions: (1) They have not been proven to be more efficient for the organization's outcome than alternatives, (2) they are not pre-scribed by the rule of law, and (3) they are not culturally grounded to an extent which makes alternatives unthinkable.[3] This may look like a tight restriction limiting the application of these arguments to a narrow field and few social phe-nomena. However, if we consider the frequency of incidences in which new practices or technologies spread in a limited organizational field although they have not or not yet been proven to be more efficient and are not required by law, there are easily sufficient phenomena which require explanation.

To explain the prevalence and the effect of these institutionalized rules, Meyer and Rowan discuss two phenomena: the process by which rules within a field become the accepted, dominant, and thereby institutionalized ways to do some-thing, and the compliance to these institutionalized rules even by actors who do not believe in the efficiency of the rules to improve the outcome.

In their early article, Meyer and Rowan described three processes through which rules spread and become institutionalized: coercion, professionalization, and imitation. Coercion is not relevant for the range of application just outlined. The first analytically helpful concept is professionalization. Professionals in organiza-tions have undergone an identical or similar education; they learned similar norms and schemata. Even if there is no standard education for specific positions, the exchange of leading personnel in an organizational field may result in the evolution of common normative and cultural-cognitive institutions. The homogeneity of the respective professionals concerning their concepts of a "good" and "successful" organization will result in isomorphism in the field. The second analytically helpful

---

[3]In fact, in their initial article Meyer and Rowan (1977) were not sufficiently clear in specifying this range of empirical application. Later work by Meyer on world society is also not explicit on these limitations. However, the choice of his empirical object, the isomorphism among nation states, fulfills these criteria. In international relations the force of law is not strong enough to guarantee this homogeneity, and change always implies that there was an alternative that was implemented before the change. Therefore neither the explanation by force of law nor by the argument that alternatives are unthinkable is convincing.

concept is imitation. In this case, a practice becomes a generally accepted model and is taken over by others.

However, why do actors follow the ideas and rules they learned either during their training or by watching and imitating others? This leads to the second core question, which asks why actors comply with institutionalized rules. This compliance is easy to explain if either coercion is strong or alternatives are unthinkable, or if the efficiency of the rule in order to achieve the intended outcome is obvious or at least strongly believed in. However, we are interested in incidences in which none of the aforementioned is the case. Meyer and Rowan ask under which conditions are institutionalized rules followed even if they become "myths and ceremonies," as their contribution to the organization's output achievement is highly questionable. They argue that compliance with rules that are considered "rational" in spite of their *inefficiency* is important for the organization to gain legitimacy. "Organizations are driven to incorporate the practices and procedures defined by prevailing rationalized concepts of organizational work and institutionalized in society. Organizations that do so increase their legitimacy and their survival prospects, independent of the immediate efficacy of the acquired practices and procedures" (Meyer and Rowan 1977, p. 340). The reference point for organizational design is therefore not only, or not even primarily, maximizing the organizational output but rather sustaining sufficient legitimacy, even if this may imply a loss in actual output. This need for legitimacy as a primary goal of organizations, in some cases even sidelining their output orientation, encourages compliance with the norms of the respective profession and fosters imitation. Other successful or otherwise dominant organizations pave the way towards a particular practice or organizational structure that then becomes an implicit standard for the organizational field. Other organizations are under the pressure to either imitate or remain behind in terms of being "modern" and "up to date," attributes that would result in a loss of legitimacy. Crucial for the argument is that this pressure for imitation may even be strong in cases where it is unclear or highly questionable whether goal attainment is improved. In order to avoid backsliding in terms of legitimacy organizations will still comply with the new implicit standard.

This approach has inspired a number of studies.[4] Particularly convincing and entertaining are studies of cases in which the lack of rationalization effects is obvious. However, one should keep in mind that the concept itself is not limited to these cases. It also has explanatory value in cases where the rationalization effect of the process is not in doubt, because the approach generally argues that fashionable

---

[4]For an overview see Scott (2008b), Schmidt (2011), or Hasse and Krücken (1999).

organizational processes are often implemented not due to this rationalization effect but rather due to the simple fact that they became the role model for organizations in this field.

2   Is Neo-Institutionalism Relevant for Social Movement Organizations?

A number of arguments and perspectives put forward by neo-institutionalism are quite familiar to social movement researchers (Campbell 2005): That the legal environment is of major impact is nothing new. The Political Opportunity Structure approach (POS approach) argued that the rise of social movements and their success is dependent on the structure of a political system, i.e., the legal situation (Kriesi 2007; Tarrow 1998). The framing approach referred to the need to interpret social situations. The "resonance" of interpretative frames, the possibility to relate the framing to ideas and arguments that are taken for granted, is regarded as crucial for successful movements (e.g., Gamson 1992; Snow and Benford 1988). Accordingly, Campbell (2005) argues that central ideas of the neo-institutionalism approach are already incorporated into classical social movement theory.

However, although these ideas from social movement research resemble aspects of the neo-institutionalism approach, they deviate in a central point. The prime reference point for developing explanations in movement research is the aim of the movement (or movement organization) to achieve progress in respect to the movement's issue: for example, improvements in environmental protection by the environmental movement or in expanding women's rights by the women's movement. Neo-institutionalism focuses on the cultural imprint of organizational activity beyond the attainment of goals related to the movement's issue. It claims that organizational practices are to an important part inspired by institutionalized rules in the organizational field and may be unrelated or even counterproductive to achieving the movement's goal.[5]

---

[5]There are two traditions that cover this argument at least to some extent. Firstly, there is the long debate about Michel's argument of an iron law of oligarchy, stating that after some time the organization's elite shifts its aims towards securing their positions only and the outcome goals are lost (Michels 1987, original 1908). References to this argument are mostly critical in a normative as well as an empirical sense (for example, Clemens and Minkoff 2007; Rucht 1999), and an elaboration of such processes is missing because the cause is solely attributed to the individuals in leading positions. Secondly, Schmitter and Streeck (1981) proposed a distinction between the logic of influence and logic of membership. They argue that organizations have to strategically follow the opportunities to influence their addressee (logic

If we accept that those neo-institutional arguments are not yet included in social movement theory, it now has to be clarified whether this approach is applicable to social movements and, if so, which puzzles it helps to solve. As we will see, both answers are closely interrelated.

In the original version of the approach, Meyer and Rowan identified types of organizations particularly prone to following sets of institutionalized rules or "scripts" regardless of the efficiency in producing their respective output (Jepperson 2002, p. 235). These were organizations that work under particularly unclear conditions and/or are confronted with unclear goals. "The uncertainties of unpredictable technical contingencies or of adapting to environmental change cannot be resolved on the basis of efficiency. Internal participants and external constituents alike call for institutionalized rules that promote trust and confidence in outputs and buffer organizations from failure" (Meyer and Rowan 1977, p. 354). Publicly financed institutions were regarded as classical examples (DiMaggio 1991). Later this assumption was relaxed, as all kinds of organizations appeared to be in desperate need of legitimacy gained by complying with institutionalized scripts (Jepperson 2002, p. 236).

Limiting the application of the approach to only specific organizations is obviously not helpful. However, identifying organizations particularly prone to the mechanism of following institutionalized scripts regardless of the effects on output efficiency seems to be an interesting way of further specifying the theory. In this regard, social movements are a particularly interesting case.

Social movements and social movement organizations are confronted with two very fundamental problems. First, they have to point out that they are legitimate actors. As they are not participating in a formally institutionalized procedure, the interference of social movements by protest (and other means) calls for justification. Even if protest as a form of political participation is widely accepted and frequently practiced, to such a point that protest can itself be regarded as institutionalized (Rucht and Roose 2001) in a movement society (Neidhardt and Rucht 1993; Meyer and Tarrow 1998), the action of a movement in respect to a specific cause still requires justification or can at least be questioned (and very frequently is

---

(Footnote 5 continued)
of influence) but also need to satisfy the expectations of their members (logic of membership) and both can be contradictory. The logic of membership resembles the longing for legitimacy proposed as a core goal of organizations by neo-institutionalism. However, Schmitter and Streeck simply state membership expectations as a factor while neo-institutionalism broadens the scope of potentially relevant reference groups and elaborates the processes of how such expectations develop, diffuse, and are incorporated in organizational practices.

questioned).[6] Presenting oneself as a legitimate actor following an institutionalized script might be a helpful component.

The second fundamental problem is probably even more pressing. Social movements have to choose strategies. Of course, all actors must decide on strategies and in nearly all cases they have to choose from a wide array of possibilities. However, for social movements, the chances of success are extremely difficult to assess and accordingly the way to achieve their stated goals is extremely unclear.

Classical social movement theory has not tackled these problems explicitly but rather ignored them by assuming by and large rational actors.[7] This applies to all of the three most prominent approaches in social movement research, the resource mobilization approach, the POS approach, and the framing approach.[8] In their first outline of the resource mobilization approach McCarthy and Zald focused on "ongoing problems and strategic dilemmas of social movements" (1977, p. 1212). According to the approach, mobilization is dependent on the clever mobilization of resources by the core actors, their tying of networks, collecting money and supporters.

The POS approach argues in a similar manner (Kriesi 2007). On first sight, it is a structural theory as it argues with reference to the macro conditions in which social movements are situated. Favorable political conditions are regarded as crucial for the chances of mobilization. Cross-country variation of movement activity is explained by the chances of the respective movements to make themselves heard in the political system. The close theoretical link between available opportunities and action is established by a concept of rational actors. "[T]he emphasis of [the POS approach, J.R.] is on relating the strategic choices and societal impacts of movements to specific properties of the external political opportunity structures that movements face" (Kitschelt 1986, p. 59f). Accordingly, rational actors are indispensable for the mechanism to work. "The opportunity theses (…) amounts to the claim that people choose those options for collective action that are (1) available and (2) expected to result in a favorable outcome" (Koopmans 1999, p. 97).

---

[6]The framing approach considered this need for self-justification (e.g., Gerhards 1992; Klandermans 1988, p. 177).

[7]This argument was critically elaborated by Pettenkofer (2010). Opp (2009) argues similarly, but from within the rational choice paradigm, that the theoretical approaches to social movements can be completely integrated into a rational choice model.

[8]For this classical enumeration of approaches see, for example, Snow et al. (2007) or della Porta and Diani (1999).

Finally, the framing approach (Benford and Snow 2000; Snow 2007) also builds upon the concept of a rational actor. The interpretation of the issue as a relevant problem with specified addressees, who are able and responsible to tackle the problem, is regarded as a task for the movement entrepreneurs. The framing approach does not target the inevitable interpretation of the social world and the cultural implications of this process. Rather, framing is regarded as a strategic task that can be accomplished with varying success affecting the movement's mobilization strength.

At first sight, these theories can comfortably explain why the variance of strategies by social movement organizations (and to some lesser extent by social movements) is fairly limited and constant over time. As movement organizations try to employ the most rational strategy they all end up close to the one best way. Isomorphism is the result.

However, a rationalistic explanation of similar strategies remaining fairly constant over time is not very plausible. It would imply that the assessment of the chance of success has quite an obvious result, which is evaluated similarly by all movement entrepreneurs independently from one another. This is in sharp contrast to the scientific discussion on movement success. Researchers found it particularly difficult to assess the effects of movements (Giugni 1998, 1999; Kolb 2007; Roose et al. 2006).

Movements usually target processes of fundamental social change, which is influenced by many factors. The mere complexity of the phenomenon of social change makes it extremely difficult to attribute the outcome to specific factors—and only some of the possibly proposed factors can plausibly be associated to social movements. Causal inferences on relevant influences are even more obscured by the fact that effects of social movements often become visible only after long periods of time. In many cases, fundamental social change is a slow process lasting even decades. Therefore, not only current situations but also relevant future changes need to be taken into account. Also, learning processes are particularly difficult, as the response in terms of success or failure is only visible in the distant future, while strategic decisions have to be made in the present.

The problem of the evaluation of success is even further complicated. The definition of success remains ambivalent in the first place. The actual aim of the movement is only on rare occasions clearly specified. Even within social movement organizations, which often have a formal charter specifying goals, the definition of short-term and long-term goals is controversial (Giugni 1998, p. 383). Accordingly, people will differ in rating something as a success or failure. These differences necessarily increase when it comes to judging partial successes (and partial failures) or compromises. Differences in judgments and the differing preparedness for compromises should have effects on the choice of strategies if a rational choice of means takes place.

Taking into account these fundamental and systematic difficulties in identifying crucial influences on the desired outcome and in assessing situations as successes or failures, the choice of strategy in a rational manner is extremely difficult. The evaluation of chances, opportunities, and adequate strategies will be fundamentally influenced by personal judgments, experiences, and preferences. As the situation is so unclear, the causal influences so hard to determine, the choice of strategies should be heterogeneous, with rapid changes over time. Social movement activists coming to similar decisions regarding their means, i.e., their protest forms and strategies, should be a rare occurrence under these circumstances. Also, a particular, stable repertoire of activities over time, chosen by a movement or a movement organization (or by an individual) is highly unlikely and, accordingly, should be seldom found.

The rational perspective of movement research leads us to expect heterogeneous choices of strategies and protest forms, rapidly changing over time. But empirical reality looks quite different. Tilly (1995a, b) identified protest repertoires that are stable over long periods of time. della Porta and Rucht (1995, p. 232) coined the phrase "movement families," which subsumes movements with a focus on different goals and different strategies but overlap in their constituency and occasional cooperation. Roose (2003) identified activity repertoires of movement organizations that are employed on different political levels, i.e., irrespective of the political system with which the organization is confronted. This evidence, as well as our general knowledge about social movements, contradicts the expectation of highly heterogeneous, quickly changing movement strategies. Rather, we find a considerable isomorphism—within a particular movement, among several overlapping movements forming a movement family, and in organizations, also over longer spans of time. The rational approach of the classical social movement theories would lead to different expectations; however, neo-institutionalism would predict exactly this.

3   Social Movements and Neo-Institutionalism— Lessons to Learn

Combining neo-institutionalism and social movement research is not a completely new idea. However, to date, neo-institutionalism's perspective has been applied to movements in a very particular way. Social movements were predominantly seen as actors who either modify or exploit the institutional structure (Campbell 2005).

This use and modification of institutionalized rules has again been regarded as a strategic activity. In their widely received analysis of transnational movement networks, Keck and Sikkink (1998) refer to the world polity approach of Meyer and others (Meyer et al. 1997; Thomas et al. 1987; Meyer 2010), which is based on neo-institutionalism, to underline the importance of norms and frames of interpretation. The particular perspective of neo-institutionalism on organizations is neglected by this account. In the following, I will first ask how the analysis of social movements can be refined by using neo-institutionalism (Sect. 3.1), before I turn to the question what neo-institutionalism may learn from its application to social movements (Sect. 3.2).

3.1 Using Neo-Institutionalism for Social Movement Analysis

What questions should we ask and what can we learn if we apply neo-institutionalism to social movement organizations and social movements? Firstly, we have to modify the theoretical assumptions about strategic reasoning in social movements and movement organizations.

An explanation of movement strategies would relate to the desired legitimacy of such strategic choice by conforming to rules and concepts considered valid in the field of movement organizations. The research question is not so much concerned with which political structures are opportunities and therefore bring movements into being; also a neo-institutionalist perspective would not look much at whether the framing convinces the public of a problem and the ways to solve it. Rather, it would ask which regulative, normative and cultural-cognitive institutions are regarded as valid, i.e., which legal rules are accepted or rejected, which norms are regarded as crucial, and which cognitive schemata guide the interpretation of the world by movement activists.

This is not to say that the choice of strategy is irrational. Neo-institutionalism does not assume irrational actors or action beyond rationality—at least the approach should not make such claims (Scott 2008a, p. 435ff). Rather, more diverse goals have to be considered and specified. Not only is the desired social change a relevant goal but some kinds of actions may also be regarded as goals in themselves. Such forms of action may be followed in a value-rational (*wertrational*) manner (Weber 1968, p. 24f). Their importance may be taken for granted as an obligatory part of movement activity. Some strategies or internal organizational structures may also be deliberately chosen, in awareness that they will not help or might even hinder the ultimate movement goals, because the measures help to stabilize the organization itself. Neo-institutionalism reminds us that the prerequisites for organizational survival are not limited to the flows of resources that are the focus of the resource mobilization approach (McCarthy and Zald 1977; Edwards and McCarthy 2007). Legitimacy among the constituency and the broader public is also a necessary prerequisite. The argument as such would probably be easily accepted among resource mobilization theorists, as it could be reformulated as basically adding a new category of preferences, but it seldom made its way into empirical research. Research inspired by neo-institutionalism would focus on exactly this aspect.[9]

Yet the importance of neo-institutionalism is not limited to raising these questions. Rather, it gives us a guideline for how to pose questions and where to look for solutions. The above-mentioned processes resulting in isomorphism could also be applied to social movements (see also Scott 2008b, p. 79ff). Here, again, coercion itself may not be a surprising factor as the rule of law is universal. However, the case of social movement organizations reminds us how interwoven regulative institutions are with normative or cultural-cognitive institutions. Social movement activists do not only act within the limits allowed by law; they also employ calculated law-breaking as a strategy (Rucht 1995). This law-breaking again follows specific rules. In many cases, there is a precise line to distinguish protest forms that are regarded as legitimate (though illegal) from other illegitimate forms. The use of violence is here of major importance. Law-breaking or breaking other kinds of rules is in itself part of the strategy. Therefore, laws and rules still have relevant influence on isomorphism, not in the sense of fixed laws which need to be obeyed but at least partly also in defining a set of norms that can be violated.

The second process, professionalization, seems not to apply to social movements at first glance. Social movement organizations and even more loosely structured protest groups often rely on volunteers with a small degree of professionalization (but see Jordan and Maloney 1997; Rucht et al. 1997; Rucht and Roose 2001). However, the process specified in the theory does not refer to paid work as such but rather to a specialization of leading personnel, a common path of training and the exchange of people in leading positions. What Lave and Wenger

---

[9]A directly linked question would be which kind of movement organization is more prone to follow institutionalized rules. However, two contradictory thoughts are possible. Either formal organizations may be strongly committed to their own survival and the permanency of paid posts while informal organizations may be more flexible, or informal organizations are more fragile and therefore are more dependent on legitimacy, and tend to comply with institutionalized rules in an even stricter manner.

(1991) describe in their analysis of personnel training also applies to social movement activists. Though not employed, they are also subject to a socialization process with learning on the job, often copying the practices of more experienced activists (see also Scott 2008b, p. 82f). There is only little research on the rank of social movement organizations available (see, however, Frantz 2005), but from the reasoning of neo-institutionalism this would be a rewarding research field.[10]

While professionalization refers to the socialization of leading personnel, imitation shifts our focus from individuals to the copying of strategies and protest forms on the organizational level. Imitation does not refer primarily to interpersonal contact and the transfer of practices on the interpersonal level, but organizations imitate each other instead by observing the visible parts of activities. There has been some research on the diffusion of movement ideas and practices (Doerr and Mattoni 2007; McAdam 1995; McAdam and Rucht 1993; Snow and Benford 1999). In the context of neo-institutionalism, this research takes a different spin. Instead of identifying sources, receivers, and connections (McAdam and Rucht 1993), the crucial question is: Under which circumstances does a strategy or an organization (with its structure and strategic repertoire) become "attractive" and "admired" in the first place?

In his comprehensive analysis of neo-institutionalism, Scott (2008b, p. 121ff) presents an overview of several studies describing the *construction* of institutions. A particular focus has been on the construction of regulatory institutions implementing scripts in a formal way (e.g., Djelic and Quack 2003; Overdevest 2010). Once these institutions have been established, their guidelines are enforced by coercion, either in a strong sense of enforcement by state power or in a weaker sense due to market forces. The question arising from this perspective is whether such institutions also exist for social movements. Obviously there is no official licensing or anything similar for movement organizations. Still there might be relevant organizations that grant legitimacy to social movement organizations depending on their compliance with a particular script. A potential candidate would be organizations that monitor the use of donations. Possibly there are also other organizations or groups that are particularly influential in defining scripts for movement organizations.

A formal organization, which defines a script and monitors its application, is of course not the only form of constructing an institution. Scott's overview documents several other examples of how specifically and idiosyncratically the processes of establishing institutions evolve. Rather than providing general rules of

---

[10]From a somewhat different angle this question is touched by research on the influence of social movement activity on activists' biographies (Giugni 2007; McAdam 1990, 1999).

how institutions are diffused and finally institutionalized, these studies are historical accounts of specific processes. Although obviously the individual interests of concerned actors play a crucial role and norms are often the result of explicit conflicts about opposing concepts or ideas, the described processes remain contingent on specific events and circumstances. It turns out to be very difficult to generalize, especially regarding the institutionalization of socio-cultural rules. It nevertheless might be rewarding to search for patterns of the institutionalization of rules in social movements.[11]

3.2 Refining Neo-Institutionalism from a Social Movement Perspective

As the approach has matured and spread during the last decades (Scott 2008a) we should not expect completely new insights for neo-institutionalism by confronting it with social movements. Rather, the perspectives might be supplemented or refocused. Two points arise from our discussion.

Firstly, a question that received little attention up to now is why people in organizations comply with the scripts. This question is at least in part different from the problem of how scripts are established (see above). The approach has always acknowledged that people in organizations may realize that following the scripts is not rational in the sense of direct output attainment, but rather it is rational in respect to public image or specific reference groups. Additionally, the concept of decoupling points out that often the scripts are only followed as ceremonies while the processes necessary for the actual goal achievement are still practiced—if necessary in secret. However, if nobody or nearly nobody believes in the rationality of the scripts why then are they still followed? The neo-institutionalism approach offers two assumptions to this question. First the scripts are held up by people who for one reason or another profit from it (DiMaggio 1988). So, even if the practice does not contribute to goal attainment it will still reward some individuals in the sense that they control relevant resources (which might become irrelevant otherwise), grant social prestige, etc. The rationale of crucial actors who lead to the implementation of a script in the first place may thus also contribute to

---

[11]Research on protest waves might be a good starting point, as part of the diffusion process seems to be a socio-cultural institutionalization of protest as a means of action in itself, often in particular contexts. For example, during the protest wave in North Africa in 2011 the "Day of Rage" was copied in several countries (Roose 2011). Similar processes of copying could be witnessed for the use of sit-ins as a form of protest (Andrews and Biggs 2006).

its stabilization. But even actors who were never involved in its implementation may find themselves in a position to profit from the application of a script.

While actors profiting from script application have received some attention within the research tradition, the second answer has been by and large neglected. Also, as is usually not explicitly stated in neo-institutionalism, there will be true believers *somewhere*. Assuming that we also find people who follow parts of scripts in a ceremonial way, this implies that others will follow the rules because they regard them as valid. But where should we expect to find true believers? In situations in which goal attainment is particularly difficult to assess it may be unclear to the actors themselves what contributes to success and what is only a myth. In these cases true believers and cynics might be found anywhere. The question is more pressing—and theoretically more interesting—in cases where the inappropriateness of a practice is quite evident, at least to well-informed crucial actors. To identify true believers under these circumstances, we probably need to focus on the reference groups. People outside the organization may have only limited knowledge of the internal processes and the practical needs for goal attainment. Yet they still have to judge the organizations' ability to be successful. These people are probably particularly prone to judgments according to scripts, irrespective of their rationality. In general, we should look for true believers among highly relevant stakeholders who have not (and cannot have) enough knowledge of the actual processes for goal attainment. These might be bank clerks in the case of economic organizations; they might be supporters of political movements without thorough knowledge of policy processes. The importance of these stakeholders for the respective organization is crucial and, at the same time, these stakeholders are severely limited in their knowledge due to systematic reasons and not due to individual failure. Accordingly, the gap between expectations and practical needs is a systematic one.

This second point is a reassessment of an earlier debate. The idea of differentiating organizations or social units with respect to their exposure to expectations formed by scripts should be taken up. The original approach from organization theory referred to institutionalized environments and complex or insecure environments (Jepperson 2002, p. 235; Scott and Meyer 1991). Thus the arguments referred to the difficulties in identifying the rational way to achieve the organization's outcome. According to this argument, organizations have to substitute the rational way of output production through compliance with a supposedly rational script in order to remain legitimate. With regard to the discussion of social movement organizations, we can add another argument. The need for legitimacy is not identical to all.

Organizations with disputed legitimacy are particularly prone to follow scripts more closely and with higher priority. This might be the reason why the approach is well suited for the behavior (at least the face work) of nation states, particularly newly formed nation states, as has been shown in studies on world culture (Meyer 2010). Accordingly, we should expect a particularly strong influence of scripts on social movement actors, as they are in need of legitimacy and act in a particularly complex and insecure environment. Another potential candidate would be the European Union, which is also in need of legitimacy while working in a very complex and insecure environment. Initiatives of the EU that are only partially popular but in line with political correctness might be the result of a tight compliance with cultural scripts.

4   Conclusion

The research agenda of neo-institutionalism is helpful if we look at the influence of social movements on script formation. It is beyond doubt that the institutionalization of scripts is highly influenced by social movements. But social movement actors themselves are also subject to specific social movement scripts. This perspective has not yet been systematically exploited. However, it is a promising perspective that could provide us with new insights. It first turns our attention to processes of professionalization and imitation in the field of social movements and social movement organizations.

For neo-institutionalism, on the other hand, the discussion of social movements directs our attention towards the questions of who actually believes in scripts (which are severely questioned by insiders) and whether the need for legitimacy leads to a stricter transposition of scripts.

Initially the notion of Meyer and Rowan's work was a reassessment of rationality. They claim that patterns that are regarded as rational are myths of rationality. At first it seems that they substitute the concept of rationality with a perspective of culturally-based institutions. A closer look shows that rationality is still the core assumption for actors. However, instead of output rationality, rational strategies for gaining legitimacy guide organizational practices. But we should keep in mind that not everything that is called "rational" can stand a systematic evaluation. It may instead be rationally chosen compliance with institutionalized rules. The consequences of this finding need to be exploited further, for neo-institutionalism and even more for social movement studies.

References

Andrews, Kenneth T., and Michael Biggs. 2006. The dynamics of protest diffusion: Movement organizations, social networks, and news media in the 1960 sit-ins. *American Sociological Review* 71: 752–777.

Benford, Robert D., and David Snow. 2000. Framing processes and social movements: An overview and assessment. *Annual Review of Sociology* 26(1): 611–639.

Berger, Joseph, and Morris Zelditch. 1998. Theoretical research programs: A reformulation. In *Status, power, and legitimacy*, ed. Joseph Berger, and Morris Zelditch, 71–93. New Brunswick: Transaction.

Berger, Peter, and Thomas Luckmann. 1967. *The social construction of reality: A treatise in the sociology of knowledge*. New York: Doubleday.

Campbell, John L. 2005. Where do we stand? In *Social movements and organization theory*, ed. Gerald F. Davis, et al., 41–68. Cambridge: Cambridge University Press.

Clemens, Elisabeth S., and Debra C. Minkoff. 2007. Beyond the iron law. Rethinking the place of organizations in social movement research. In *The Blackwell companion to social movements*, ed. David Snow, Sarah Soule, and Hanspeter Kriesi, 155–170. Malden, Oxford: Blackwell.

Davis, Gerald F., et al. (eds.). 2005. *Social movements and organization theory*. Cambridge: Cambridge University Press.

della Porta, Donatella, and Mario Diani. 1999. *Social movements: An introduction*. Oxford: Blackwell Publishers.

della Porta, Donatella, and Dieter Rucht. 1995. Left-libertarian movements in context: A comparison of Italy and West Germany, 1965–1990. In *The politics of social protest: Comparative perspectives on states and social movements*, ed. Bert Klandermans, and Craig J. Jenkins, 229–272. Minneapolis: University of Minnesota Press.

DiMaggio, Paul J. 1983. State expansion and organizational fields. In *Organizational theory and public policy*, eds. R. H. Hall, R. E. Quinn, 147–161. Beverly Hills.

DiMaggio, Paul J. 1988. Interest and agency in institutional theory. In *Institutional patterns and organizations: Culture and environment*, ed. Lynne G. Zucker, 3–21. Cambridge: Ballinger.

DiMaggio, Paul J. 1991. Constructing an organizational field as a professional project: U.S. art museums, 1920–1940. In *The new institutionalism in organizational analysis*, eds. Walter W. Powell, Paul J. DiMaggio, 267–292. Chicago, London.

Djelic, Marie-Laure, and Sigrid Quack (eds.). 2003. *Globalization and Institutions. Redefining the Rules of the Economic Game*. Cheltenham: Edward Elgar.

Doerr, Nicole, and Alice Mattoni. 2007. Activists communicating across the European space: The diffusion of the Euromayday campaign against precarity, ECPR General Conference. Pisa.

Edwards, Bob, and John D. McCarthy. 2007. Resources and social movement mobilization. In *The Blackwell companion to social movements*, ed. David Snow, Sarah Soule, and Hanspeter Kriesi, 116–152. Malden, Oxford: Blackwell.

Frantz, Christiane. 2005. *Karriere in NGOs. Politik als Beruf jenseits der Parteien*. Wiesbaden: VS Verlag für Sozialwissenschaften.

Gamson, William A. 1992. *Talking politics*. Cambridge: Cambridge University Press.

Gerhards, Jürgen. 1992. Dimensionen und Strategien öffentlicher Diskurse. *Journal für Sozialforschung* 32: 307–318.

Giddens, Anthony. 1986. The constitution of society: Outline of the theory of structuration. Berkeley et al.: University of California Press.

Giugni, Marco. 1998. Was it worth the effort? The outcomes and consequences of social movements. *Annual Review of Sociology* 98: 371–393.

Giugni, Marco. 1999. How social movements matter: Past research, present problems, future developments. In *How social movements matter*, ed. Marco Giugni, Doug McAdam, and Sidney Tarrow, xiii–xxxii. Minneapolis, London: University of Minnesota Press.

Giugni, Marco. 2007. Personal and biographical consequences. In *The Blackwell companion to social movements*, ed. David Snow, Sarah Soule, and Hanspeter Kriesi, 489–507. Malden, Oxford: Blackwell.

Hasse, Raimund, and Georg Krücken. 1999. *Neo-Institutionalismus*. Bielefeld: transcript.

Hoffmann, Andrew W. 1997. *From heresy to dogma: An institutional history of corporate environmentalism*. San Francisco: New Lexington Press.

Jepperson, Ronald L. 2002. The development and application of sociological neoinstitutionalism. In *New directions in contemporary sociological theory*, ed. Joseph Berger, and Morris Zelditch, 229–266. Lanham, Boulder u.a: Rowman & Littlefield.

Jordan, Grant, and William Maloney. 1997. *The protest business? Mobilizing campaign groups*. Manchester, New York: Manchester University Press.

Keck, Margaret E., and Kathryn Sikkink. 1998. *Activists beyond borders: Advocacy networks in international politics*. Ithaca: Cornell University Press.

Kitschelt, Herbert P. 1986. Political opportunity structures and political protest: Anti-nuclear movements in four democracies. *British Journal of Political Science* 16: 57–85.

Klandermans, Bert. 1988. The formation and mobilization of consensus. S. 219–246. In *From structure to action: Comparing social movement across cultures*, ed. Bert u a Klandermans. London.

Kolb, Felix. 2007. *Protest and opportunities. The political outcomes of social movements*. Frankfurt/M., New York: Campus.

Koopmans, Ruud. 1999. Political. Opportunity. Structure. Some splitting to balance the lumping. *Sociological Forum* 14: 93–106.

Kriesi, Hanspeter. 2007. Political context and opportunity. In *The Blackwell companion to social movements*, ed. David Snow, Sarah Soule, and Hanspeter Kriesi, 67–90. Malden, Oxford: Blackwell.

Lave, Jean, and Etienne Wenger (eds.). 1991. *Situated learning: Legitimate peripheral participation*. Cambridge: Cambridge University Press.

McAdam, Doug. 1990. *Freedom summer*. Oxford: Oxford University Press.

McAdam, Doug. 1995. "Initiator" and "Spin-off" movements: Diffusion process in protest cycles. In *Repertoires and cycles of collective action*, ed. Mark Traugott, 217–239. Durham, London.

McAdam, Doug. 1999. The biographical impact of activism. In *How social movements matter*, ed. Marco Giugni, Doug McAdam, and Charles Tilly, 117–146. Minneapolis, London: University of Minnesota Press.

McAdam, Doug, and Dieter Rucht. 1993. The cross-national diffusion of movement ideas. In *Citizens, protest, and democracy*, ed. Russel J. Dalton, 56–74. Newbury Park, London, Neu Dehli.

McCarthy, John D., and Mayer N. Zald. 1977. Resource mobilization and social movements: A partial theory. *American Journal of Sociology* 82: 1212–1241.

Meyer, David S., and Sidney Tarrow (eds.). 1998. *The social movement society: Contentious politics for a new century*. Lanham, Boulder, New York, Oxford: Rowman and Littlefield Publishers Inc.

Meyer, John W. 2010. World society, institutional theories, and the actor. *Annual Review of Sociology* 36: 1–20.

Meyer, John W., John Boli, George M. Thomas, and Francisco O. Ramirez. 1997. World society and the nation-state. *American Journal of Sociology* 103(1): 144–181.

Meyer, John W., and B. Rowan. 1977. Institutionalized organizations: Formal structure as myth and ceremony. *American Journal of Sociology* 83: 340–363.

Michels, Robert. 1987. Die oligarchischen Tendenzen der Gesellschaft. In *Masse, Führer, Intellektuelle. Politisch-soziologische Aufsätze 1906–1933*, ed. Robert Michels, 133–187. Frankfurt/M: Campus.

Neidhardt, Friedhelm, and Dieter Rucht. 1993. Auf dem Weg in die "Bewegungsgesellschaft"? Über die Stabilisierbarkeit sozialer Bewegungen. *Soziale Welt* 44: 305–326.

Opp, Karl-Dieter. 2009. *Theories of political protest and social movements. A multidisciplinary introduction, critique, and synthesis*. London, New York: Routledge.

Overdevest, Christine. 2010. Comparing forest certification schemes. The case of ratcheting standards in the forest sector. *Socio-Economic Review* 8: 47–76.

Pettenkofer, Andreas. 2010. *Radikaler Protest: Zur soziologischen Theorie politischer Bewegungen*. Frankfurt/M., New York: Campus.

Roose, Jochen. 2003. *Die Europäisierung von Umweltorganisationen. Die Umweltbewegung auf dem langen Weg nach Brüssel*. Wiesbaden: Westdeutscher Verlag.

Roose, Jochen. 2011. Nordafrika 2011: Revolutions- und Bewegungstheorien und die (Un-) Vorhersehbarkeit von Protest. *Forschungsjournal Soziale Bewegungen* 24: 7–18.

Roose, Jochen, Karin Urich, and Stephanie Schmoliner. 2006. Immer in Bewegung - nie am Ziel. Was bewirken soziale Bewegungen? *Forschungsjournal Neue Soziale Bewegungen* 19: 2–4.

Rucht, Dieter. 1995. Ecological protest as calculated law-breaking: Greenpeace and earth first! In comparative perspective. In *Green politics three*, ed. Wolfgang Rüdig, 66–89. Edinburgh.

Rucht, Dieter. 1999. Linking organization and mobilization: Michels' 'Iron law of oligarchy' reconsidered. *Mobilization* 4(2): 151–169.

Rucht, Dieter, Barbara Blattert, and Dieter Rink. 1997. *Soziale Bewegungen auf dem Weg zur Institutionalisierung. Zum Strukturwandel "alternativer" Gruppen in beiden Teilen Deutschlands*. Frankfurt/M., New York: Campus.

Rucht, Dieter, and Jochen Roose. 2001. Zur Institutionalisierung von Bewegungen: Umweltverbände und Umweltproteste in der Bundesrepublik. In *Verbände und Demokratie in Deutschland*, ed. Bernhard Weßels, and Annette Zimmer, 261–290. Opladen: Leske + Budrich.

Schmidt, Vivien A. 2011. Discursive institutionalism: The explanatory power of ideas and discourse. *Annual Review of Political Science* 11: 303–326.

Schmitter, Philippe C., and Streeck Wolfgang. 1981. *The organization of business interests. a research design to study the associative action of business in advanced industrial societies of Western Europe.* Berlin: Wissenschaftszentrum, Arbeitspapier IIMV dp 81-13.

Scott, W. Richard. 2008a. Approaching adulthood. The maturing of institutional theory. *Theory and Society* 37: 427–442.

Scott, W. Richard. 2008b. *Institutions and organizations. Ideas and interests.* Los Angeles, London, New Delhi, Singapore: Sage.

Scott, W. Richard, and John W. Meyer. 1991. The organization of societal sectors: Propositions and early evidence. In: *The new institutionalism in organizational analysis*, eds. Walter W. Powell, and Paul J. DiMaggio, 108–140. Chicago, London.

Scott, W. Richard, and John W. Meyer. 1994. *Institutional environments and organizations.* London: Sage.

Snow, David. 2007. Framing processes, ideology, and discursive fields. In *The Blackwell companion to social movements*, ed. David Snow, Sarah Soule, and Hanspeter Kriesi, 380–412. Malden, Oxford: Blackwell.

Snow, David A., and Robert D. Benford. 1988. Ideology, frame resonance and participant mobilization. In *From structure to action: Comparing social movement across cultures*, ed. Bert Klandermans, Hanspeter Kriesi, and Sidney Tarrow, 197–218. London: Jai Press.

Snow, David A., and Robert D. Benford. 1999. Alternative types of cross-national diffusion in the social movement arena. In *Social movements in a globalizing world*, ed. Donatella della Porta, Hanspeter Kriesi, and Dieter Rucht, 23–39. Basingstoke, London: Macmillan.

Snow, David, Sarah Soule, and Hanspeter Kriesi (eds.). 2007. *The Blackwell companion to social movements.* Oxford: Blackwell.

Tarrow, Sidney. 1998. *Power in movement: Social movements and contentious politics.* Cambridge: Cambridge University Press.

Thomas, George M., et al. (eds.). 1987. *Institutional structure: Constituting states, society, and the individual.* Newbury Park: Sage.

Tilly, Charles. 1995a. Contentious repertoires in Great Britain. In *Repertoires and cycles of collective action*, ed. Mark Traugott, 15–42. Durham, London: Duke University Press.

Tilly, Charles. 1995b. *Popular contention in Great Britain, 1758–1834.* Cambridge, Massachusetts, London: Harvard University Press.

Weber, Max (ed.). 1968. *Economy and society. An outline to interpretive sociology. 3 Volumes.* New York: Bedminster Press.

Author Biography

Dr. Jochen Roose is Professor for Social Sciences at the Willy Brandt Center for German and European Studies, University of Wrocław and researcher at the Institute for Protest and Social Movement Studies (ipb). His research interests are participation, Europeanisation and research methodology. Recent publications are „Empirische Kultursoziologie" (edited with J. Rössel, Springer VS 2015), „Culture and Movement Strength from a Quantitative Perspective" (in: Baumgarten et al. Conceptualizing Culture, Palgrave 2014), „How European is European Identification?" (Journal of Common Market Studies 2013), „Fehlermultiplikation und Pfadabhängigkeit" (Kölner Zeitschrift für Soziologie und Sozialpsychologie 2013).

Judith Butler and the Politics of Protest

Dorothea Reinmuth

What can social movement theory learn by taking some points of Butler's theoretical work into consideration? At first sight it seems that there are no compelling reasons for social movement theory to deal with Butler. The very different rhetoric of the two approaches is only a first sign of their different ways of dealing with social movements. So, why should social movement theory engage with Judith Butler's theoretical work? What could be learnt? Normally, Butler is introduced because of her importance in the understanding of queer movements. But in this article I want to argue that her contribution goes beyond that. We gain from her work an understanding of other protest phenomena, too.

In what follows I would like to discuss Butler's theoretical approach with regard to its contribution to social movement theory. Although Butler does not offer a social theory framework that was meant to be used in the specialized social movement scholarship, it is my objective within this article to examine the aspects of her approach that could be helpful for social movement theory. To outline my argument, I divide the article into three sections. First, I will sketch the relation between Butler's presumptions that are rooted in discourse theory and her understanding of recognition. To illuminate her position I will contrast it with the conventional discourse on recognition. Second, I will broaden the *post*-structuralist perspective by introducing the concept of performativity as a key to evade the power of discourse. Third, I will propose in which way new social movements could be understood according to these theoretical findings. To conclude, I would like to focus on the protest activities that are centered on the resignification of speech acts.

D. Reinmuth (✉)
Universität Erfurt, Erfurt, Germany
e-mail: dorothea.reinmuth@uni-erfurt.de

© Springer Fachmedien Wiesbaden 2016   135
J. Roose and H. Dietz (eds.), *Social Theory and Social Movements*,
DOI 10.1007/978-3-658-13381-8_8

1 Subordination and Existence at Once: Recognition Within the Order of Discourse

According to Butler every claim that is articulated by a protest movement could be understood as a claim for recognition. To understand the relationship between the relevance of recognition and the possibility to protest I would like to sketch out very briefly Butler's post-structuralist perspective, which is influenced by Foucault and Althusser. This perspective critically and radically succeeds the *structuralist* starting point. According to this tradition getting recognition is limited to the specific order of the discourse. Every order of the discourse entails specific recognizable positions. According to Butler's account, the subject is *subjugated* under the norm of recognition. The subject is constituted as a formation of powerful and less powerful discourses: "Subjectivation signifies the process of becoming subordinated by power *as well as* the process of becoming a subject" (Butler 1997c, p. 2, my emphasis). Butler's understanding of recognition is centered on this idea. With reference to Althusser's concept of interpellation, Butler proposes that "the act of recognition becomes an act of constitution: the address animates the subject into being" (Butler 1997b, p. 25). And Butler goes on:

> Bound to seek recognition of its own existence in categories, terms, and names that are not of its own making, the subject seeks the sign of its own existence outside itself, in a discourse that is at once dominant and indifferent. Social categories signify subordination and existence at once. In other words, within subjection the price of existence is subordination. (Butler 1997c, p. 20)

If someone is recognized they are always recognized *as somebody*. Although those names could hurt, the subconscious longs continuously for subject formation by naming.[1] Existing as a subject depends on the continuous repetition of some contents of discourse and the exclusion of others: "There is no power that acts, but only a reiterated acting that is power in its persistence and instability" (Butler 1993, p. 9). The discourse of identity neglects this contingency (Butler 1993, p. 53, 1997c, pp. 10–11). By contrast, according to Butler's perspective identity could be understood as "a sedimented effect of a reiterative or ritual practice" (Butler 1993, p. 10).

---

[1]With reference to psychoanalysis, Butler explains: "Called by an injurious name, I come into social being, and because I have a certain inevitable attachment to my existence, because a certain narcissism takes hold of any term that confers existence, I am led to embrace the terms that injure me because they constitute me socially" (Butler 1997c, p. 104).

For Butler, the subject "ought to be designated as a linguistic category, a place-holder, a structure in formation" (Butler 1997c, p. 10). It is not interchangeable with the individual or the person. Individuals "enjoy intelligibility only to the extent that they are, as it were, first established in language. The subject is the linguistic occasion for the individual to achieve and reproduce intelligibility, the linguistic condition of its existence and agency" (Butler 1997c, p. 11). Because recognition ascribes some qualities while it marginalizes others, recognition is also part of a process of producing invisibility (Butler 1997c). Besides the exclusionary effects of every interpellation Butler highlights the totalizing effect of an interpellation: "The more specific identities become, the more totalized an identity becomes by that very specificity" (Butler 1997c, p. 100).[2]

As Butler wants to highlight the effects of ideological recognition, she pays attention to the *doing* of recognition (Butler 1997a, 2005). That means Butler applies the theoretical position on performativity to discourse theory and to the discourse on recognition. Different to Austin who "assumes a subject who speaks" (Butler 1997b, p. 25), Butler understands performativity in accordance with Derrida's reformulation of Austin's approach "as the reiterative or citational practice by which discourse produces the effects that it names" (Butler 1993, p. 2). I would like to come back to this point later.

The subject is not free to choose when and what kind of performative act it wants to execute. The recognized are committed to the citation of the norms that include the recognized identity. According to Butler a performative speech act includes the effects of discourse in two ways. First, it determines the way a person is perceived and treated. Second, the discourse also materializes itself "from within," which means that the discourse expresses the demand for a performance. By analyzing the twofold effects of performative speech acts the "contingent foundations" of every subject can be focused (Butler 1992). Hence, an act of recognition ascribes specific qualities, while it marginalizes or neglects or denies other qualities (Butler 2003). Therefore, every order of the discourse entails specific recognizable positions.

What does this imply for protest movements? From this perspective protest movements are only significant in a way that they promote adaptations to a

---

[2]With reference to Foucault, Butler goes on: "Indeed, we might understand this contemporary phenomenon as the movement by which a juridical apparatus produces the field of possible political subject. [...] In this sense, what we call identity politics is produced by a state which can only allocate recognition and rights to subjects totalized by the particularity that constitutes their plaintiff status" (Butler 1997a, p. 100).

changing environment that is structured by hegemonic discourses. Actually, it seems hard to imagine that demands will be recognized that are situated outside the order of discourse. To that extent the success of a recognition demand could coincide with the *subjugation* to the order of discourse—and it implies not simply a gaining of emancipation and autonomy. From this point of view recognition efforts fail much more frequently than might appear at first sight. Contrary to the conventional approaches of recognition that assume an essential positive meaning of recognition (Honneth 2007, p. 329), Butler represents an approach diametrically opposite to Axel Honneth, Charles Taylor, and Nancy Fraser in order to theorize the subject and to refer to the concept of performative speech acts.

In order to characterize the essential points of dissent this section starts by very briefly presenting the main arguments of conventional recognition theory. Thereafter, I would like to contrast them with Butler's position by summarizing the most important points of her theoretical framework with regard to the performativity of recognition.

Challenged by the many voices that claimed political, social, and cultural rights in the name of various political movements that may be described as identity politics, the social theorists Taylor (1992), Honneth (1995, 2003), and Fraser (1995, 2000, 2003) aimed to develop theoretical frameworks of recognition. Even though these approaches differ significantly, the authors all focus on discussing the normative dimension of recognition. They develop the idea of reciprocal or mutual recognition with respect to the discourse of a just society and ask for the legitimacy of demands for recognition. Consequently, Taylor, Fraser, and Honneth elaborate complex frameworks around the norm of recognition. These frameworks allow the political and social present to be analyzed and the dynamics of social change with the expanding claims for mutual recognition to be explained. Thus, the debate over recognition refers to two questions. First—with recourse to the Hegelian formulation of the "struggle for recognition"—the participants discuss the question of the dynamics of social, cultural, and political change and the change of normative conceptions. Second, the discourse on recognition provides a contribution to the question of the conditions for the communication about values because recognition is understood both as the precondition of these dialogues and as their result.

For Honneth claims of recognition are raised for two reasons. First, because of anthropological reasons. Recognition is a basic need of human subjects. Second, Honneth argues that persons, groups, or social movements demand the application of a prevailing norm of recognition for themselves when it is valid for other members of a society.[3] Therefore, Honneth distinguishes legitimate and illegitimate claims for recognition. He conceptualizes recognition in two ways. On the one hand mutual recognition is a condition of integrity, identity, understanding, and interaction. Thus, recognition is defined as an attitude, as a "recognitional stance" (Honneth 2004, p. 107, 2005, p. 126). On the other hand, according to Taylor's, Fraser's, and Honneth's approach, recognition is understood as an action (Honneth 2007, p. 329). This dual conceptualization of recognition both as an attitude and as an action is summarized in the formulation of recognition "as an attitude realized in concrete action" (Honneth 2007, p. 330). I think this dual conceptualization of recognition as an attitude and as an action leads to a number of problems. It does not look at the mechanisms by which the norm of recognition becomes manifest in the practice of recognition. Furthermore it is deficient in conceptualizing the establishment, the stabilization, and the change of recognition relations. Thus, this perspective does not include the *process* by which the norm of recognition is expressed. Following the argumentation of Taylor, Honneth, and Fraser, awarding, doing, and gaining recognition coincide. However, their differentiation is crucial for the following reason: it is entirely possible for a discrepancy between a recognition act that is supposed to express the norm of recognition and its effects to occur.

The recognition theories of Taylor, Honneth, and Fraser lead to insufficient statements on the relationship of subjectivity, identity, and embodiment and the effects of relations of recognition for those involved. In addition, the relation between normative change and social, cultural, and political developments and the conditions of a dialogue about recognizable values are spelled out unsatisfactorily. They would therefore need to be supplemented by focusing both the *struggle* for recognition and the *implementation* of recognition as a social process.

When discussing the *struggle* for recognition as a social process it immediately raises the question of the nature of this process: is it an open discussion with the goal of reaching a consensus on the basis of the better argument or is it rather a violent struggle? Although Honneth is aware of the possibility that social change can occur as violent eruptions there is not a systematical place in his theoretical approach to take into account the possible violent character of struggles for recognition or at least integrating the conflict-driven character of demands and

---

[3]Honneth explains as follows: "[…] thanks to their underlying principles, the social spheres of recognition that together make up the socio-moral order of bourgeois-capitalist society possess a surplus of validity, which those affected can rationally assert against actual recognition relations" (Honneth 2003, pp. 149–150).

claims for recognition.[4] Provided that these struggles end in expanded relations of recognition, Honneth identifies struggles for recognition as progress (Honneth 2003).

With regard to this consensus-oriented understanding of struggles for recognition, what is the role of power within Honneth's approach? Honneth's way of conceptualizing recognition says that it cannot be implemented by coercion or discursive hegemony. Following Honneth's approach, recognition has an essential positive meaning (Honneth 2007, p. 329). However, Honneth's conceptualization of recognition does not integrate the reasons and causes for possible breakdowns of relations of recognition. According to Honneth, recognition is supposed to be a rational response to the valuable qualities of other persons. Precisely because Honneth takes the essential need for recognition into account, the struggle for recognition as a discussion about the surplus of the recognition principle's validity can only be *one* version of fighting for recognition. To extend the focus on different shapes of struggles for recognition it is useful to reconsider the procedural character of a struggle for recognition and its enforcement.[5] Regarding the procedural character of struggles for recognition neither Honneth nor Butler offer a theoretical approach that could explain—according to their specific frameworks—the way a struggle for recognition proceeds. For Butler's as for Honneth's contrary theoretical work it would be interesting to discuss in which way social movement theory could help to analyze the process of demanding and negotiating/fighting for recognition.

With respect to the *implementation* of recognition Honneth was challenged to discuss this issue because of Butler's questioning that recognition ends with autonomy and emancipation. As a response Honneth discusses the possibility that recognition could fail. In doing so, he wants to reply especially to the critique of Markell (2003) and Butler that recognition can affirm ideology (Honneth 2007). According to Honneth, recognition as ideology can be established *only* in the case of institutionally granted recognition. Ideologies of recognition motivate to an "individual self-conception that suits the existing dominant order" (Honneth 2007, p. 337). Let me summarize Honneth's criteria of ideological forms of recognition:

---

[4]In direct response and contrast to Honneth, Robin Celikates bases his interpretation of struggles for recognition on conflict theory. According to Celikates, struggles for recognition can never be solved or ended (Celikates 2007). For a further discussion also see Pettenkofer (2010).

[5]James Tully emphasizes the circumstances of struggles for recognition in a democratic society (Tully 2000).

First, there could be a lack of legitimacy of recognition. Honneth mentions the possibility for persons to resist accepting a new form of recognition. Vice versa, persons have to be convinced of the legitimacy of recognition for it to be granted. Honneth does not share Butler's (and Althusser's) view on recognition as subordination and existence at once. In contrast to Butler's perspective these resisting persons are not constituted by these forms of recognition in an existential sense. Second, ideologies of recognition could be identified by "a gap between an evaluative promise and its material fulfilment" of recognition (Honneth 2007, p. 346). That means recognition has two components. The evaluative component—mentioned above—means that recognition is a rational attitude on behalf of valuable qualities. According to Honneth, recognition has to be completed by the second "material" component. This material component consists of changed behavior in intersubjective recognition relationships or of adequate measure in the case of institutional recognition. This means that the institutional framework has to be changed to convince someone that they are recognized in a new way. Nevertheless, there could be a temporal gap between the fulfilments of these two components. When Honneth introduces his model of two components, he explicitly refers to Austin. Since Austin's concept of performative speech acts says that things happen when a speech act was felicitous, Honneth wants to transfer this idea: "With my notion of 'material fulfillment' I am applying his analysis of performative statements to the specific case of 'recognition'" (Honneth 2007, p. 345).

Third, this point includes a criterion dealing with the implementation of recognition that is based on Honneth's own conclusion concerning ideological recognition. Instead of differentiating between legitimate or illegitimate recognition, Honneth suggests distinguishing between open or closed forms of recognition:

> The more a certain form of recognition ties the addressees down to a specific identity and keeps them from the chance of applying to the normative surplus, the more they tend to a just ideological practice of public addressing (Althusser). (Honneth 2004, pp. 117–118, own translation)

In contrast to Butler, Honneth does not understand recognition as something that links the existence and subordination of the subject. He excludes relationships that contradict the positive meaning of recognition by definition. In order to at least identify the problem of ideological recognition Honneth integrates a material component into his definition of institutionally granted recognition. In doing so, he establishes a criterion that addresses the recognized to evaluate if the new form of recognition is "sufficiently rational as to be 'credible' enough" (Honneth 2007,

p. 344).[6] Thus, he designates a criterion for felicitous recognition that is contingent according to speech act theory. It is evident that the implementation of acts of recognition and their evaluative and material components can only be evaluated retrospectively. But, according to Austin's account, one can "do things with words" without changing "material" things. For instance, an apology of a representative of an institution can be successful without changing any material matters.

Ultimately, Butler represents an approach diametrically opposite to Honneth, Taylor, and Fraser in order to theorize the subject and to refer to the concept of performative speech acts. As we recall, according to her account, the subject is subjugated under the norm of recognition. Honneth does not want to take part in "hermeneutics of suspicion that is all too certain of itself" (Honneth 2007, p. 346), whereas Butler questions that recognition ends with emancipation. According to the conventional discourse on recognition there is only a very small systematic place to identify this issue.

To summarize: Taking Butler's perspective into account means that different forms of failed recognition become visible. But it also raises a new problem: it seems to be difficult to identify in which way the power of discourse could be evaded. And this leads to the question of how to define the role of protest activities.

2   Evading the Power of Discourse

There seem to be only a few opportunities to integrate protest into Butler's theoretical framework. It is hardly conceivable that the demand for recognition could drive protest activities that do not aim at getting recognition within the existing orders of discourse. Why should the subject risk claiming recognition that does not fit into the orders of discourse? And in which way could the stabilized order of discourse be evaded? This section turns to the second question. However, the first one will be discussed later.

The existence and stability of orders of discourse depend on the ongoing repetition of appropriate performances. They do not remain stable from within. Butler applies the theoretical findings on performativity to the discourse on recognition. As Butler wants to highlight the effects of ideological recognition, she pays attention to the *doing* of recognition (Butler 1997a, 2005). She refers not only to Foucault and Althusser but also to Austin and Derrida for explicating the performativity of recognition. To introduce this part of Butler's approach regarding the

---

[6]For a further discussion see Bedorf (2010, p. 96).

stability/instability of orders of discourse I would like to go one step back to take into account John L. Austin's concept of performative speech acts.

In his early version Austin classified a performative speech act as an utterance that performs a particular action. Later on in his lectures "How to do things with words" (1955) Austin introduced the term *speech act* to emphasize that we do something in speaking. According to Austin a performative speech act can be assessed as either "felicitous" or "infelicitous" (Austin 1975). Austin was interested in the conditions "that allow something to be done through the saying of a particular set of words" (Loxley 2007, p. 167). He focused on the effect that an utterance achieves "*in* being said" (Loxley 2007, p. 168, original emphasis).

By analogy with Austin's speech act theory, an act of recognition can also be assessed as either "felicitous" or "infelicitous"—and it cannot be assessed as either "true" or "false". The performative perspective opens up the opportunity to make the unpredictable consequences of recognition acts visible. These acts can fail or be undermined, too. According to Butler, recognition has to be understood as a performative act that constitutes an identity by naming it (Butler 1997b, see also 1990, 1993).

Butler starts to theorize performativity—as we recall—by dealing with Derrida's reformulation of Austin's concept of the performative. According to Butler, Derrida points out that the power of the performative "is not the function of an originating will, but is always derivative" (Butler 1993, p. 13). Although the rhetoric of citation implies that the performative act refers to an original this would not be the case for two reasons. First, there is no pre-discursive original. For example, the discourse on *the female* cannot declare an existing female body as the original that only has to be cited. Second, the meaning of an utterance cannot be finalized. Therefore, a significate cannot be declared as the original. Rather, it depends on social processes, so it has to be negotiated constantly. What an utterance means depends on the setting in which a speaking subject is situated, and it depends on performing this utterance. With recourse to Derrida, Butler understands a speech act as an iteration that could never be repeated identically. Both the performative speech act and the act of recognition are constituted by repetition/citation, institutionalization, and standardization. In this regard, the two concepts can be combined.

For Butler, ritualization and conventionality imply the continuous repetition of discursive norms. They do not simply stand for performing social, political, or religious ceremonies (Butler 1997b, p. 25). Thus, the subject's identity has to be produced and constituted constantly by the citation of the referred identity discourse through performative speech acts.

As a process of continuous repetition of discourses performativity has a historical dimension. Butler asserts the aspects of memory and repetition. She stresses the temporal dimension of every identity. Thus, the discourses on identity have another temporal dimension than the identity of a subject that is configured by these discourses. Each performative speech act that relates to discourses of identity can succeed only when it refers to the previous effective performative speech acts of these discourses. At the same time, the sedimented meanings would be lost if they were not continuously repeated.

In accordance with Butler, I would like to understand recognition as a performative act in order to conceptualize recognition with regard to its succeeding or failing. By analogy with Austin's speech act theory, an act of recognition can also be assessed as either "felicitous" or "infelicitous". Consequently, it is a crucial point to think about the conditions that have to be fulfilled for gaining recognition by its doing. Just like Austin asks "How to do things with words?" one can ask "How to do recognition with words or acts?"

Because of its citational practice a speech act can fail. Herein Butler acknowledges several opportunities to lose the connection of discourse and its performativity. The failure of a performative leads to an effect that is different to its intention. Thereby it works as subversive. Furthermore, the reiterative character of performatives can be highlighted. Its failure shows that there are no stipulated quasi natural meanings. The ambiguity of every utterance and the impossibility to determine meanings once and for all become evident, which shows that they are contested.[7]

Evading the implication of a speech act is only possible when it is allowed to cite this (possibly injurious) speech act in a new context. Thus, it is not surprising that Butler rejects censorship and other statutory prohibition of humiliating speech acts like hate speech (Butler 1997b). According to her the state should not be an authority to stop the contest on the meaning of an utterance. And the state should not be the authority to define what was done when an utterance was made.[8] In contrast to the conventional discourse on recognition, agency refers to the

---

[7]Butler goes on: "The critical task is […] to locate strategies of subversive repetition that are enabled by those constructions, to affirm the local possibilities of intervention through participating in precisely those practices that constitute identity and, therefore, present the immanent possibility of contesting them" (Butler 1999, p. 188).

[8]For instance Butler was critical when the US army declared that to say you are homosexual meant to act homosexual. Likewise she questions that pornography effects relationships that represent the gender norms of pornography (Butler 1997b).

possibility to modify meanings by citation; agency can be located in the performative act.

Possibilities of failing the stabilizing performances provide starting points for targeted protest. Although Butler connects recognition, performativity, and subjectivity with regard to more or less powerful discourses, she insists that subjects can cause political change. And she does not want to rule out that in accordance with her concept of performativity responsible persons can be identified (Butler 2005, pp. 83–136). At the same time the lack of sovereignty to govern the effects of speech acts causes the potential to evade the power of discourses (Butler 1990). So, what is the contribution of Butler's perspective on recognition and performativity for the study of phenomena of protest?

3 Understanding New Social Movements

Butler has a specific perspective on protest movements. She wrote her early key texts in the context of feminism and the gay and lesbian movement of the 1970s and 1980s. If one is interested in the relation between the philosopher Judith Butler and the social movements we have to illuminate a very special relationship. On the one hand, Butler is an inspiring writer for several social movements. Her work was adopted by some social movements to redefine the way these social movements see themselves. Furthermore, Butler is a writer who is politically involved in several fields of critique. On the other hand, Butler is critical of some aspects of the very same social movements.[9]

This special relationship could be described as a "temporary identification" (Butler 1997a, p. 266). To imply a concurrence of the political and the theoretical involvement based on the same set of convictions seems to be too simple because that would result in a risky simplifying psychological evaluation. However, in a *gedankenexperiment* we could ask if there are some themes that plausibly link Butler's theoretical and political involvement. Is there a systematic connection between the attraction of some theoretical aspects for the social movements and Butler's own dissociation from these movements by questioning the way social movements see themselves?

---

[9]An example of this ambivalent relationship is Butler's rejection of the award Preis für Zivilcourage at the Berlin Christopher Street Day in 2010. Butler declared to the audience at the Brandenburger Tor that the event was too commercial and that the organizers are not sufficiently active against racism (www.spiegel.de/panorama/eklat-bei-christopher-street-day-butler-lehnt-preis-ab-a-701729.html, accessed November 11, 2015).

I would like to argue that her theoretical framework is a key to a better understanding of these mutual (critical) interests. Butler is generally interested in recognition. Who is recognized? Who is not? What is recognizable and what will be excluded from recognition? How is recognition accomplished? These are the underlying questions when commenting on many different political issues at her heart, like feminism, the gay/lesbian movement, the anti-racism movement, and the intersex/transgender movements. Furthermore, she criticizes the debates on hate speech and pornography. In recent times, Butler has focused on the American war against terror, the conflict between Israel and Palestine, and Islamophobia.[10] Butler's position on all these issues is based on a close relation with queer politics and queer theory. She comments on her political commitment as follows:

> What moves me politically, and that for which I want to make room, is the moment in which a subject—a person, a collective—asserts a right or entitlement to a livable life when no such prior authorization exists, when no clearly enabling convention is in place (Butler 2004b, p. 224).

If one understands recognition as a performative act that creates certain norms and stabilizes them by its repetition, how do these norms become manifest but also change in acts of recognition? By conceptualizing performativity in this way, it is obvious why collective or individual identities cannot be circumscribed as a specific set of qualities that have to be recognized. Instead, every act of recognition constitutes the identity that this act confirms.

The disputes over performativity and recognition in recent years can therefore also be interpreted as different responses to the perceived characteristics of identity movements: People with a feeling of injury, humiliation, or disrespect confronted societies with the claim to recognize the specific identity of a group or an individual person. That identity could be defined by gender, class, and race or by age, religion, and/or sexuality. Simultaneously, protesters raised the demand that the suppressive effects of identification which were connected to the naturalization of discourse have to be revealed and that they could be subverted. Based on the different conceptualization of the subject and its ability to act, Butler thus answers the questions about the dynamics of normative change and its reference to the political, social, and cultural development and to the communication about recognizable values in a very different way than Taylor, Honneth, and Fraser. Nevertheless, both perspectives relate protest with orientations that are identity based.

---

[10]For an overview of Butler's work, see: www.egs.edu/faculty/judith-butler/bibliography/, accessed November 11, 2015.

However, both perspectives try to explain the origins of these identity-based orientations in different ways.

Indeed, some features of the new social movements could be understood as a reaction to the dilemma of recognition that was focused by Butler: Because raising a protest claim seems to compel the protesters to subjugate to an order of discourse that coincides with specific identity-related impositions the problem of identity was explicitly addressed within these protest movements. Butler highlights a dilemma that captures contemporary protest movements on an analytical level. On the one hand, the participants of new social movements claim to be recognized on the base of the prevailing norms. On the other hand, movements contest the norms that define what can be recognized because the movement members do not want to be reduced to the identity framed by these norms. In her article "Merely Cultural" (1997) Butler concentrates on a critique of relegating new social movements to a sphere that is called "merely cultural." Butler criticizes the "material/cultural distinction" (Fraser 1997, p. 281). She wants to deconstruct this distinction as "unstable" (Butler). Butler suggests a specific understanding of the new social movements. She refers to new social movements that mobilize for the recognition of social categories and that therefore relate to the norms that circumscribe "the sphere of the humanly intelligible [...] and this circumscription is consequential for any ethics and any conception of social transformation" (Butler 2004b, p. 222).

The dilemma that captures subjects who demand recognition concerns also those who are engaged in a protest movement. Hence, new social movements could be defined as follows: New social movements are collectivities of activists who long for recognition and who thereby question the universality of the norm because they do not feel included by this norm. "One who is excluded from the universal, and yet belongs to it nevertheless, speaks from a split situation of being at once authorized and deauthorized [...]" (Butler 1997b, p. 91). The protest activities of new social movements can be partly understood as attempts to deal with the described dilemma. They do not want to submit to the identity scheme nor do they want to give up on articulating their protest claims completely. If you become aware of these phenomena in this particularly clear case of new social movements, they could be identified in other protest movements, too.

Butler maintains a "doubled truth" of normativity "that although we need norms in order to live, and to live well, and to know in what direction to transform our social world, we are also constrained by norms in ways that sometimes do violence to us and which, for reasons of social justice, we must oppose" (Butler 2004b,

p. 206).[11] To link this precarious relation with social transformation Butler wants to show "even if we cannot do without them, it will be seen that we also cannot accept them as they are" (Butler 2004b, p. 207). Although Butler analyzes this dilemma in detail, she does not conclude that this line of argument ends up in aporia which is impassable with regard to the ability to act. For Butler it is essential that humans have the "capacity to distinction between enabling violations and disabling ones" (Butler 2004b, p. 214). The following statement illustrates how Butler combines theoretical work and political commitment:

> One must make substantive decisions about what will be a less violent future, what will be a more inclusive population, what will help to fulfill, in substantive terms, the claims of universality and justice that we seek to understand in their cultural specificity and social meaning. When we come to deciding right and wrong courses of action in that context, it is crucial to ask: what forms of community have been created, and through what violences and exclusions have they been created? [...] What resources must we have in order to bring into the human community those humans who have not been considered part of the recognizably human? That is the task of a radical democratic theory and practice that seeks to extend the norms that sustain viable life to previously disenfranchised communities (Butler 2004b, p. 225).

Obviously, Butler has an expansion of social categories in mind. These categories shall be "more inclusive and more responsive" to all cultural populations. That is to say "that the category itself must be subjected to a reworking from myriad directions, that it must emerge anew as a result of the cultural translations it undergoes" (Butler 2004b, p. 224).

By introducing radical democratic theory, Butler engages an external framework that evaluates claims and their justification with regard to recognition and performativity. Coming to this point Butler's approach reveals an implicit tension. On the one hand, Butler emphasizes the opportunity to protest and to change. On the other hand, if one follows Butler's arguments on subjectivity it is difficult to distinguish between failed recognition and recognition that succeeded. Rather, following Butler's argument we should answer two more paradox questions. Either, according to an understanding of emancipatory recognition, when does recognition fail and when does it fail more? Or, according to an understanding of recognition that executes power, when does recognition succeed and when does it

---

[11]Butler goes on "[...] consider that normativity has this double meaning. On the one hand, it refers to the aims and aspirations that guide us, the precepts by which we are compelled to act or speak to one another, the commonly held presuppositions by which we are oriented, and which give direction to our actions. On the other hand, normativity refers to the process of normalization, the way that certain norms, ideas and ideals hold sway over embodied life, provide coercive criteria for normal 'men' and 'women'. (Butler 2004b, p. 206).

succeed more? Obviously, Austin, Honneth, and Butler focus on different types of the failure of recognition. Whereas Austin collects different types of failed speech acts as elements of ordinary language, Honneth discusses failed recognition as an ethically failed recognition in case of ideological recognition. In contrast Butler has speech acts in mind that make marginal life visible because the conventional correct citing of an act of recognition fails.

Butler focuses on performances that attempt to undermine the existing category scheme. Besides the specific understanding of new social movements, analyzing performativity opens a horizon to comprehend specific forms of protest and their functioning that could be identified as speech acts. Most prominently, Butler discusses the effects of "resignification". Every discursive citation implies shifting the sedimented meaning of speech acts. Thus, every speech act has the potential for resignification and subversion. Over the last two decades Butler has discussed resignification from different perspectives that are not systematized. That means she stresses different opportunities that could cause the resignification of speech acts. For instance by doing these acts subjects move "from Parody to Politics," as the final chapter of "Gender Trouble" is called. Over the last two decades, the discussion of drag has been the most prominent example of "practices of parody" (Butler 1999, p. 186). Drag shall show "that the naturalized knowledge of gender operates as a preemptive and violent circumscription of reality".

Besides those practices of parody Butler stresses the option of performative contradictions that "constitute valuable contestations crucial to the continuing elaboration of the universal" (Butler 1997b, p. 89). The point of "performative politics" is to undermine the existing category scheme (Butler and Spivak 2007, pp. 66–67).

> Consider, for example, that situation in which subjects who have been excluded from enfranchisement by existing conventions governing the exclusionary definition of the universal seize the language of enfranchisement and set into motion a 'performative contradiction', claiming to be covered by that universal, thereby exposing the contradictory character of previous conventional formulations of the universal (Butler 1997b, p. 89).

This perspective provides insights why it could be sensible for protesting illegal immigrants to sing the Star Spangled Banner in Spanish although singing the English text could appear as the better strategy in terms of the opportunity structure. According to Butler this is a telling example of a performative contradiction. Butler "entertains the […] thesis" that there are no politics of transformation without performative contradictions (Butler and Spivak 2007, pp. 66–67). To enforce one's claim to freedom and equality against an authority that denies both means showing that freedom and equality move beyond its positive articulation (Butler and Spivak 2007). This heightening of performative contradictions as an essential part of *all* politics of transformation does not really convince. An action to reach resignification is not necessarily structured like a logical contradiction.

For instance Butler deals with mourning as a form of protest. In contrast to the national mourning of the victims of September 11 she asks "Is our capacity to mourn in global dimensions foreclosed precisely by the failure to conceive of Muslim or Arab lives *as lives?"* (Butler 2004a, p. 12, original emphasis). As an example Butler mentions a memorial submitted by an Arab Christian group to the San Francisco Chronicle remembering Palestinians who were killed by Israeli troops. The newspaper declined to publish the memorial (Butler 2004a, p. 37). According to Butler these lives should find recognition by mourning their death. Butler states: "To grieve, and to make grief itself into a resource for politics, is not to be resigned to inaction, but it may be understood as the slow process by which we develop a point of identification with suffering itself" (Butler 2004a, p. 30). In "Frames of War" (Butler 2009) Butler asks "when is life grievable?" Butler argues that grief "furnishes a sense of political community of a complex order, and it does this first of all by bringing to the fore the relational ties that have implications for theorizing fundamental dependency and ethical responsibility" (Butler 2004a, p. 22).

Once again, it is not easy to define the status of resignification with regard to the examples of drag, immigration politics, or global justice. On the one hand resignification shall be "a means of exposing illusory claims to naturalness, as if the revelation of an act's citationality were enough to make the critical intervention stick" (Loxley 2007, pp. 127–128). On the other hand it shall be "the term of a more generalised form of political work" (Loxley 2007, p. 128).

However, following Butler's view activities could be identified as protest forms that would not be characterized as political action according to the mainstream social movement theory.

Thus, applying Butler's approach to new social movements we could link collective and individual identity concerns that drive protest movements by analyzing the diverse demands for recognition. If Butler transcends the duality of acting rationally and irrationally, how are the themes of protest structured? Butler deals with the precarious status of *misrecognized* that hinders them from protesting. It is the closeness to others that causes our vulnerability: "Loss and vulnerability seem to follow from our being socially constituted bodies, attached to others, at risk of losing those attachments, exposed to others, at risk of violence by virtue of that exposure" (Butler 2004a, p. 20). The dilemma of recognition that Butler describes could also help to understand why the protesters have a stark individual motive to act out these types of performances. For Butler, "one can risk serious disenfranchisement and physical violence for the pleasure one seeks, the fantasy one embodies, the gender one performs" (Butler 2004b, p. 214).

Still, why should someone risk losing those attachments by protesting against the prevailing relations of recognition? Butler does not answer this question with an elaborated set of conditions that has to be fulfilled before someone starts to protest. Instead, as mentioned above, she proposes paying attention to the subject's capacity to distinguish "between enabling violations and disabling ones" (Butler 2004b, p. 214). In line with this suggestion, her concept of subjectivity has to contain the subject's potential to transcend his status. This is because the subject reflects his binds to violations and anticipates a more inclusive future state that is worth protesting for. Consequently, who is able to undermine the power of discourse? And if every speech act can fail and can never be repeated identically what is the difference between the intended failing of speech acts to protest and the failing of speech acts by chance?

There seems to be another ambivalence regarding the role of speech acts in Butler's theoretical framework: On the one hand the performativity of speech acts establishes the power of discourse while on the other hand the performativity of speech acts shall offer the key to undermining the order of discourse. As for the understanding of the aims of social movements again, it is the radical democratic theory that shall offer the normative framework to evaluate practices of resignification. For evaluating action and innovation radical democratic theory contextualizes resignification (Butler 2004b, p. 224).

Butler's view on the relation of performativity and recognition contains an alternative to interrogate a protest movement as a coherent collective actor. Instead, this perspective offers a possibility to focus not only on the claims for recognition that are raised by a social movement, but also the relations of recognition within a movement that has to be performed continuously. Following Butler's perspective on performativity the origin of a protest movement has to be seen as a constant performance. Since Butler published "Gender Trouble" (1990), an analysis that catapulted her into international prominence, she claims to question a collective actor that shares a coherent collective identity. For instance, she contests the universality of the human rights discourse by highlighting its contingent foundation (Butler 1992). Butler stresses that to recognize simultaneously means to define what is not recognized. "This raises the political question of the cost of articulating a coherent identity position by producing, excluding, and repudiating a domain of abjected specters that threaten the arbitrarily closed domain of subject positions" (Butler 1997c, p. 149).

Thus, applying Butler's approach to social movements we could link collective and individual identity concerns that drive protest movements by analyzing the diverse demands for recognition. Taking these insights into account opens an unconventional way to explain why protest emerges, although it is unlikely in view of the opportunity structure—and why protest does not emerge.

4 Conclusion

Butler's propositions on the performativity of recognition help to understand new social movements. Butler's account does not fit into the rationalistic and structure-oriented paradigm of social movement theory. How do we apply this to protest activities? Butler's perspective on the constitution of identity opens the horizon to analyze the protest activities of resignification that are motivated by performative politics. The routines of protest could be understood. For instance, holding your shoes in the air is a way to protest that is meaningful just because of the meaning that is cited by its doing.

There are several points that are worth discussing in more detail. First, in which way does Butler's approach offer the tools for analyzing not only new social movements? Second, with reference to discourse theory Butler highlights the subject's dependency on the constant repetition of performances that fit into the ruling norms. Does everybody take the same risks when they do not pass this order or when they try to resist by undermining these hegemonic discourses? Because Butler highlights the situation of people who are forced into extreme rigid practices to become intelligible it is difficult to develop a differentiated view on this issue. Third, as mentioned above, although Butler is greatly interested in struggles for recognition her approach does not include a procedural understanding of these struggles. Hence, it would be worthwhile to discuss in which way Judith Butler's theoretical framework could gain from social movement theory.

References

Austin, John L. 1975. *How to do things with words: The William James lectures delivered at Harvard University in 1955*. Cambridge MA: Harvard University Press.
Bedorf, Thomas. 2010. *Verkennende Anerkennung*. Berlin: Suhrkamp.
Butler, Judith. 1992. Contingent foundations. In *Feminists theorize the political*, ed. Judith Butler, and Joan Scott, 3–21. New York: Routledge.

Butler, Judith. 1993. *Bodies that matter: On the discursive limits of 'sex'*. New York: Routledge.

Butler, Judith. 1997a. Merely cultural. *Social text. Queer transexions on race, nation, and gender* 0(52/53): 279–289.

Butler, Judith. 1997b. *Excitable speech. A politics of the performative*. New York: Routledge.

Butler, Judith. 1997c. *The psychic life of power. Theories in subjection*. Stanford: Stanford University Press.

Butler, Judith. 1999 [1990]. *Gender Trouble: Feminism and the Subversion of Identity*. New York: Routledge.

Butler, Judith 2003. Imitation und die Aufsässigkeit der Geschlechtsidentität. In *Queer Denken. Gegen die Ordnung der Sexualität*, ed. Andreas Kraß, 144–170. Frankfurt/M.: Suhrkamp.

Butler, Judith. 2004a. *Precarious life: The powers of mourning and violence*. London: Verso.

Butler, Judith. 2004b. *Undoing gender*. New York: Routledge.

Butler, Judith. 2005. *Giving an account of oneself*. New York: Fordham University Press.

Butler, Judith. 2009. *Frames of war? When is life grievable?*. London: Verso.

Butler, Judith, and Gayatri Chakravorty Spivak. 2007. *Who sings the Nation-State? Language, Politics, Belonging*. Oxford: Seagull Books.

Celikates, Robin. 2007. Nicht versöhnt. Wo bleibt der Kampf im ‚Kampf um Anerkennung'? In *Socialité et reconnaissance. Grammaires de l'humain*, ed. Georg W. Bertram, 213–228. Paris: L'Harmattan.

Fraser, Nancy. 1995. From redistribution to recognition? Dilemmas of justice in a 'post-Socialist' age. *New Left Review* I(212): 68–93.

Fraser, Nancy. 1997. Heterosexism, misrecognition, and capitalism: A response to Judith Butler. *Social text. Queer transexions on race, nation, and gender* 0(52/53): 279–289.

Fraser, Nancy. 2000. Rethinking recognition. *New Left Review* 3: 107–120.

Fraser, Nancy 2003. Social justice in the age of identity politics: Redistribution, recognition, and participation. In *Redistribution or recognition? A political–philosophical exchange*, eds. Nancy Fraser, and Axel Honneth, 7–109. London: Verso.

Honneth, Axel. 1995. *The struggle for recognition: The moral grammar of social conflicts*. Cambridge: Polity.

Honneth, Axel. 2003. Redistribution as recognition: A response to Nancy Fraser. In *Redistribution or recognition? A political–philosophical exchange*, eds. Nancy Fraser, and Axel Honneth, 110–197. London: Verso.

Honneth, Axel. 2004. Antworten auf die Beiträge der Kolloquiumsteilnehmer. In *Axel Honneth: Sozialphilosophie zwischen Kritik und Anerkennung*, eds. Christoph Halbig, and Michael Quante, 99–121. Münster LIT-Verlag.

Honneth, Axel. 2005. *Reification: A recognition–theoretical view*. The tanner lectures on human values. Delivered at University of California, Berkeley March 14–16, 2005. http://tannerlectures.utah.edu/_documents/a-to-z/h/Honneth_2006.pdf, Accessed 4 Nov 2015.

Honneth, Axel. 2007. Recognition as ideology. In *Recognition and power: Axel Honneth and the tradition of critical social theory*, eds. Bert van den Brink, and David Owen, 323–347. Cambridge: Cambridge University Press.

Loxley, James. 2007. *Performativity*. London: Routledge.
Markell, Patchen. 2003. *Bound by recognition*. Princeton: Princeton University Press.
Pettenkofer, Andreas. 2010. *Radikaler Protest: Zur soziologischen Theorie politischer Bewegungen*. Frankfurt/M.: Campus.
Taylor, Charles. 1992. The politics of recognition. In *Multiculturalism and "the politics of recognition"*, ed. Amy Gutmann, 25–73. Princeton: Princeton University Press.
Tully, James. 2000. Struggles over recognition and distribution. *Constellations* 7(4): 469–482.

Author Biography

Dorothea Reinmuth M.A. is a Ph.D. student at the Max Weber Center for Advanced Cultural and Social Studies at the University of Erfurt and she works for the European Foundation for Education EuSiB gAG. Her Ph.D. research explores the performativity of recognition. She is interested in the issues of recognition, age, gender, and urban development.

Networks, Interaction, and Conflict: A Relational Sociology of Social Movements and Protest

Nick Crossley

There are many aspects of relational sociology that could be highlighted in a discussion of this kind. For this chapter I focus specifically upon networks. I hope that I will say enough about relational sociology more widely, however, to indicate some of the other key concepts and concerns of the approach.

Relational sociology is not my idea. A number of contemporary sociologists identify their work in this way, often making claims to a heritage which extends back to the very beginning of the discipline (e.g. Emirbayer 1997; Elias 1978). And there is a strong strand of relational thinking in social movement studies (e.g. Tilly 2006; Gould 1993a, 1995; Diani and McAdam 2003; McAdam et al. 2001; Saunders 2008). Definitions and types of relational sociology vary, however. In this chapter I describe my own variant (see also Crossley 2011). The paper begins with a brief account of the central tenets of the approach.

1 Defining Relational Sociology

Relational sociology, as I define it, is a challenge to both individualism and holism (ibid.). Social life can neither be reduced downwards to the individual, for the relationalist, nor reduced upwards to a whole. Social life consists in networks of interaction between actors, both human and corporate; networks which, qua networks of interaction, are always in process. And sociologists must analyze it as such.

N. Crossley (✉)
University of Manchester, Manchester, UK
e-mail: nick.crossley@manchester.ac.uk

© Springer Fachmedien Wiesbaden 2016
J. Roose and H. Dietz (eds.), *Social Theory and Social Movements*,
DOI 10.1007/978-3-658-13381-8_9

Interaction presupposes actors, of course, but human and *a fortiori* corporate[1] actors, as commonly understood, are defined by properties whose acquisition presupposes prior (human) social interaction: e.g. language and symbol use, a sense of self, empathic and moral sense, fundamental body techniques, etc. The newly born infant, notwithstanding the fact that they grow for nine months within the body of their mother, whose own body feeds and shapes them in numerous ways, is a limit case here. Even if we accept that the newly born is an inter-actor, however, they are clearly limited as such and only acquire the properties most commonly associated with human actors in philosophical and social scientific discourse as an effect of interactions with others in their immediate environment. They acquire language, and a sense of self/other, a moral sense, etc. by way of social interaction.

Furthermore, abstracting the actor qua individual from the networks of alters with whom they regularly interact or indeed from the specific context of any given interaction situation is precisely to create an abstraction and one which is very often unhelpful. We would not expect to understand and explain the actions of a football player independently of the flow of the game in which they were involved, with the various actions of other players, nor would we expect to adequately grasp a conversation through the utterances of one of its participants alone. The point applies to social life more generally. Actors respond to and anticipate the actions of others and most of what we do is shaped in some part by the network of significant others involved in whatever it is we are doing. Consequently it is the network of actors rather than the actor alone which should be the focus of our analyses.

Individuals qua actors are not thereby rendered irrelevant, however. Networks of interaction are 'wholes' of a sort and they are more than the sum of their parts; interactions manifest *sui generis* dynamics and generate various emergent properties including relations, conventions, and exchange values. But these are not the teleological or historicist wholes often invoked in sociological holisms. They are not entities with their own historical destiny and laws of development, to which individuals, insofar as they figure at all, are subordinated. They do not have functional prerequisites which are met in virtue of a force of necessity independent of human agency. Networks have properties distinct from those of the actors who belong to them. They constrain and enable interaction, influencing and shaping both interaction and interactors in ways that are sometimes quite subtle and almost

---

[1]A firm or organization may be regarded as an actor in its own right (a corporate actor) when it involves decision-making processes, resources, and/or a legal status which is irreducible to any given individual human actor or to a simple aggregate of human actors.

imperceptible, other times not so subtle. But networks have no existence independently of the actors whose interactions and relations (understood as lived histories of interaction[2]) constitute them. Networks qua social structures are not "above" actors, to invoke a classical sociological representation of structure, but rather *between* them. They are structures of *relations* and *interactions*.

Furthermore, network structure, along with the other emergent properties generated within networks, whilst sometimes temporally stable, survives only in virtue of interactions which have the capacity to transform it. A relational ontology is also a processual ontology, conceptualizing the social world in a state of perpetual becoming, motored by social interaction. As such network structure is constantly subject to a pressure to change, on varying scales, as interaction dynamics veer in new directions and ties between actors are formed, broken, and transformed.

The interactions involved in such networks may assume very different forms, from relations of conflict and war in a global political-military network of nations (understood as corporate actors), through highly formalized and routinized relations such as those of the taxpayer to the government revenue office, to the informal ties of friends and lovers. Furthermore, most interactions combine a range of different aspects: e.g. affect, exchange of goods/resources, strategy, convention, etc. (Crossley 2011). Whether the nodes of the network in question are nations, multinational corporations, trade unions, or schoolchildren in a playground, however, and whether the relations between them are multi-stranded ('multiplex') and legally binding or a simple matter of "who plays with whom," we are dealing with networks of interaction all the same; there will be important similarities in the ways in which we approach an analysis of them and we would expect to find, at an abstract level, similar mechanisms underlying their structure and dynamics.

In terms of social networks and protest at least two forms of interaction are important. Much of what I discuss below is focused upon interaction and relations of solidarity between activists and I will be suggesting, following Melucci (1989), that the alternative worlds constructed through interaction within activist networks are crucial to a proper understanding of social movements. No less important and in many ways more obvious, however, are relations of conflict and contention between activists, their adversaries, and sometimes also the police. Demonstrations, petitions, sit-ins, and more extreme acts of political violence are all

---

[2]To say that two actors are tied or related, as I use those terms, is to say that they have an ongoing history of interaction (or active avoidance) and that how they interact in the present is shaped both by their history of interaction and their anticipation of future interaction (or the lack of it).

interactions—in fact they are usually quite complex webs of interaction. And relations of conflict, as Simmel (1955) in particular reminds us, are irreducibly social relations. Moreover, the dynamic of the dialogue between adversaries is often a key factor determining the trajectory of a campaign or movement. Adversaries who each "step up" their levels of hostility as the other does likewise can become locked in a dynamic of escalation, for example (Schelling 1981), and on a more subtle level the tactics adopted by competing parties and the pace of and necessity for innovation can all be driven by the contingencies of tit-for-tat exchanges (McAdam 1983). All involved may find themselves thinking and acting in ways that they could not have envisaged at the start of the struggle as they are driven along by the dia-logic of conflict.

The importance of interaction is also underlined by recent discussion of the role of new communication technologies upon protest. The invention of the World Wide Web and more especially more recent Web 2.0 innovations potentially open up whole new ways of forming and maintaining ties, perhaps even whole new forms of ties. In recent work, for example, Sageman (2008) argues that the possibility of virtual connection has allowed for a major transformation in the structure of global Islamic militancy. The court is still out with respect to other activist contexts. Although strong claims have been made for the revolutionary potential (literally) of new communication technologies and though such technologies appear, anecdotally, to have played a significant role in recent protests, not least the Arab Spring of 2011, the academic evidence is more mixed (see Garret 2006; Gillan et al. 2008). Whatever the balance of evidence, however, nobody denies that communication technologies are significant in relation to protest and this is important because it underlines the relational contention that communicative interaction is at the heart of activism.

It is important, lest this approach seem insensitive to inequalities and power, to note that many established relations involve the former and most involve the latter. Interaction tends to stabilize in the form of enduring relations where partners to it benefit in some way from it and come to depend upon one another for the goods from which they benefit (which might range from love, friendship, and conversation to money and political influence). Relations entail exchange and interdependence. And interdependence is a basis of power because the prospect of losing access to valued goods upon which one has become dependent is an incentive for compliance to the wishes of the other. We do what others want, in many instances, because and to the extent that they are in a position to reward or punish us through their control over resources which we desire. The power balance between interdependent parties may be relatively even and may concern goods which are either low in importance or easy to procure from other sources but they may not, with one party being more dependent upon the other for something of importance to them. Furthermore, such imbalances of power may be mobilized even where the actor who benefits is not aware of the fact: e.g. one party in a romantic relationship may put much more effort into maintaining the relationship and keeping the other happy than the other is aware of because they are more dependent upon the other than the other is upon them. Such power is ubiquitous in the networks that comprise the social fabric: from the crying baby whose parents jump somersaults in pursuit of its recognition, through employment relations to international trade and diplomacy. And it is an integral consideration in relational sociology.

Making sense of complex webs and processes which have no obvious beginnings or ends is a challenge. One useful way of constructing explanatory accounts, however, is by seeking to identify "mechanisms" which appear to constrain actors, afford them opportunities, and/or exert a steering effect on the course of interactions. There may be many such relational mechanisms (see Tilly 2006; McAdam et al. 2001) but for present purposes it must suffice to focus upon (some of) those attaching to the properties of networks. Before doing this we must define networks.

2 Defining Networks

Following Wasserman and Faust (1994), networks comprise two sets: (1) a set of nodes, which in our case will be either human or corporate actors, and (2) a set (or sets) of "ties" (relationships) between those nodes. Some nodes may lack ties to anyone ("isolates") and in theory all nodes in a given network could be isolates but in most networks of interest a majority of nodes enjoy ties with at least some others.

What counts as a tie depends upon our research question and what we are interested in. For some purposes casual acquaintance may suffice. In other cases we may be interested in economic exchanges. In other cases still we may be interested in sexual contact. And it may be that we are interested in a number of different tie types. Furthermore, ties can be conceived in either binary terms, as present or absent, or weighted according to a variable (e.g. strength or frequency of contact) in ordinal or continuous terms.

Who or what is included in our node set is similarly dependent upon research questions and interests. Nodes must be capable of the type of relationship being focused upon and, for single-mode[3] networks, must be capable, in theory, of enjoying that type of relationship with any other members of the set, but beyond that inclusion is at the discretion of the researcher. Defining the relevant node set for any given project is often fraught with difficulties and various established strategies for dealing with these difficulties exist (Diani 1992) but there are relatively few constraints within the networks concept itself.

Smaller networks can be visualized.[4] Figure 1 is a network of 53 student political activists at the University of Manchester (for more details on the study from which this graph is taken see Crossley and Ibrahim 2012, forthcoming). Each activist is represented by a small square ("vertex") and these vertices are colored according to the type of politics in which the activists are engaged[5]: the white nodes are active members of Trotskyist groups; the grey nodes are active members of "new social movement" groups; and the black nodes are members of mainstream political parties and/or pressure groups/charities (the latter being distinguished from "social movement organizations" (SMOs) by their decision not to use direct action tactics). Relations, which are represented on the graph by lines connecting nodes ("edges"), were deemed present where the researchers had evidence that the nodes in question both cooperated on political actions and socialized together.

The location of the nodes along the two dimensions of Fig. 1 has no meaning.[6] The space of the graph is defined exclusively by reference to the ties between its

---

[3]Two-mode networks involve two types of nodes which can only enjoy direct ties with nodes of a different type to their self: e.g. we might have a network of actors and events, recording relations of participation between given actors and given events. A single-mode network, by contrast, involves nodes of one type only and relations between those nodes.

[4]All network graphs used in this chapter were drawn, and all network measures derived, using the Ucinet software package (Borgatti et al. 2002).

[5]As defined here some activists could have fallen into more than one camp. Some "Trotskyists", for example, also belonged to new social movement (NSM) groups, and some NSM activists also belonged to charitable pressure groups. To make the categories mutually exclusive it was decided that members of Trotskyist groups would be categorized as "Trotskyists" whatever other groups they belonged to (a decision which accords with the strong tendency for Trotskyism to be the master frame through which they who subscribe to it appropriate other issues and concerns); non-Trotskyists who participated in direct action protests were categorized as "NSM activists," such that mainstream actors were defined by their decision not to engage in extra-parliamentary activities. Again this categorization resonates with qualitative observations—that the identity and modus operandi of NSM activism tends to prevail amongst those who combine this type of activism with more mainstream forms of involvement.

[6]This is not entirely true. In network theory the location of nodes in two-dimensional Euclidean/Cartesian space has no meaning and is not interpreted. In practice, however, nodes

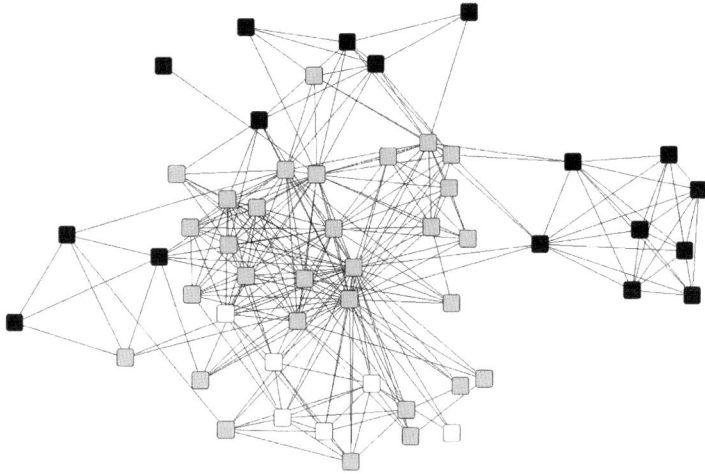

Fig. 1 Cooperation between 53 student activists (*Source* Author's own data, drawn with Ucinet)

nodes. The distance between any two nodes, for example, is defined as the number of intermediary relations ("degrees") which separate them, and any two nodes are said to be in the same "position" in the network where they have ties to the same alters, irrespective of where they may happen to be located on the plot.

Defined thus, networks have a wide range of sociologically meaningful, measurable properties. For example, we can measure the density of the network by counting the number of ties and expressing this as a proportion of the number of ties that are possible. Density always ranges between 0 (nobody is connected to anybody else) and 1 (everybody is connected to everybody else). Figure 1 has a density of 0.2, meaning that 20 % of the ties that are possible within it have been actualized. This, in turn, is important because it tells us how cohesive or close-knit the network is, a variable which, as noted below, has been found to be associated with levels of solidarity and trust, as well as the possibility for communication and coordination, and thus with the capacity of a set of actors for collective action. At a

(Footnote 6 continued)
are often positioned using algorithms and techniques (e.g. multidimensional scaling) which locate nodes close to others which have a similar profile of connections (although locations can and may be altered, for esthetic reasons, by analysts).

somewhat obvious extreme, actors who are not tied to one another and do not communicate cannot orchestrate their actions in collective action.

To give another example, each activist's pattern of connections affords them different opportunities (and constraints) for taking the lead in collective action. Generally, the more central an actor is to a network the greater their opportunity for being a key player within it. However, there are different ways of "being central" in a network, as the numerous centrality measures of social network analysis attest (Scott 2000; Wasserman and Faust 1994). To give only the three most commonly used measures: an actor may enjoy a higher number of ties than any other (*degree centrality*); the cumulative path distances connecting them to every other node in the network may be shorter (*closeness centrality*); or they may find themselves more often positioned between alters who are not otherwise connected (*betweenness centrality*). These types of centrality each effect distinct opportunities and constraints for the actor and they do not necessarily correlate. An actor might be very central in one respect and much less so in the others. In Fig. 1, however, the same two actors, both officers within the Students Union, were most central for each of the three measures just defined.

Centrality within a network can be visualized on a graph. In Fig. 2, for example, which visualizes relations of cooperation between the 23 political groups

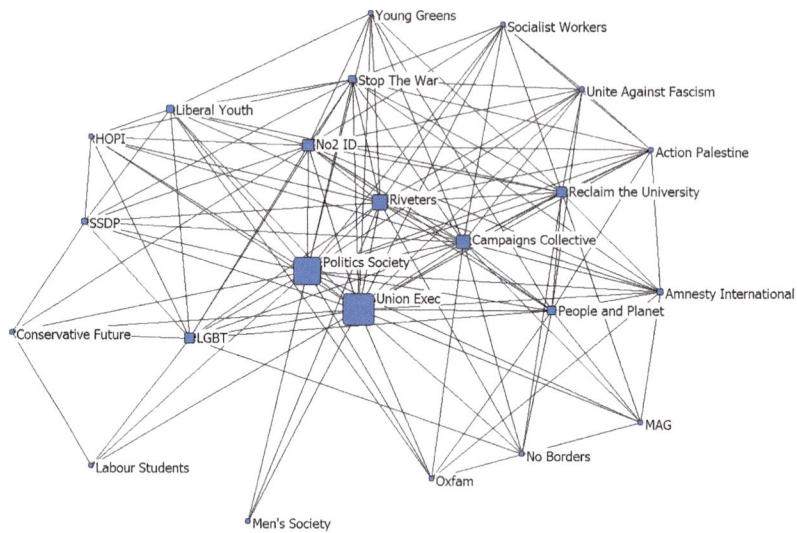

Fig. 2 Cooperation and overlapping membership between 23 student activist groups (*Source* Author's own data, drawn with Ucinet)

that the activists in Fig. 1 variously belonged to, nodes are sized in accordance with betweenness centrality.

Centrality measures, to reiterate, can be an important way of identifying "key players" in a network, both because being central in a network affords an actor the opportunity to play a key role and because playing a key role will tend to make one central: political activity and network position are mutually affecting. This contention was borne out in the research from which the two networks above were taken. The Students Union (whose *Executive* and *Campaigns Collective* are both represented in Fig. 2) was a key site of activity for student activists and the two abovementioned union officers were repeatedly identified by other activists as the "movers and shakers" of the campus political world.

The networks discussed above are both, in the jargon, "whole networks." The nodes included were selected independently of one another, on account of individual attributes and activities which defined them, collectively, as a population (i.e. "political activists/organizations active on the Manchester University campus"). Another way of approaching networks, however, which has been used in a number of recent studies of political discussion and its effects upon individual political behavior, is to select a number of individuals and trace the network of contacts that forms around them: their ego-net. Typically the seed individuals are asked to identify the people with whom they enjoy a particular type of relationship and they are then asked a number of questions about those alters, including whether the alters enjoy the same type of relationship to one another as they enjoy with ego: e.g. "which of your named friends are friends with one another?" Ego-net research, which has the advantage of meeting the assumptions of standard survey and statistical methodologies, has been used in a number of recent studies of voting behavior (see Zuckerman 2005). Its proponents within psephology argue that traditional survey approaches treat the voter as an isolated atom who makes their decisions and acts within a social vacuum and that this is problematic. Their studies suggest that discussion of political matters in ego-nets and the properties of those ego-nets, that is to say, the embedding and activity of the actor in a network and the structure of that network, make a big difference to their political behavior.

Typically an actor's ego-net will involve alters from the various different social worlds which, to paraphrase Simmel (1955), they intersect, and it may be segregated as a consequence. Ego might keep their family, workmates, and friends strictly separated, for example. There is no necessity to this, however; ego-nets, like whole nets, vary in sociologically significant ways which we can explore.

3 Networks and Social Movements

Networks do not only make a difference in relation to conventional forms of political behavior. They make a difference in relation to protest and social movements too. Indeed, by some definitions social movements are networks: networks of individual activists connected through (histories of) cooperative activity and the sense of trust and *esprit de corps* this generates (Blumer 1969); networks of the "social movement organizations" (SMOs), loosely defined, to which such activists belong, which are linked again by way of cooperation and by overlaps in their membership; and networks of events (e.g. protests) linked by the involvement of a common set of activists and SMOs in them.

If we accept that movements are networks then the above techniques of visualizing and measuring networks can be invaluable means of mapping and exploring them, allowing us to address issues and test claims which are often assumed but seldom directly analyzed in empirical research (Diani 1990, 1995; Rosenthal et al. 1985; Saunders 2005, 2007). Claims regarding inclusivity, for example, can be examined by way of network ties and a consideration of who links to whom; splits and factions can be detected and correlated against salient attributes (e.g. ideological affiliation). What appears to be a cohesive movement might, by means of network analysis, prove to be internally segregated into relatively distinct camps (Sageman 2004; Rosenthal et al. 1985), for example, whilst apparently quite diverse struggles and groups might be found to form a cohesive network and thus to constitute a single (if multifaceted) movement. Furthermore, where data are available we may map and model the evolution of such networks over time; the ways and bases upon which ties are made, maintained, broken, or allowed to become latent (Diani 1990; Saunders 2007).

No less importantly, it has been observed that collective action and social movements are only able to emerge where their participants or would-be participants are in contact with one another and form a network (Oliver and Marwell 1993; Marwell et al. 1988). On one level this is necessary to coordination. Actors can only coordinate collective action if they communicate, which presupposes some form of contact between them and thus a (communication) network. And different network structures will both affect the ease with which coordination can be achieved and give rise to wider "side effects." In networks where density is low and average path lengths are long, for example, information will take longer to diffuse, as it must pass through many mouths to reach everybody. For the same reason, moreover, it will be subject to greater degradation. Networks with higher density would be expected to perform better in this sense but even relatively low-density networks might avoid these problems if highly centralized: that is, if most actors in the network enjoy ties to a small number of hubs who can pool and disseminate all relevant information. This, in turn, will tend to generate a power imbalance, however, as the hubs effectively control a scarce resource (information), which may run contrary to the democratic aspirations of many direct action networks.

As this suggests, the importance attached to "resource mobilization" by some movement scholars (Jenkins 1983) also implies networks because mobilization of resources entails exchange, which is a form of interaction and thereby either presupposes or forges a network. The donor–recipient relation is a network tie, indeed a crucial network tie in relation to movements and protests. Furthermore, research by both Diani (1990, 1995) and Saunders (2007) suggests that ties between SMOs—and thus the density of the networks of such SMOs—tend to be fostered, maintained, and dropped instrumentally, in accordance with resource needs.

In addition, where action is risky activists may feel the need for the support of others whom they trust (although see Ray et al. 2003). They may need a sense of solidarity and *esprit de corps* to spur them on (Fantasia 1988). And in a context where "free riding" is common and tempting or where movement aims are not widely shared in the general population, would-be activists may find it much easier to sustain their commitment if they belong to relatively dense and perhaps even closed networks of likeminded others (Coleman 1988, 1990). Dense networks of likeminded actors tend to maintain salient identities and situational definitions, keeping their members "in the frame" and reinforcing valued (by network members) practices, even where the "outside world" is skeptical and critical—and not only in relation to political activity (Bott 1957; Milroy 1987). This appears to be what Melucci (1989) is suggesting when he refers to social movements as "submerged networks" of everyday life which transcend the high-profile protest events focused upon in much movement-related research. The work of activism is not confined to big (and usually) infrequent protest events, for Melucci. It is as much a matter of everyday interaction and conversation which, over time, generates alternative spaces within an existing society and, no less importantly, cultivates the commitment and belief of activists. Furthermore, as Taylor's (1989) work on "abeyance structures" suggests, this may work over extended periods; networks of activists may re-engage with protest activities after long periods of abstinence if, during this period, they maintained social ties with one another.

Some of these ideas were supported empirically in the abovementioned work on student politics (Crossley and Ibrahim 2011a, b). For example, we found that what Tilly (2006) calls "contentious politics" (i.e. Trotskyist and NSM activism) was much more prominent on campus and seemingly easier to organize, and also that those activists involved in such politics formed a much denser sub-network than their counterparts pursuing more mainstream political activity. In other words, collective action was more evident where density was higher. And there are many other good case study examples. It has been shown, for example, that the black civil rights movement in the USA in the 1950s and 1960s grew out of pre-existing networks: specifically out of church and college networks (Morris 1984; McAdam 1982; although see also Biggs 2006). And in its early stages this movement borrowed certain of the existing organizational forms of these networks; the tendency for church leaders to become political leaders—e.g. the Rev Martin Luther King—being a clear example of this (McAdam 1982). Furthermore, Gould (1991) has shown that, in the context of the Paris Commune, those brigades of the National Guard whose members were exclusively drawn from specific arrondissements, that is, who were neighbors and who therefore likely enjoyed informal social ties, were the brigades who demonstrated higher levels of solidarity (for a wider relational account of this uprising see also Gould 1993b, 1995).

Density alone may not suffice to create the solidarity necessary for collective action in such situations. Building upon White's (1965/2008) concept of "catnets", for example, Tilly (1978) has argued that a population is most conducive to collective action when its members are both densely networked and belong to a common "category" which they can invoke as a collective identity. This is clearly the case in relation to the aforementioned civil rights movement, whose participatory networks both formed and mobilized around a black identity (McAdam 1982). Likewise, Gould (esp. 1995) goes into some detail to explore the salience of neighborhood as a basis for collective identity formation within the revolutionary groupings of the Paris Commune. These points remind us both of the symbolic work that goes on within networks and of the importance for relational-sociological research to (qualitatively) explore such symbolic interaction, in addition to mapping and measuring networks in quantitative terms (on qualitative/quantitative considerations in network analysis see Emirbayer and Goodwin 1994; Mische 2003; Crossley 2010a, b; Edwards and Crossley 2009).

4   Recruitment

In addition, many studies have pointed to the significance of networks in relation to recruitment to social movements (Snow et al. 1980, 1983; McAdam 1986; McAdam and Paulsen 1993; Sageman 2004; Opp and Gern 1993). Activists often claim both to have been recruited by a friend and to recruit their friends, and would-be activists are more likely to become involved if their "significant others" do too. Analyzing the differences between individuals who registered to take part in the 1964 "Freedom Summer[7]" campaign but dropped out before the campaign and those who participated in it, for example, McAdam (1986) notes that those who followed through on their initial commitment were distinguished from those who did not by their pre-existing ties to others who also followed through. Moreover, in work with Fernandez, he adds, firstly, that following through is more common amongst those who enjoy particular structural positions within a network ("prominence"[8]), but also, secondly, that this effect is mediated by local context (Fernandez and McAdam 1988). Fernandez and McAdam compared rates of following through for students recruited at Berkeley and Wisconsin respectively, finding that "prominence" had a much greater effect at the latter. This, they hypothesize, is because levels of activism at Wisconsin were considerably lower than at Berkeley, and there was little history of activism on campus. Network prominence gave Wisconsin students extra reinforcement to participate, which was not necessary at Berkeley because levels of mobilization on campus were higher there.

In addition, work by Passy (2001) suggests that connection to an activist shapes the way in which individuals perceive activism and encourages assimilation of a (positive) activist identity.

Again these accounts and processes remind us of the need to focus qualitatively upon the symbolic dimension of the interactions comprising a network, in addition to its measurable, structural properties. The considerable importance attached to framing in contemporary social movement studies, following Snow et al.'s (1986) seminal article, is a useful reference point here. Framing is precisely a facet of communication and thus of interaction. It is one aspect of the symbolic work comprising the networks involved in social movements and protest.

It is not networks per se that are important in recruitment, however. As Snow et al. (1980, 1983) argue, relationships can hinder recruitment efforts. They might do so indirectly: for example, when the demands of relations with non-activist alters compete with those of activism. Alternatively, they might do so directly: e.g. when significant others disapprove of protest participation and seek to prevent an

---

[7]Freedom Summer was a project, in 1964, which involved bringing affluent college students from elite universities in the north of the USA down to the south to help the efforts of civil rights groups there: e.g. by helping with voter registration and political education. Three volunteers were killed by the Ku Klux Klan within the first few days of the project and most participants experienced considerable hostility and often violence.

[8]I do not have space to engage in technicalities here. Suffice it to say that "prominence" entails being both central in a network and linked to others who are also central.

actor from becoming involved (see also Kitts 2000; McAdam and Paulsen 1993). This does not undermine claims regarding the importance of networks. It specifies them. Agents are most available for recruitment when their personal network ("ego-net") is rich in ties to those who support involvement and contains few who discourage it.

A related argument has been made for relations between collectives. If dominated groups enjoy relations with those who dominate them, additional to those which form the basis of their domination (e.g. employment relations), they are less likely to mobilize. Social mixing and friendship temper hostility and generate a controlling effect (Cloward and Piven 1992). McAdam (1982), for example, observes that mobilization during the heyday of the black civil rights movement in the USA was more prevalent in areas of greater racial segregation; that is, where there were less sociable ties between blacks and whites. Again, it is not networks per se which are important but their *composition and configuration*.

Similarly, Sageman (2004) has observed that the segregation of particular Islamic terror groups from the political networks of the wider societies in which they are located has allowed them to transcend local concerns and develop a global agenda. Osama Bin Laden's relative disconnection from the Taliban, whilst resident in Afghanistan, for example, allowed him and his followers to avoid becoming embroiled in the local politics of their host country and to focus rather upon global jihad. Local connections, on this account, may control agendas and divert resources. Relative segregation, by contrast, liberates them.

5   Network Formation and Covert Networks

As the focus upon recruitment indicates, networks are shaped by mobilization processes as much as they shape those processes. In particular, beyond direct recruitment, protest events and groups constitute what Feld (1981, 1982) refers to as "foci": they attract likeminded actors to the same spaces, at specific times, increasing the probability that those actors will meet and form links. Thus, where networks facilitate events, those events reciprocate by attracting new participants into networks.

This process takes on new aspects, however, when the movement in question is outlawed within the context in which it is operating or aims to engage in illegal activity and must therefore act covertly. The rise to prominence of al-Qaeda and related groups has prompted considerable interest in "covert networks" amongst some academics and lots of theories; some of which, at least, directly conflict with one another. Where some argue that high density is necessary to sustain the very high levels of commitment necessary to such action, for example, others argue that high density poses a major security risk which network members are likely to seek to avoid, i.e. if everybody knows everybody else then one compromised individual could compromise the whole network (Coleman 1988, 1990; Erikson 1981; Morselli 2009; Morselli et al. 2007). Covert networks, it is argued from this latter perspective, tend to have a very low density. Likewise, whilst some claim that high levels of centralization in a network maximize security others make this same claim for very low levels of centralization (Ender and Su 2007; Lindelauf et al. 2009; Morselli 2009; Morselli et al. 2007).[9]

These ideas and debates are very much in their infancy and little good empirical data exists to allow us to decide on competing hypotheses. In work which tracked activist networks of British suffragettes through an escalation process in which they become ever more militant and also more covert, however, I and colleagues found clear evidence of a reduction in both network density and centralization (Crossley et al. 2011).

The need for secrecy and security is just one example of the kinds of constraints which might affect and thereby shape processes of network formation. And the abovementioned "foci" are just one example of a mechanism of network formation important in the social movements context. A relational approach to social movements and collective action, as I envisage it, is committed to identifying and analyzing all such mechanisms and constraints.

6   Conclusion

I have done little more in this chapter than signal a few key concerns of relational sociology, in relation to social movement studies, and identify a number of important studies that demonstrate the salience of these concerns. There is much more to relational sociology than I have been able to discuss here and much more that is of relevance to the understanding of social movements and protest. If the chapter has made a persuasive case for the claim that social life comprises

---

[9]Briefly stated, the argument for a high degree of centralization is that it keeps path lengths short in a network (since most nodes are linked through a central hub), therefore reduces the number of transactions, which in turn reduces vulnerability because each transaction exposes the network to risk. The argument for a low degree of centralization, by contrast, is that hubs are very vulnerable since they could be betrayed by any of the many alters with whom they are connected, and that this makes the network vulnerable since the hubs are so central to the network.

networks of interaction between actors, who are simultaneously shaped by those networks/interactions, that it can be studied as such and that social movements and protest, in particular, can be studied in that way, with significant and interesting results, then it has achieved about as much as could be hoped for.

References

Biggs, M. 2006. Who joined the sit ins and why? *Mobilisation* 11(3): 241–256.

Blumer, H. 1969. Collective behaviour. In *Principles of sociology*, ed. A. McClung-Lee, 166–222. New York: Barnes and Noble.

Borgatti, S.P., M.G. Everett, and L.C. Freeman. 2002. *Ucinet for Windows: Software for social network analysis*. Harvard, MA: Analytic Technologies.

Bott, E. 1957. *Family and social network*. London: Tavistock.

Coleman, J. 1988. Free riders and zealots: The role of social networks. *Sociological Theory* 6 (1): 52–57.

Coleman, J. 1990. *Foundations of social theory*. Cambridge: Harvard, Belknap.

Crossley, N. 2010a. Networks, interactions and complexity. *Symbolic Interaction* 33(3): 341–63.

Crossley, N. 2010b. The social world of the network: qualitative aspects of network analysis. *Sociologica* 2010 (1). www.sociologica.mulino.it/doi/10.2383/32049. Accessed 4 Nov 2015.

Crossley, N. 2011. *Towards relational sociology*. London: Routledge.

Crossley, N., and Y. Ibrahim. 2012. Critical Mass, Social Networks and Collective Action: the Case of Student Political Worlds. *Sociology* 46(4): 596–612.

Crossley, N., and Y. Ibrahim. forthcoming. Network Formation in Student Political Worlds. In *Student Politics and Protest*, ed. Brooks, R., London: Routledge.

Crossley, N., G. Edwards, E. Harries, and R. Stevenson. 2011. *Covert Social Movement Networks and the Secrecy-Efficiency Trade Off: The case of the UK suffragettes (1906–1914)*. Working Paper, Department of Sociology and Mitchell Centre for Social Network Analysis, Manchester: University of Manchester.

Diani, M. 1990. The network structure of the Italian ecology movement. *Social Science Information* 29(1): 5–31.

Diani, M. 1992. Analysing movement networks. In *Studying collective action*, ed. M. Diani, and R. Eyerman, 107–135. London: Sage.

Diani, M. 1995. *Green networks*. Edinburgh: Edinburgh University Press.

Diani, M., and D. McAdam. 2003. *Social movements and networks*. Oxford: Oxford University Press.

Edwards, G., and N. Crossley. 2009. Measures and meanings: Exploring the ego-net of Helen Kirkpatrick Watts, Militant Suffragette. *Methodological Innovations On-Line* 3(2).

Elias, N. 1978. *What is sociology?*. London: Hutchinson.

Emirbayer, M. 1997. Manifesto for a relational sociology. *American Journal of Sociology* 103(2): 281–317.

Emirbayer, M., and J. Goodwin. 1994. Network analysis, culture and the problem of agency. *American Journal of Sociology* 99(6): 1411–1454.

Enders, W., and X. Su. 2007. Rational terrorists and optimal network structure. *The Journal of Conflict Resolution* 51(1): 33–57.

Erikson, B. 1981. Secret societies and social structure. *Social Forces* 60(1): 188–210.

Fantasia, R. 1988. *Cultures of solidarity*. Berkeley: University of California Press.

Feld, S. 1981. The focused organisation of social ties. *American Journal of Sociology* 86(5): 1015–1035.

Feld, S. 1982. Social structural determinants of similarity among associates. *American Sociological Review* 47(6): 797–801.

Fernandez, R., and D. McAdam. 1988. Social networks and social movements. *Sociological Forum* 3(3): 357–382.

Garrett, R.K. 2006. Protest in an information society: A review of literature on social movements and new ICTs. *Information, Communication and Society* 9(2): 202–224.

Gillan, K., J. Pickerall, and F. Webster. 2008. *Anti-war activism: New media and protest in the information age*. London: Palgrave.

Gould, R. 1991. Multiple networks and mobilisation in the Paris Commune, 1871. *American Sociological Review* 56(6): 716–729.

Gould, R. 1993a. Collective action and network structure. *American Sociological Review* 58 (2): 182–196.

Gould, R. 1993b. Trade cohesion, class unity and urban insurrection. *American Journal of Sociology* 98(4): 721–754.

Gould, R. 1995. *Insurgent identities*. Chicago: Chicago University Press.

Jenkins, C. 1983. Resource mobilisation theory and the study of social movements. *Annual Review of Sociology* 9(1): 527–553.

Kitts, J. 2000. Mobilizing in black boxes. *Mobilization* 5(2): 241–258.

Lindelauf, R., P. Borm, and H. Hamers. 2009. The influence of secrecy on the communication structure of covert networks. *Social Networks* 31(2): 126–137.

Marwell, G., P. Oliver, and R. Prahl. 1988. Social networks and collective action: A theory of critical mass III. *American Journal of Sociology* 94(3): 502–534.

McAdam, D. 1982. *Political process and the development of black insurgency*. Chicago: University of Chicago Press.

McAdam, D. 1983. Tactical innovation and the pace of insurgency. *American Sociological Review* 48(6): 735–754.

McAdam, D. 1986. Recruitment to high risk activism: The case of freedom summer. *American Journal of Sociology* 92(1): 64–90.

McAdam, D., and R. Paulsen. 1993. Specifying the relationship between ties and activism. *American Journal of Sociology* 99(3): 640–667.

McAdam, D., S. Tarrow, and C. Tilly. 2001. *Dynamics of contention*. Cambridge: Cambridge University Press.

Melucci, A. 1989. *Nomads of the present*. London: Radius.

Milroy, L. 1987. *Language and social networks*. Oxford: Blackwell.

Morris, A. 1984. *The origin of the civil rights movement*. New York: Free Press.

Mische, A. 2003. Cross-talk in movements. In *Social movements and networks*, ed. M. Diani, and D. McAdam, 258–280. Oxford: Oxford University Press.

Morselli, C. 2009. *Inside criminal networks*. New York: Springer.

Morselli, C., C. Giguère, and K. Petit. 2007. The efficiency/security trade-off in criminal networks. *Social Networks* 29(1): 143–153.

Oliver, P., and G. Marwell. 1993. *The critical mass in collective action*. Cambridge: Cambridge University Press.

Opp, K.-D., and C. Gern. 1993. Dissident groups, personal networks and spontaneous cooperation: The East German revolution of 1989. *American Sociological Review* 58(5): 659–680.

Passy, F. 2001. Socialisation, connection and the structure/agency gap. *Mobilization* 6(2): 173–192.

Piven, F., and R. Cloward. 1992. Normalising collective protest. In *Frontiers in social movement theory*, ed. A. Morris, and C.McClurg Mueller, 301–325. New Haven: Yale University Press.

Ray, K., M. Savage, G. Tampubolon, A. Warde, M. Longhurst, and M. Tomlinson. 2003. The exclusiveness of the political field. *Social Movement Studies* 2(1): 37–60.

Rosenthal, N., M. Fingrutd, M. Ethier, R. Karant, and D. McDonald. 1985. Social movements and network analysis. *American Journal of Sociology* 90(5): 1022–1054.

Sageman, M. 2004. *Understanding terror networks*. Philadelphia: University of Pennsylvania Press.

Sageman, M. 2008. *Leaderless jihad*. Philadelphia: University of Pennsylvania Press.

Saunders, C. 2005. The configuration of the Global Justice Movement in Britain. Paper presented at 'Genealogies of the Global Justice Movement', Paris 30 Sept–1 March 2005.

Saunders, C. 2007. Comparing environmental movement networks in periods of latency and visibility. *Graduate Journal of Social Science* 4(1): 109–139.

Saunders, C. 2008. Using social network analysis to explore social movements: A relational approach. *Social Movement Studies* 6(3): 227–243.

Schelling, T. 1981. *The strategy of conflict*. Cambridge: Harvard University Press.

Scott, J. 2000. *Social network analysis: A handbook*. London: Sage.

Simmel, G. 1955. *Conflict and the web of group affiliations*. New York: Free Press.

Snow, D., L. Zurcher, and S. Ekland-Olson. 1980. Social networks and social movements: A microstructural approach to differential recruitment. *American Sociological Review* 45 (5): 787–801.

Snow, D., L. Zurcher, and S. Ekland-Olson. 1983. Further thoughts on social networks and movement recruitment. *Sociology* 17(1): 112–120.

Snow, D., E. Rochford, S. Worden, and R. Benford. 1986. Frame alignment processes, micromobilisation and movement participation. *American Sociological Review* 51(4): 464–481.

Taylor, V. 1989. Social movement continuity: The women's movement in abeyance. *American Sociological Review* 54(5): 761–775.

Tilly, C. 1978. *Mobilisation to revolution*. Reading: Addison-Wesley.

Tilly, C. 2006. *Identities, boundaries and social ties*. New York: Paradigm.

Wasserman, S., and K. Faust. 1994. *Social network analysis*. Cambridge: Cambridge University Press.

White, H. 1965/2008. Notes on the constituents of social structure. *Sociologica* 1. www.sociologica.mulino.it/doi/10.2383/26576. Accessed 4 Nov 2015.

Zuckerman, A. (ed.). 2005. *The social logic of politics: Personal networks as contexts for political behaviour*. Philadelphia: Temple University Press.

Author Biography

Professor Nick Crossley is based in the Department of Sociology at the University of Manchester (UK) and is the co-founder/co-director of the university's Mitchell Centre for Social Network Analysis. His research interests include: collective action; social networks and network analysis; music; and embodiment. His most recent book is: Networks of Sound, Style and Subversion: the Punk and Post-Punk Worlds of Manchester, London, Liverpool and Sheffield, 1975–1980 (Manchester 2015).